HEART *of the* CARIBOO-CHILCOTIN

VANCOUVER • VICTORIA • CALGARY

HEART *of the* CARIBOO-CHILCOTIN

MORE STORIES WORTH KEEPING

edited by DIANA WILSON

Heritage House Publishing Co. Ltd.
#108 – 17665 66A Avenue
Surrey, BC V3S 2A7
www.heritagehouse.ca

Heritage House Publishing Co. Ltd.
PO Box 468
Custer, WA
98240-0468

LIBRARY AND ARCHIVES CANADA CATALOGUING IN PUBLICATION
Heart of the Cariboo-Chilcotin: more stories worth keeping/edited by Diana Wilson.

Includes bibliographical references.
ISBN 978-1-894974-28-8

1. Cariboo Region (B.C.)—Literary collections. 2. Chilcotin River Region (B.C.)—
Literary collections. I. Wilson, Diana, 1958– II. Title.

FC3845.C3H42 2007   971.1'75   C2007-900866-6

LIBRARY OF CONGRESS CONTROL NUMBER: 2006940146

Edited by Diana Wilson and Karla Decker
Book design by Frances Hunter
Cover design by Jacqui Thomas
Cover photo by Chris Harris

Printed in Canada

Heritage House acknowledges the financial support for its publishing program from the
Government of Canada through the Book Publishing Industry Development Program
(BPIDP), Canada Council for the Arts, and the province of British Columbia through the
British Columbia Arts Council and the Book Publishing Tax Credit.

The Canada Council | Le Conseil des Arts
for the Arts | du Canada

BRITISH COLUMBIA
ARTS COUNCIL
Supported by the Province of British Columbia

This book has been printed on 100% post-consumer recycled paper,
processed chlorine free and printed with vegetable-based dyes.

Contents

*Dedicated to the pioneer families and First Nations
peoples of the Cariboo–Chilcotin*

FOREWORD

Modern book publishing in British Columbia started about 50 years ago, 100 years after the Cariboo gold rush of 1858 that led to Great Britain establishing a new colony. Fittingly, the book that launched this era, *British Columbia: A History* was written by Cariboo-born historian Margaret Ormsby and published by Macmillan & Co. The centennial itself spurred local interest in both writing and regional publishing.

Among the forefathers of modern publishing in B.C. were Vancouver printer Howard Mitchell; Quesnel River valley farm boy, environmentalist and magazine publisher Art Downs; former Mountie, RCAF war vet and cattle rancher Gray Campbell; and Scottish-Canadian book salesman Jim Douglas. During their careers, all published books linked to the Cariboo–Chilcotin.

"The most notable B.C.-published book to follow the 1958 breakthrough," wrote SFU professor Rowland Lorimer for the *Encyclopedia of British Columbia*, "was *Wagon Road North* by Art Downs [1960]." Inspired by the positive reaction to his book, Art Downs founded the company that became Heritage House Publishing.

While the fledgling Heritage program of the 1960s has become a successful western Canadian enterprise supported by Canadians from coast to coast, our roots have remained in the heartlands of B.C. Every year, Heritage publishes at least one book either set in the Cariboo–Chilcotin or written by one of the region's authors.

The body of work available to our editor, Diana Wilson, was rich, deep and far-reaching. In his foreword to the first volume, publisher and author Alan Twigg described it as a "literary terrain ... [where] much of the writing is uplifting, bemused and anecdotal, but that doesn't mean it's not also sophisticated." Sophisticated or not, the writing is most lively and enjoyable when both the land and its people are part of the stories. Whether the narratives unfold in an autobiographical or a third-person voice, much of what has been written celebrates individuality and a high regard for dry humour.

For newcomers to the region or others, like myself, who have enjoyed only sporadic visits, it is the literature of the Cariboo–Chilcotin, generated over 150 years, that gives us an affinity for the people, a sense of belonging and fond memories of the awe-inspiring landscapes.

It is most fitting that Diana chose to include an excerpt from *The Promise*, Bill Gallaher's creative non-fiction gold-rush drama set in the Cariboo—a story of immense gains and tragic losses, of love, friendship, honour and mourning. Gallaher's lyrical writing made for what Victoria *Times Colonist* editor and reviewer Dave Obee called "a compelling read, and a worthy addition to books that record the early years of B.C. history."

Certainly the mix of voices in this volume is nothing if not eclectic—even, occasionally, eccentric. Robin Skelton, for example, was best known as a poet and long-time University of Victoria professor, but was also one of Canada's most famous witches. And before heading into the remote Chilcotin backcountry, Chilco Choate had all of his perfectly healthy teeth replaced with a set of "choppers" so that he would never have to deal with a toothache.

Then there are the doctors, brilliant men who recorded the history they had lived and the human struggles they had witnessed. Mark Wade served patients along the Cariboo Road and later, as owner of Kamloops' *Inland Sentinel*, blended his own recollections with stories from old issues to compile an entertaining—if not always accurate—manuscript that came to light nearly 50 years after his death.

Like Wade, Dr. Al Holley never lived to see his *Don't Shoot from the Saddle* in print (he died weeks before its release), but his sense of humour and yarn-spinning live on forever in one of the most entertaining collections of stories by a single Cariboo–Chilcotin voice.

Retired obstetrician Eldon Lee is said to have delivered 8,000 babies throughout the Interior before retiring in Prince George, where he wrote many books about his experiences and ranch life south of Williams lake with his brother Todd. Todd became a minister, and the prolific Reverend Lee wrote more than 400 children's stories in addition to his narrative of Cariboo stories, *He Saw With Other Eyes*, published in 1992.

Policeman Bill Riley felt he needed assistance to record the stories of his professional life, so at age 85, he retained Laura Leake, a journalism student, to help write a memoir that is now a classic record of B.C. police life before the provincial force even had uniforms.

Many of these authors were born, raised and found their heroes on the land they loved. Jean Speare, along with her pioneering family, lived with the Shuswap people as neighbours and, fortunately for all of us, she prepared a photo-essay tribute to a woman she greatly admired, Mary Augusta Tappage, who was born at Soda Creek in 1888.

Another writer's girlhood idol was a gent named Tex. Raised on ranches near Kamloops and Williams Lake, Karen Piffko first met Texas Fosbery in 1945, when she was three. When she met up with him again in the 1960s, their friendship led to their collaboration on Karen's entertaining biography *The Life and Times of Texas Fosbery*.

Karen, like many Cariboo writers, worked for the *Williams Lake Tribune*, the newspaper founded by Clive Stangoe and one of my all-time favourite Cariboo writers, his wife Irene. I spoke by telephone with Irene recently and, at 89, her voice still sounds girlish and her spirit is relentless, in spite of a long battle with osteoporosis. Her two stories in this volume are from one of her three anecdotal bestsellers about the Cariboo–Chilcotin, and Irene hopes to give us one or two new stories for the next volume.

Raconteur and musician Hilary Place grew up in Dog Creek. Hilary's stories, like Irene's, are full of empathy and humour, and have been retold or reread over campfires every summer since they were published. His latest, about the Alkali Lake Hockey Team, will join their ranks.

In the Dirty '30s, the B.C. Interior became a haven for many people. Cariboo-raised Earl Baity survived the Depression by escaping a big-city welfare existence and returning home to live off the land. Also in the '30s, a very pregnant Olive Spencer Loggins and her husband Arthur, greenhorns to the core, sought refuge on an isolated homestead near Deka Lake. American-born Rich Hobson, devastated by the crash of 1929, roamed the American West before teaming up with his pal Panhandle Phillips and establishing the Home Ranch, north of Anahim Lake. Fred Ludditt came to the Quesnel River area as a prospector when the Depression set in and then rushed with a horde of like minds to

Zeballos when the cry of "Gold!" came from Vancouver Island; he then returned to start a campaign to save Barkerville as a historic site.

Other wanderers discovered the Cariboo–Chilcotin by chance as they traipsed around the world. Sage Birchwater, for example, a native of Victoria, crossed the continent before settling into Chilcotin life as a trapper, educator and newspaper correspondent.

Many Cariboo authors had English roots. One of the best known was Eric Collier, who was sent to live with his cousin, Cariboo rancher Harry Marriott. Eric's famous *Three Against the Wilderness* received international attention when it was released in 1959, whereas Harry's memoir enjoyed a more regional readership when it appeared seven years later.

Another fine writer of homestead lore is Alan Fry, born on a ranch east of Lac La Hache. Fry's 1962 memoir *The Ranch On the Cariboo* followed in the footsteps of Collier's book, and was likewise published in New York, and Great Britain, as a fascination with the Canadian West continued to grow.

Ann Walsh is primarily known for her young adult books, but her short essay about a mother's love and Cariboo sunflowers is a fitting inclusion here. (After all, the word "anthology," derived from the Greek, is defined as a collection of flowers.) Heidi Redl grew up on a Cariboo cattle ranch pioneered by her grandfather. Continuing in that line of work, Heidi brings a fresh, humourous perspective to the hard work and nitty-gritty involved in operating a large ranch.

No anthology of Cariboo–Chilcotin literature would be complete without a contribution from that dean of contemporary B.C. storytelling Paul St. Pierre. These excerpts deal with horses and, of course, a horseman—in this case, pioneer rancher Duane Witte. And Duane gets the last word, in the concluding story written with his sister Veera Bonner.

Rodger Touchie, Publisher
Victoria, 2007

Note: ABCBookworld is the source of much of the information about these authors. Our thanks to publisher Alan Twigg.

The Promise

from *The Promise: Love, Loyalty and the Lure of Gold*
The Story of "Cariboo" Cameron
by Bill Gallaher

*Bill Gallaher has worked at all manner of jobs, from wrestling
a bear in Winnipeg to teaching high school in Surrey. A stint
in Ireland fired up the natural poet in him and he began
writing songs and performing them. When he returned home to
Vancouver, Gallaher wrote songs about Canada and its history,
singing them across the nation at concerts and folk festivals,
on television and radio, and in venues ranging from saloons
to a prison for the criminally insane. As his reputation grew,
Gallaher expanded his passion for weaving historical tales
to novels and works of creative non-fiction, all breathing new
life into old legends of that most storied setting, the Cariboo.
Gallaher now lives in Victoria with his wife, and devotes most of
his time to writing historical books.*

What follows is a condensed extract from The Promise,
*Gallaher's creative non-fiction book dramatizing the amazing
trek of Cariboo Cameron, who risked life and limb to fulfill a
deathbed promise to his wife. The story is narrated by Cameron's
friend and partner, Robert Stevenson, who accompanied
Cameron and his macabre cargo on an extraordinary journey.
We begin with their chance meeting in gold-fevered Victoria.*

Robert Stevenson (left) met John and Sophia Cameron in Victoria in 1862. He and John became partners in their search for Cariboo gold.

first met the Camerons in the early spring of 1862. Had I been able to foresee the extraordinary events our meeting would lead to, that we would forge a tale that would survive long after their departure from this earth, and will likely do so long after mine, I would have thought it the wildest of dreams.

We all three were raised by Loyalist families in Glengarry County in Canada West. We had grown up within just a few miles of each other but had never met. Ironically, that would have to wait for another time and another place—one nearly 3,000 miles away.

I speak of Victoria, that strangest of towns in the colony of Vancouver Island. By strange, I mean that beyond the collection of buildings that stood on the slope above the harbour, it was virtually a city of tents and shanties. Low peaks of canvas tilted every which way alongside slapdash plank shelters, all lodgings for miners waiting for winter to pass and the trails to Cariboo to be free of snow.

I was there for the same reason but could afford to take a room at the Royal Hotel. My room was small but adequate. A window overlooked Wharf Street and I welcomed the noise of creaking wagons, chuffing horses, and chattering people, for I was invigorated to have civilization so near at hand. On any given weekday, the town was busy with the hustle and bustle of commerce and the general transactions of humanity. And the topic of most conversations was gold.

I had four months to spend before the mining season reopened, and I began making preparations for Cariboo. There appeared to be no end of business opportunities for a man with a clear view of the road ahead of him and some capital behind. I could also see that the most profitable of them would require a partner, yet so far, I'd not met anyone with whom I wished to embark on such a relationship. That ended on a particularly dull day at the beginning of March when I was resting in my room, impatient for the snow and ice to give way to spring so that I could be moving on.

I was surprised by a knock at the door. I had made no appointments and was therefore not expecting anyone. I opened the door to a handsome but sober-looking man, about 40, with wavy brown hair receding from his forehead, and a full beard that hung to the lapels of his jacket. There was an uncommon air of assurance about him, but what commanded my attention was his eyes, an unusually deep brown, with a gaze that gripped as tight as his handshake, yet hid the man behind them. He introduced himself as John Cameron from Glengarry County, Canada West. He had arrived the day before from San Francisco with his wife and infant daughter. Upon registering at the desk, he was told by the hotel's owner that another guest was also from Glengarry and he was kindly given my room number.

His arrival boosted my spirits immensely. I was heartened to meet someone from home in a town that teemed with strangers. We exchanged pleasantries, after which he led me to his room to meet his wife. Sophia Cameron was nearly as tall as her husband. Her face was a harmony of lovely, soft features accented by long, raven-black hair tied in a bun. Her skin seemed so smooth that I thought silk merchants might scour the Orient forever and not find a cloth as fine. I was hopelessly drawn to her, though her mahogany eyes promised nothing more than the moment.

She smiled easily, but looked haggard after their long sea journey and lines of worry marked her exquisite face. Their daughter had come down with a fever and even though they'd obtained medicine in San Francisco, her condition hadn't improved. Sophia had just put the little girl down to sleep.

I suggested to Cameron that the two of us might walk up to the Boomerang for a whiskey. He asked Sophia if she minded some time on her own, to which she replied wearily, "After five days in steerage, John? I think not."

The day had turned remarkably brighter in the company of this man, and I don't think I stopped chattering as we cut through Waddington Alley and up Yates to the Boomerang. In the convivial atmosphere of the bar, thick with the smell of men, liquor, tobacco smoke and camphor, Cameron and I began forging the bonds of a friendship that neither of us knew would last a lifetime. Before long he was insisting on knowing the road that had brought me to Victoria.

Cameron was impressed with my resumé, commenting that I had accomplished much for so young a man. My story had taken us through a few whiskeys and we both felt in need of a walk to clear our heads. We left the Boomerang and walked up Chancery Lane to Government Street. Our footsteps thudded on the wooden sidewalk but I scarcely paid attention to where we were walking as Cameron related the events that had brought him to Victoria.

He had grown up with a head full of dreams, and couldn't remember when he first became aware that dreams of adventure and fortune were among them. Perhaps they had always been there, nurturing a restless spirit and stirring his soul, pushing him inexorably toward the day when he would abandon farm life to go in search of something better. Consequently, when news arrived that gold had been found in great quantities in California, it was news he'd been born to hear.

Before he finished, I had reached a decision. Not only had he accumulated an enviable knowledge of placer mining, he was as hardy as the Highland stock from which he was descended. He was forthright in his opinions, and though I did not necessarily agree with all that he said, I certainly appreciated his zeal. He openly admitted possessing a stubborn streak that would put a mule to shame, although I wouldn't find out till later how much of an understatement that was. I knew beyond a doubt that he was exactly the man I needed for the task I had in mind.

On our way back to the hotel, I laid out my plan. It had been my intention to return to Antler with a pack train of supplies that I would sell there out of my recently purchased building. The profits from that venture would help finance my mining operation. However, to do that I would have to wait until the snow had melted sufficiently on the Cariboo trails to allow horses to get through. Also, since there were 2,000 miners anxious to get to the creeks, and a limited number of packers to get them there, I might have to wait my turn and would therefore arrive later than was desirable.

On the other hand, if I entrusted that job to Cameron, I could leave sooner, be on the creeks in time for the arrival of the first packers and sell their merchandise out of my building for a commission. To this end, I offered to stake Cameron to $2,000 worth of provisions for himself that he would bring up by pack train along with my merchandise and mining equipment. We shook hands on our new partnership and arranged to meet the following morning when I would take him to the Hudson's Bay Company store and introduce him to the trader.

At breakfast, the Camerons were conspicuous by their absence. I ran into them afterward as they were descending the narrow staircase to the lobby. Their daughter's condition had worsened. Cameron asked to delay our meeting while they took the child to see a doctor. Upon their return, it was apparent that little had been done to alleviate their concern, but the doctor had prescribed medicine and they were hopeful it would work. Cameron and I went directly to the Hudson's Bay warehouse, where I introduced him to the chief trader with whom we discussed our plans.

We met again the next day and made a list of supplies for our venture. It included everything from nails to candles: anything that a miner might purchase to make his quest for gold a trifle easier. Some smaller items had to be purchased at other stores and so we made the rounds, arguing good-naturedly over this and that, as plump with enthusiasm as two men can be. This cheerfulness was to be short-lived, tempered by devastating news.

Shortly after daybreak on Monday morning, a loud knocking startled me awake. I pulled on my trousers and swung open the door. It was Cameron, and the look in his eyes made my heart leap.

"Come quickly," he said. "It's Mary."

I followed him down the short hallway to his room. The half-light of morning through the window cast shadows on Sophia's face as she sat on the edge of the bed, slowly rocking back and forth, holding the lifeless form of their daughter in her arms. To this day, I see Sophia's face as clearly as I did then, a study in pain and grief. It was all I could do to keep from enfolding her in my arms. Cameron did his best to provide comfort, but was so grief-stricken himself that I thought I would never again see a more pathetic sight. But I was more wrong than I could imagine.

Mary's death was an immense blow to the Camerons. I began to wonder if their despair was more than they could bear. During her worst moments, Sophia would insist that John must try to raise money for them to catch the first steamer bound anywhere out of Victoria, as long as their ultimate destination was Canada and home. I offered them the cost of the tickets in the form of a loan, but Cameron was determined not to return home empty-handed. He had come this far and he would see it through. Sophia was his wife and so would she. They would find consolation, he insisted, in the fact that Sophia was with child again and would give birth sometime in the fall. Slowly, they began busying themselves in preparation for the long journey to British Columbia's interior.

After a good storm at the beginning of March, the weather had warmed and spring flowers were beginning to show their colour. By the middle of the month the river was clear. Miners were packing up and leaving, heedless of warnings in the newspapers that because of the prolonged winter, provisions were low at the roadhouses and the trails were still thick with snow. It was recommended that everyone wait until the middle of April before trying to get to the creeks.

I had no intention of waiting. It made good business sense to be on the creeks ahead of everyone else so on April 1, I was up as day was breaking in the eastern sky. I had my packboard, filled with the supplies needed for the journey, and to it was tied a pair of snowshoes.

At Yale, 45 of us set out on foot together for the creeks. There was still much snow and it wasn't long before the group was strung out over a great distance along the trail as it rose and fell beside the river. Three weeks later I reached Antler Creek.

The snow lay seven feet deep, but the spring thaw was well under way. I set to work preparing my building for the arrival of the packers. Meanwhile, other merchants and miners arrived and filled the air around Antler with the sounds of industry. Soon the creek grew murky from dirt washed through sluices. When the pack trains pulled in, I began a booming commission business. Most items went for more than double the cost to get them there. By the time the Camerons arrived on Antler Creek, near the end of July, I had cleared $11,000.

It was a fiercely hot day, the sky streaked with mares' tails. Sophia looked exhausted from the long trip, and her expectant condition was now quite apparent. Since Antler Creek appeared to be petering out, I sold my business for a modest profit and, with the Camerons, made haste across the mountain.

Word of "colour" was a clarion call to miners everywhere, many of whom went dashing off immediately upon hearing the smallest bit of news, without ever verifying it. Some of the more cunning would send out fake reports of good prospects on non-gold-bearing creeks so that others would rush there to stake claims, leaving the paying creek to the discoverers. But there was nothing remotely fake about Williams Creek. It would prove to be one of the richest creeks of all time and, for a few, the Eldorado they sought.

When we arrived at Williams Creek, it was a storm of human activity in the middle of an indifferent wilderness. Several thousand men worked along a mile or so of creek and only a close look would show the order that was in it. The creek itself was no longer recognizable as a creek, diverted as it was in so many places by ditches, channels, wing dams, and wooden flumes with rickety supports. The forest on the surrounding hillsides had been reduced to stumps, yet most of the trees were still there, resurrected as houses, stores, restaurants, hotels, saloons, grog shops, sidewalks, sluices and flumes.

One of the most persistent myths of Cariboo is that there were no women in those early days. There were a number of them, mostly wives, including Sophia Cameron. Then there were the prostitutes. My God, but those women were a vile lot. Most of them dressed like men and emulated our worst habits of cursing, smoking, chewing tobacco, spitting, and drinking more whiskey than any decent person ought to. But men need women and that is the way of the world, so their presence was tolerated.

While making the rounds selling candles, I met a Doc Crane—he wasn't a medical doctor, the title was only a nickname—who told me about an unclaimed stretch along Williams Creek. I immediately set up a company that included the Camerons, Alan McDonald, Dick Rivers, Charles and James Clendenning and myself. Everything was in place and all that was left to do was stake the claim. But, unbelievably, Cameron refused. It was Friday, and Fridays were unlucky. He would not make a move till Saturday.

Cameron's superstition tried my patience. If we didn't move quickly, we might be unable to move at all. Yet, something held me back from asserting my position. Maybe it was those eyes that seemed to look right through a person. Whatever the reason, I acquiesced. Saturday it was. On August 25, in the Year of Our Lord 1862, we officially registered our claim. Since Cameron chose the spot, we named it after him.

We could barely contain our excitement because on that "unlucky" Friday, less than a half-mile up the creek, Billy Barker struck it rich. We moiled away what was left of the summer, encouraged by Barker's uncanny luck. But summer soon turned into the shortest fall I'd ever reckoned with and a heavy snowfall blanketed us by late September. The miners began disappearing in droves, heading down to Victoria for the winter, until there was only a smattering of us left.

We'd sunk a shaft that reached bedrock but found nothing. That completely demoralized the Clendennings, who left for Victoria. They refused to leave behind any money to help start a new shaft, which was a hardship because our expenses had been as high as $7,000 for a single week. We started one anyway, but each day that we toiled and came away empty-handed not only chipped away at our pocketbooks, it also eroded our pride and optimism. To make matters worse, typhoid, or "mountain fever" as we called it, found Williams Creek to be a pretty good place to stake a claim too. We'd dug holes in the ground for toilets and when it rained or flooded, the waste seeped into our drinking water and poisoned some of us with that awful disease. We had no idea what we were doing to ourselves.

Sophia Cameron was having a devil of a time. Not long after her arrival on the creeks she went into labour prematurely and gave birth to a stillborn baby. Since there was no cemetery on Williams Creek, the baby was wrapped in a cloth, taken up the hillside, and buried in a shallow grave.

The Camerons were shattered. They had hoped the baby would help fill the void caused by losing Mary. The stubborn streak Cameron possessed was never more evident than in his determination to carry on. As for Sophia, it was simply more pain added to an already painful situation.

It might have been tolerable had she not hated Cariboo. The mountains penned her in like walls of a prison, and when dark, heavy clouds slid down the ravaged slopes to fill the valley, she thought she might suffocate. She longed for the broad sweep of the skies above Glengarry and Cornwall, the farms, and the great river that rolled by. Most of all, she longed for her family. Yet, through all her suffering, I never once heard her complain. She was usually first up in the morning and the last in bed at night, filling her day with preparing meals, cleaning up, fetching water from the creek, and doing laundry for almost any man on our claim who asked.

She deserved something far better than thankless menial chores, yet she conducted herself with grace in the face of adversities. Then one day, out of the blue, she voiced her first complaint. She said that she had a terrible headache and was feeling quite feverish. She took to her bed earlier than usual, and when she was not at her chores first thing in the morning, and was gasping from abdominal pain, we knew it was mountain fever.

Luckily, there was a doctor in Richfield. Cameron called on Dr. Wilkinson, who visited Sophia and performed the rituals known only to men of that profession. He prescribed some medicine and gave us directions as to how and when to administer it. From that point on, Cameron spent many of his waking hours tending to his wife. We set up an irregular schedule and took turns so that someone was with Sophia day and night. During that period the weather turned so brutally cold that the air felt brittle and the snow crunched under my feet like gravel.

One night as Cameron was relieving me, Sophia had one of her brief lucid moments and pleaded with him that if she died, he must promise not to leave her in that God-forsaken place. "It is not death I'm afraid of," she said hoarsely, the words nearly lost among the eerie sounds emitted by the cabin's logs as they contracted in the frigid weather. "My only fear is of spending eternity here among these wretched mountains. I know that what I ask may seem impossible, but I beg of you, John, please take me home."

The desperation in her voice was such that Cameron did not hesitate. He reached for her hand and clasped it between both of his. "I will do it," he said, his voice cracking. "If it's my last earthly act, I will do it. As God is my witness, I will take you home. You have my word on it."

How Cameron was able to contain himself, I cannot say, but I believe that if there were a power that would have allowed him to exchange places with her, he would not have delayed a moment. I could see a slight trembling in his shoulders as he reached for a cloth, and also in the hand that began to wipe Sophia's brow.

On the night Sophia died the wind howled up Williams Creek like a wolf gone mad. The thermometer stood at 30 below zero. I had gone to their cabin about midnight, tramping through the deep snow, to relieve Cameron. It was cold inside, despite the wood fire we always kept blazing. That mattered little to Sophia; she was herself on fire. Soon after I arrived, her fever began to subside and her skin grew as pale as if her blood were leaking from her body. I felt her pulse and it was weak and slow. By three o'clock in the morning, her face had taken on a peaceful cast and her breathing grew shallow, so I awoke Cameron to say she was slipping away and that he should prepare himself for her departure.

He sat on the edge of the bed, a simple pallet on a platform, and took her hands in his. "They are so cold," he whispered, and in that instant, it seemed, life left her. He laid his head on her breast, grief spilling from his eyes, as if the entire world had been lost to him, which, in a sense, I suppose it had.

By daybreak, the storm had blown itself out. A thin band of light was slowly widening above the eastern ridges as I sought out a tinsmith and a carpenter. If Cameron was indeed going to return Sophia's remains to her childhood home, a specially adapted coffin would be needed. I called on Jim Griffin, a skilled carpenter, and Henry Lightfoot, an equally adept tinsmith, and had them make two coffins, one from tin that would fit inside another made from wood. Griffin and I placed Sophia in the metal casket ourselves. I folded a beautiful knitted shawl, one that was a gift from her mother, and placed it under her head as a pillow, then stuffed some old clothing around her so that she would not be battered on the rough trip that awaited her. Lightfoot sealed the tin case shut and Griffin nailed the wooden lid on top.

The funeral service was held in the small chapel in Richfield and of the 90 miners and the handful of women who had stayed in camp that winter, all attended. Afterward, her remains were placed in an empty, unheated cabin where the sub-zero temperatures would preserve her until it came time to move her to the coast. It was a long and difficult road she'd travelled to reach this far-off place, but she would soon be going home. Cameron had promised her, and he'd proven to be a man of his word.

We went back to work—there was nothing else we could do. Cameron worked feverishly. I knew his sorrow and kept pace with him, pushing myself to the outer limits of my abilities and energy until it seemed exhaustion was all I'd ever known. In those low moments, I despaired that we'd ever find anything.

December 22 dawned clear, with the air so cold it could scarcely be breathed. I met Dick Rivers and a hired hand named Bill Halpenny at the digging, and we set ourselves to another long day's toil. We got down to 22 feet, with Rivers at the bottom of the shaft filling the barrels with earth while Halpenny and I operated the windlass. Cameron, who was working another shaft, had just arrived on the scene when Dick hollered up that we should get down there at once. "The place," he exclaimed, "is yellow with gold!"

I lay down on the platform and peered into the depths just as Rivers held up a flat rock the size of a dinner plate. Even in the candlelight, the gold was as plain as ears on a mule. "We've done it, Stevenson! We've hit pay dirt, and even if the streak doesn't go beyond what I can see of it, we'll be rich men!"

We gripped each other by the arms, and swung about in a half-circle that from a distance must have looked like a strange dance, which I suppose it was—the dance of two men who dreamed a dream and lived it. Or perhaps it was the dance of two men who didn't quite know the right steps, for Cameron's eyes spoke of what I felt: that while we had achieved something great, it would always be incomplete without the one person we needed to share it with the most.

Over the ensuing days we sank the shaft down to bedrock at 38 feet and found gold every inch of the way. Williams Creek had just yielded what would ultimately prove to be its richest pay streak ever. And as we worked the days away, a question weighed as heavy as gold on our hearts: how might things have turned out had this discovery been made sooner? The answer was too painful to contemplate.

Cameron was anxious to get Sophia's remains to the coast. Not only could he afford it now, but he needed to beat the spring thaw so that she would stay preserved. He put out an offer in the camp, stating that he would pay any man $12 a day, with a bonus of $2,000, for help in transporting the coffin, but no one took him up on his offer. Smallpox lay in ambush all the way to Victoria and the miners feared for their lives.

Cameron came to me in a quandary. He told me of the men's fears, adding that he didn't blame them. Hardly a day went by that we didn't hear of somebody being stricken with that terrible disease. I immediately offered my services. He refused, protesting, "You have never had the smallpox and I would not forgive myself if you caught it."

"That's a risk I'm willing to take," I said, and when he objected on the grounds that we needed someone to run the claim, I suggested a mutual friend we both trusted. Cameron hesitated, then he locked his eyes on mine and sighed. "Well, if you will go, Stevenson, I would rather have you than any man in Cariboo."

Well before daylight on January 31, 1863, we pulled a sled to the door of the cabin that held Sophia's remains. Our breath puffed out as ice clouds in the still morning air that felt as fragile as crystal. We had to lean our shoulders into the door because it had frozen shut. It suddenly sprang open and scraped over the rough plank floor with a sound that might have wakened the dead. The coffin sat forlornly in the gloom and Cameron paused beside it, a gloved hand resting on top. I gave him a moment, then together we carried it outside, placed it on the sled and covered it with a canvas tarpaulin before securing it with ropes. Then we eased the awkward load down the short slope to the flat road bisecting the town. From Cameron's cabin we fetched the gold poke, a two-gallon keg of Hudson's Bay rum, several blankets, sundry supplies that included an axe and as much grub as we could manage, and lashed it all on the top of the coffin. Lastly, we attached a long lead rope to the front. Altogether, it was a preposterously top-heavy load, for the sled's runners were only 14 inches apart. Yet somehow we had to haul that cumbersome thing several hundred miles through the mountains to the coast.

The first obstacle was right at our front door: a mountain of no small size. Cameron and I could not get that load up there by ourselves, but several of the miners had offered to help us get at least as far as Tom Maloney's roadhouse, in a small valley below Bald Mountain. A few others said they would go as far as Beaver Lake. That was where the smallpox was waging war against the Indians.

We all wore snowshoes, for there were two feet of freshly fallen snow on top of six feet of old, compacted snow. The going was tough, and stretching up before us was the mountain, the lower reaches stripped of trees, the upper thickly forested.

We zigzagged up the steep slope along a switchback trail that was barely visible, 26 of us pulling on the long rope attached to the sled. Several times the load tipped over and slid down to the last traverse and we'd have to start again. Finally, we stationed men on the sides and behind and with considerable effort and perseverance, reached the trees where the snow wasn't as deep. As the trail rose along the mountainside it became more difficult to follow, and higher up it petered out altogether. By noon we had managed to cover only a scant three and a half miles and it became evident that if we did not pick up our pace we would be unlikely to reach the safety and shelter of Maloney's roadhouse. The higher we climbed the colder it got, and by the time we crossed a ridge the temperature had fallen to 25 below. The sky was leaden, and the wind moaned in the branches overhead. Without a trail to follow, or the sun to offer direction, some of the men became disoriented. I had been appointed leader and guide, though, and felt certain I knew where we were. I bore off to the left amongst the dense green timber until we came to a winding, snow-smothered notch that I knew had to be Grouse Creek. Everyone worried that I was leading us deeper into the maze of the forest from which there'd be no escape. Night fell and the wind pummelled us and piled the snow up like ocean waves. At last we broke out of the trees into an open flat and saw through the blowing snow the flicker of light from the windows of Tom Maloney's house. We arrived exhausted and staggering, our enormous expenditure of energy having brought us a mere eight miles.

We passed the night in comparative luxury, bodies scattered about the floor. The next morning we awoke to the sound of the wind, still blowing a gale, while the temperature had sunk to 35 below. The entire flat around Maloney's was piled high with great drifts of snow, and the cabin itself was nearly buried. Fourteen of the miners turned back for Richfield with our profuse thanks. The rest of us struck out through the dry, loose snow to see what further hardship we could inflict upon ourselves.

Our mufflers were wound around our heads so that only our eyes were exposed. The wind blew powdery snow from the drift crests like spindrift on a stormy sea. It was as if some great angry giant was pelting us with sand. The snow contained so little moisture that it wouldn't support our weight. With much sweat and strain we soon were away from the open flat and among the trees. Conditions improved slightly, but we still had to deal with that confounded sled. Every little slant on our path threatened to upset it and usually did. Then we'd heave it upright again—all 500 pounds of it. We moved at a snail's pace up over a barren, windswept plateau where the world turned so white from blowing snow it was as if the very heavens had descended upon us, though God himself seemed far away. The trees on the far slope were a welcome refuge in which to make camp for the night.

We came upon a great lichen-covered rock with level ground on its lee side. While I knocked as much snow as I could from the limbs of the trees overhead, so that it wouldn't melt and fall on top of our fire, others gathered wood and cut boughs for mattresses. Using our snowshoes as shovels, we dug our campsite out of the deep snow, building a rampart around the edge for an added windbreak. We got a good fire blazing and set up a watch schedule to keep it that way. Then exhaustion overtook us, the men nodding off one by one, their snores mixing with the crackling fire. That night Cameron hung his spirit thermometer from a nearby tree and in the morning it registered 50 below.

The days piled on top of each other as we reached the Swift River and left it behind, turning south over a ridge toward Snowshoe Creek that would eventually lead us to Davis' Crossing on Keithley Creek. As we climbed, the snow lay deeper and every step forward was a battle won. It was along that God-forsaken stretch that our food ran out.

There was little we could do but press on and ignore the hunger pangs. Still, we had one important consolation: the two-gallon keg of rum lashed to the top of the coffin. Its contents wouldn't fill our bellies but it would give us the luxury of forgetting our hunger, if only for a brief time.

We were working our way along the rim of a steep embankment when the sled toppled over like a shot deer. It went skidding down the slope a short way until it dug in and stopped, but the ropes holding the keg snapped like old twine. We scrambled to grab it but were too late and watched in horror as it careered down the long incline and struck a tree. The bung popped out and the precious liquid gushed into the snow. Cameron and I fairly tumbled down the slope to salvage a cup or two, but our efforts were in vain. In the time it took us to reach it, the keg had emptied completely.

Cameron cursed our luck as we scrambled back up the slippery slope to the sled. By the time we got it righted and back on track, a few more of us were cursing too. Then we discovered that all of our matches had somehow been soaked and rendered useless. If our situation was desperate before, it had suddenly become deadly.

A heatless, dying sun was skirting the tops of the trees, and the forest was suffused with a combination of long shadows and pink-tinged light. The bone-numbing wind had so far not returned, and the forest was as silent as a mausoleum. We stopped to consider our options. A labyrinthine forest engulfed us and provided not a single hint of a trail. There was some confusion as to where we were. Since we'd been moving with the sun to our right, I reckoned we had to be somewhere between the Swift River and Snowshoe Creek. If my estimate was correct, we were probably about six or seven miles from Davis' Crossing. In order to survive this journey, we needed to find the roadhouse there as quickly as possible. After some discussion, we concluded that one man with a good sense of direction should go ahead, unencumbered, to find the roadhouse and thus establish a trail that the rest could follow. When I asked who would do this, not a single one of my companions volunteered. To a man, they were afraid they'd get lost, and in doing so place all our lives in jeopardy. They were, however, not without an alternative, and turned their eyes toward me.

"You could find it," they said.

It ruffled me that they would place such an onerous responsibility upon my youthful shoulders. I was reasonably sure that I knew where we were, but it was only instinct and not absolute knowledge. Dr. Wilkinson, who had been with us from the start, and Cameron took me aside.

"You must go," they pleaded. "You are our best bet."

Such was the desperation in their eyes that I did not dare refuse. It was my youth and stamina that was needed, along with what they believed was an unerring sense of direction.

"Will you go?" Cameron asked, and I replied with much more confidence than I felt, "Yes, and I'll find it too. You needn't worry. I won't make the least mistake."

Never a man to mince words, Dr. Wilkinson said bluntly, "If you do, we are all dead men."

I paced myself to conserve energy, keeping the red ball of the sinking sun on my right shoulder. Soon, even the twilight faded and I trudged on under a ghostly light cast by a gibbous moon on the mantle of snow. Then I came upon a wide cut in the trees and sensed a vague familiarity about it, even in the gloom. I had passed this way before in better times. It must be, it had to be, the headwaters of Snowshoe Creek, and that meant I hadn't much farther to go.

I descended down the frozen, twisting channel, my confidence waxing and waning with the rounding of each bend. The soft contours of the pale snow hid the sharp angles of boulders and deadfalls, and glimmering stars lit the heavens. Despite my precarious situation it seemed a lovely place. I reached a larger stream that I knew for certain was Keithley Creek, and soon, like a miracle, there was a faint smell of woodsmoke in the air. Minutes later I was banging on the door of the roadhouse at Davis' Crossing.

The old German greeted me with much surprise that someone would be arriving at his door at so late an hour in the dead of winter. A log fire blazed on the hearth and the room felt uncomfortably warm. My story, since time was crucial, spilled past my lips rather quickly. The old man insisted that I eat something, then he loaded me up with bread, meat and matches. He saw me out the door into the frozen night, and I headed back through the slit in the forest wall to find my companions.

Cold is a seductress. She seems to promise sleep and warmth, but it is only death in an alluring disguise. Luckily, no such fate had befallen any of our party and we met up about two miles from the roadhouse. They were practically crawling along, barely able to discern my tracks well enough to follow them. Concerned only for their survival, they had abandoned the coffin soon after we'd parted company, and were travelling light, one man carrying the blankets and another the gold. Never had I known a group of men so glad to see me. They crowded around and Cameron grabbed my hand.

"God bless you, Stevenson," he exulted.

While I got a fire going, the others wolfed down some of the food. We spent a restful night in that brutally cold wilderness, grateful to be alive, and at daybreak, went back for the coffin.

The following morning, we descended to the mouth of Keithley Creek, where there was a small store and a house. We bade farewell to eight more men. French Joe and Indian Jim elected to stay on and help until the danger of smallpox was imminent.

From Keithley Creek there was a well-established trail to Quesnelle Forks, and the going was much easier. We pushed and pulled the sled, righting it every time it fell over, for a dozen miles until at last we were dropping down the winding, precarious hill into the Forks.

When we left the following morning, we struck out for Beaver Lake, some 15 miles to the south, and arrived there after the supper hour. We had been on the trail 11 days, yet we had covered only 72 miles. But we were moving faster now, over better roads, which was a good thing, for French Joe and Indian Jim had reached the end of the trail. In the morning, they would return to Richfield. Meanwhile, the weather remained frigid, with overnight temperatures between 40 and 50 below.

Beaver Lake was a white field of death. The area undulated with small mounds, all snow graves. Smallpox had struck the local Indian tribe and wiped out every man, woman and child, except for one bewildered old man. Altogether, I counted 90 graves, but there may have been more.

Cameron dug into the gold poke and bought a sturdy mare and a harness rig for $300. We hitched the sled to the animal and set off. Down through Deep Creek and Williams Lake the snow wasn't much more than a couple of feet deep, not counting the drifts; nevertheless, the horse struggled with the load, which kept digging in and upsetting. There were signs of smallpox everywhere. Small Indian villages devastated by the disease were eerily characterized by the ubiquitous hummocks of snow. At Williams Lake I counted 120, and found only three Indians alive. They were a sorry-looking lot, as silent as the graves they stood beside.

The road was much improved, but it was still a hard grind, descending into deep hollows and rising up killing grades. Given the slightest excuse the sled would tip over and was the scourge of our existence. There was evidence of smallpox all the way down the road, so much that I gave up counting the snow graves. With surprising ease we took the long hill down into 100 Mile House and continued on, passing roadhouses every 10 to 15 miles. The road then made a long and gradual ascent to a rolling tableland.

The horse began to struggle with the weight of the load and slowed down alarmingly, steam rising from her rump. Near 70 Mile House, she refused to move another step. No amount of coaxing would budge her. Suddenly she collapsed to her knees, paused for a moment, then fell over onto the snow. She lay there panting. Then her eyes rolled back in her head and she died. Cameron and I undid the harness and shafts and got between them ourselves, but we made a poor pair of draft animals. Between the two of us, we had nowhere near the strength of a single horse. Fortunately, the last stretch of road was downhill and we made the next roadhouse before almost falling over dead ourselves. Cameron wasted no time in opening the poke to buy another horse, this time a rather ragged-looking chestnut stallion.

From 70 Mile House the road tended to descend. Soon, even the Great Chasm was at our backs. We reached 47 Mile House with relative ease. Beyond the house the road turned southwest and remained fairly level for several miles as it ran along the floor of Cut-Off Valley and past a frozen lake. From there we could see it snaking toward the top of Pavilion Mountain. It looked so much like a serpent as it wound its way in six sweeping turns up the flank of the mountain that it had been named "Rattlesnake Grade." Here and there, it stuck out over the appallingly steep mountainside on platforms supported by a cribwork of wooden beams. The ease of travel we'd been enjoying for several miles had come to a decidedly abrupt end.

As we began our ascent up that slippery, narrow trail, my one fervent wish was for a railing to prevent us from plummeting to our deaths. But there was nothing except empty space, so we hugged the mountainside. A light, grainy snow began to fall while a variable wind picked up and blew the flakes helter-skelter. Thank God the visibility remained fair. Cameron and I took turns leading the horse, while the other pushed the sled from behind and tried to keep it from tumbling over the edge. Looking down in places made my stomach flutter. Our snowshoes proved useless on the hard-packed snow so we removed them. Still, I lost track of the times our feet skidded out from under us and we fell flat on our faces. The horse strained up the grade with the heavy load, far more sure-footed than either Cameron or I, but with great difficulty. Every step up that long, steep road was a contest between ourselves and the mountain. When we reached the top all three of us were about done in.

Our altitude gain must have been at least 2,000 feet, with the mountaintop well over 5,000 feet above sea level. Even with the weather conditions, the view was panoramic. Before us, the road began a modest descent to a flat, snow-covered expanse that sloped away to our right for some distance before falling off rather dramatically toward the Fraser River. It was as if the gods had taken pity on us for our recent exhausting toil and were rewarding us with easy travel for the time being. The wind was strong and bitter but it was on our backs, and we set a good pace to a roadhouse about four miles from the Rattlesnake Grade.

We were now only 29 miles from Lillooet, but from where we were on that plateau, surrounded by snow-covered mountain peaks, it might have been a million. I've never been one to complain, but on that night I was grateful a roadhouse existed in such a lonely place, that a cheery fire crackled in its fireplace, and that we were sheltered from the arctic wind that howled unhindered across the mountaintop.

Still, I found the utter isolation of that spot, so high above everything else, strangely unsettling. As weary as I felt, I looked forward to the morning, when we could leave that desolation behind. Our host sensed my impatience and suggested that I not be so eager. Some of those 29 miles to Lillooet, he assured me, might very well have me wishing I hadn't left the sanctuary of his roadhouse.

The grey light of the morning saw us some three miles across the flat top of the mountain to the perilous trail that zigzagged down to the valley floor 1,500 feet below. This trail was much steeper than the Rattlesnake Grade, and both Cameron and I thanked our lucky stars that we weren't travelling in the opposite direction with his wife's coffin. We might not have made it up that grade with two horses, let alone one. Still, going down provided its own set of challenges. We had to be extremely careful, lest we found ourselves taking a much faster route to the bottom than we would have liked. The owner of the roadhouse had told us that wagon-masters negotiating the downgrade in the summertime would drag heavy logs behind their rigs, like sea anchors, to act as brakes.

At the top of the hill there was a pile of logs awaiting the wagons in the spring. We selected a small one and tied it to the sled, then with some trepidation started down the three-mile slope, the pitch so steep in places that we seemed in constant danger of losing everything over the side, including ourselves. On the hairpin curves we looped a rope around the rear stanchions of the runners and eased the sled around the corner by pulling it in toward the mountainside. The blunt end of the log kept digging into the snow, working as a brake, and kept the sled from getting away on us. It was excruciatingly difficult work and the tension on our backs, particularly on the backs of our legs, was punishing. We panted and groaned down that grade for a dog's age before we got to the bottom. By that time my legs were trembling from fatigue. Cameron looked completely worn out but voiced not a single complaint.

Much of the rest of the day slipped by in a fog, and just as the sky was giving up to darkness, we came to a roadhouse high above the Fraser River and some 15 miles from Lillooet. By that time, neither man nor beast was fit for another inch of travel.

As we prepared for our departure the next morning we found

consolation in the fact that Pavilion Mountain was a good distance behind us and a small town with decent food and drink was not far ahead. The road down the Fraser was in good shape so we pushed hard, hoping to reach Lillooet before nightfall. Following the course of the river, the road rose and fell in waves as it wound in great looping turns among the folds of the sagebrush-covered hillsides. The closer we got to Lillooet the more forested the hillsides became, while the rocky outcrops gleamed red in the light of a welcome sun.

The horse grew winded, but we forced him on and by suppertime were moving gingerly down a long switchback to the river's edge. A winch ferry sat there, as if waiting expressly for us, and we rode the current across the narrow channel to the far side. Climbing up the opposite bank to the terrace upon which Lillooet sat was a Herculean struggle for the horse, but we thrashed his rump with a stripped branch. Somehow, the poor beast made it to the top. I said a silent prayer of thanks that the day's journey was nearly at an end.

If the spectre of smallpox hanging over it was disregarded, Lillooet was an oasis in a desert of snow. The main street was wide enough to turn a team of oxen around in, and, even better, it was smooth and level. There were more than a dozen saloons, but we managed to find a livery stable among them and put the horse up for the night. We took rooms at the Stage Hotel and were late for supper, but the cook took pity on us and warmed up leftover potatoes, salted ham, biscuits and gravy that we washed down with scalding coffee. Then, for the first time on our journey, we slept in a proper bed.

Lest it be thought that the roadhouses we'd stopped at were as respectable as the Stage Hotel, let me dispel that notion right now. They were hovels—usually single-roomed log cabins with a fireplace at one end and a countertop at the other—that offered little more than a place out of the wind and rain in summer, and a modest opportunity to reduce the risk of frostbite in winter. And I never stayed in one that wasn't also inhabited by a large population of lice and bedbugs. In fact, the miners often held racing competitions with the vermin; they were placed on plates and the first to reach the far side was the winner. Few miners would disagree with me when I say that in the beginning, the only thing remotely comforting in those houses was the liquor. After a hard day's slog on the trail, it would send a most joyous flood of warmth and well-being through your entire body.

At the livery stable in the morning, the owner informed us that our horse was not likely to survive the day. That news held no surprise. We opened up the gold poke and bought another, for the one thing we could not do without was a horse. The stable owner assured us the animal was a fine one. He charged us accordingly.

We set off before first light in deep snow. It was only a few miles to Seton Lake, which was covered in places by a thin, watery layer of ice, though not enough to stop the small paddlewheeler that plied its length. It bore us down the lake between steep mountains that plunged straight into the green depths. At the far end, a small tram on wooden rails carried us and our cargo over a short portage connecting Seton with Anderson Lake, and we were soon steaming down the dark waters against a light chop. The vessel moved slowly, taking three hours to run the 16-mile length of the lake.

We stayed that night at a roadhouse run by a loquacious Frenchman who charged us two dollars each for our meals and beds and a dollar for livery for the horse. This was expensive, but he kept a clean establishment and for that we were grateful. We each enjoyed a jug of mulled wine to celebrate the easiest day of travel we had had so far, then turned in.

There was much less snow on the ground from that point on and the air temperature was substantially warmer. Neither of these improvements, however, did anything to prevent the sled from pitching onto its side at the slightest provocation. It was a long, tough pull amongst the thickly forested mountains and over some pretty rugged terrain that more than made up for the ease of the previous days travel. By late afternoon, we caught a glimpse of woodsmoke rising from Ketterel's Halfway House.

Compared to the roadhouses north of Lillooet, places like Ketterel's were relatively luxurious, providing good food, good drink and comfortable beds. After a good night's sleep, we were off early and moved quickly through to Pemberton, the last few miles being flat as a billiard table. Peter Smith's roadhouse at Pemberton was a fine establishment and, like Ketterel's, was an indication of how accommodations along this route were changing for the better. At the roadhouse there was a man who had just finished digging a coal pit for Smith. His name was Jim Cummings, and though he'd spent the summer on Williams Creek, we hadn't met before. Cameron asked him about the road to Port Douglas. It was in reasonably good shape, Cummings said, adding that he was about to embark upon it himself come the morning. Cameron thought that an extra hand wouldn't hurt our circumstances and suggested we travel together. Cummings eagerly agreed.

In the morning, we hauled the sled down to the steamboat landing on Lillooet Lake and boarded the *Prince of Wales*, which took us down to the Douglas Portage. Once we got onto it, the road was accommodatingly wide and in better shape than we'd expected. We made good time until the afternoon, when conditions worsened and the surface hardened with ice. We slipped and staggered down the treacherous track, Cameron using his axe to cut stakes that he used at the side of the sled to prevent it from sliding off the shoulder. While I led the horse, Cummings helped Cameron, but in places, our progress was painstakingly slow. Several times the stakes proved useless and the sled went off the road anyway. But we'd seen it turn turtle so many times by then that it had long ceased to bother us. Cummings hadn't, though. Finally, he suggested that he carry the gold on his back to make the load less top-heavy. We quickly agreed. From then on, there were fewer problems trying to keep the sled upright.

We reached 20 Mile House and whiled away the evening soothing our weary muscles in the mineral hot springs over which a part of the house was built. The next day, we pushed on to Port Douglas at the top end of Harrison Lake, and got there before daylight was spent. We'd come to the end of the overland part of out journey, which might have been good cause for celebration had it not been for the horrific sight that greeted our eyes as we entered the community.

Both sides of the road were lined with tents, and the door flaps were turned back far enough to allow us a glimpse of their occupants. We saw Indians in just about every stage of smallpox that could be imagined, some so far gone their skin had turned black. The stink of the dead and the dying hung in the air like dust on a windless day, so thick it seemed to embrace us. We hurried by, fearing the air itself was poisoned, hiding our faces in the crooks of our arms so that we wouldn't have to breathe it.

We were now less than a hundred miles from New Westminster, all of which could be travelled by boat. The next morning, for the last time, we hitched the sled to the horse and made our way to the small paddlewheeler *Henrietta*, tied up at the lake's edge. We left the horse under the care of the roadhouse owner, and gave him the sled as a gift. Then we hoisted the coffin on rope slings strung between poles and carried it on board. When the whistle blew and the vessel eased away from the landing, I could scarcely believe our travail was all but over.

The journey down Harrison Lake was pleasant. We had an ample supply of Hudson's Bay brandy to pass the time. The next day's end saw us offloading our cargo on the pier at New Westminster, notable only for its lack of snow.

The steamer *Enterprise* departed at first light the following day, and we were happily aboard it, our precious cargo under canvas and lashed securely to the foredeck. The weather was turning sour just as we rounded Ogden Point, too late to cause us any grief, and the coffin was soon being winched onto a wet and windswept Hudson's Bay wharf in Victoria harbour. It was March 6, nearly five weeks after we'd left Williams Creek.

We went straight away to the Royal Hotel, where the Wilcoxes greeted us as if we were family. Sophia's coffin was stored for the night in the same back room her daughter had occupied almost exactly a year ago. This had a visible effect on Cameron, yet he said nothing.

Before calling it a night, Cameron and I walked up to the Boomerang for a hot whiskey. Victoria had changed remarkably. Most notable were the new brick buildings and the gas lamps lighting some of the streets. There was no less mud, but the boardwalks and crosswalks were more plentiful and in better condition. More numerous, too, were the faces we saw pitted by smallpox.

Richard Lewis was the undertaker who had attended to Mary, so our first order of business in the morning was to visit his premises. Though Sophia's body was still in a frozen state, it wouldn't remain that way for very long. If Cameron was to fulfill his promise, her body needed somehow to be preserved so that it could be transported through the hot tropical climate of Panama and the Caribbean. Mr. Lewis had the perfect solution. Alcohol, he said, would do the job, but it had to be at least 95 proof, and at least 25 gallons would be required. Cameron instructed Lewis to do whatever was necessary to see the job through.

Just before noon, the undertaker's wagon pulled up in front of the hotel. He had with him a large keg of alcohol and a tinsmith, a lanky man in ill-fitting clothes wearing a bowler hat and sporting an enormous moustache. Together we moved the keg to the room containing Sophia's remains. The wooden lid was carefully removed and the tradesman cut a small hole through the top of the sealed tin coffin. Over the next two and a half hours, Lewis carefully poured the alcohol through the opening, until it bubbled over the top. With a rag, he mopped up the excess liquid and had the tinsmith seal the hole. We could do nothing more but wait for the funeral.

Meanwhile, Cameron and I had become celebrities around town. News of our huge gold strike had preceded our arrival and it seemed everyone was eager to catch a glimpse of us, so that they could tell their friends. And speaking of friends, we discovered we had more than we had ever known about, and many people scrambled to win our favour. An indication of our new-found popularity was the size of Sophia's funeral cortege on Sunday, which was not surpassed in that century until they buried Sir James Douglas in 1877. Then there was the amount of space devoted to Sophia in the *British Colonist* on Monday. She had gone from relative obscurity to the limelight simply by being the dead wife of a rich man.

Postscript: *Sophia Cameron's preserved remains were buried in Victoria. Cameron then returned to the Cariboo to work his claim. Months later, he had Sophia's and Mary's coffins exhumed and took them by boat, via Panama and New York, back to Glengarry, thus fulfilling his promise to his beloved wife: he had taken Sophia home.*

Cataline, Camels, and the Cariboo Road

from *They call it the Cariboo*
by Robin Skelton

Indigenous Natives had refined their transportation system through the interior over thousands of years, figuring out the best places to go and the easiest ways to get there, but newcomers had to reinvent the wheel, or at least the paths on which their wheels could travel. Robin Skelton became fascinated by the Cariboo–Chilcotin region in 1963 when he visited his uncle, Will Robins, a Caribooo settler since 1907. Skelton later spent summers travelling there, delving into its history to write They Call it the Cariboo. *In the following excerpt, Skelton explores some of the transportation problem-solving that went on. As a writer, editor, teacher, historian, biographer, art and literary critic, initiated witch and occultist, Skelton became a major force in shaping the literature and thought of British Columbia. He taught at the University of Victoria for almost 30 years, founding the Creative Writing department, and he co-founded* The Malahat Review, *one of Canada's most respected literary journals, editing it until 1982. He was a fellow of the Royal Society of Literature, and a chairman of the Writers' Union of Canada. Skelton died in 1997.*

Jean Caux, or "Cataline" (top), was a Spaniard from Catalonia and the Cariboo's most famous packer. Frank Laumeister was a partner in the ill-fated "Dromedary Express."

The great Cariboo Road of the 1860s bore little resemblance to the highways of today [1980]. At 18 feet, it was wide enough for wagon trains to pass each other, and could accommodate cattle drives of considerable size. It was, however, stony, dusty, muddy, pitted with holes, and constantly subject to slides, washouts, and other hazards. During the summer the dust was ferocious; cattle drives in particular would raise such a huge sand-brown choking cloud that citizens in Clinton would rush to close all doors and windows when the cattle were going through, and the houses did not have the conventional front porches but rather balconies above the dust level.

Moreover, because the road had to be made quickly, it did not always take the most direct route. Rather than cut slowly and laboriously through hills, [road builder Gustavus Blin] Wright took the road over them; rather than face the problems of a bridge, he would detour the road. Much of the territory was swampy and the road had to be built up, usually on a bed of logs laid side by side like the ribs in corduroy; often the rains would wash away the topsoil and gravel, and the road would be worn down to the logs themselves. The bumps on the roads and the rocky surface so belaboured the iron rims of the wagons that they expanded with the heat, and mechanical tire shrinkers had to be provided at stopping places. Each wagon train took care to carry a jack to ease the wagons out of mudholes. The gradients were so steep and the wagons so heavy and cumbersome that each train had to be hauled by a team of oxen, horses, or (sometimes) mules, ranging from 6 to 10 or even 12 in number.

Blacksmiths were needed at each stopping place to repair broken chains, to reshoe horses, and even, on occasions, reweld axles. There was no way of controlling each animal in a train by means of an individual rein, all reins being gathered together in the two hands of the driver, and cleanly separated from each other as with stagecoach driving. Therefore, highly trained lead animals were used on a single "jerk line" which could signal instructions by the number of jerks given. These animals were extraordinarily adept, could step over their own chains at sharp corners to keep the wagon on the road, and could even lead the team right off the road at sharp bends, so as to keep the wagon from rolling over the outside of the curve.

The wagon trains, hauled by either oxen or horses, were not the only traffic on the new road. Ever since the gold rush began, mule trains had packed in provisions over the trails, and the most famous of these packers was Jean Caux, or "Cataline." He had begun as a packer on the fur-brigade trails, and then turned to serving the goldfields, taking a train of 16 to 48 mules first along the rough trails and then along the road. It took him a month to reach the goldfields from Yale and he packed anything and everything from mine machinery to champagne, from crates of chickens to millinery. Cataline was a short, broad-shouldered man, bearded, with shoulder-length hair. To establish his position he wore a starched white shirt, always, and it is said that his crew never contained any white men, but Chinese, Indians, Mexicans, and Negroes. He himself was a Spaniard from Catalonia. The mule train was led by a white bell mare, each animal walking free, not linked to any other in case one animal falling might bring down others over the precipices or into the swamps. A leading mule would be ridden or accompanied by the cook so that he would arrive first at the stopping place for the day and be able to prepare the meal for the cargo packers, one to every eight beasts, while the long, single-file train came in and the mules, each carrying between 250 and 400 pounds of freight, were being unloaded. Cataline was famous for always sleeping in the open, wrapped up in a blanket, even when there was snow on the ground. He drank rum (or cognac), which he also rubbed into his hair, saying "a little inside and a little outside." He marked the conclusion of each trip by taking off his shirt, hanging it on a handy fence post, and buying a new one for the return journey. Twice during his career his mule train was almost destroyed by a series of accidents but, intent upon keeping to his packing contract, he hired Indian women who back-packed the loads to the end of the trail. The coming of the wagon road took much of Cataline's custom away from him, but he continued for a while and then moved up to the northern part of the country, packing in Northwestern British Columbia and was well known in Quesnel until he retired in 1913. He died in Hazelton in 1922, at the age of 80 (or 93).

Cataline was not the only packer on the road. Frank Way, who also owned a stopping station on Deep Creek, packed as well, as did "Redhead" Davis, and there were a number of others. The most memorable packing venture of all perhaps was that organized by John C. Callbreath (or Calbreath) of Lillooet, who had partnered Gus Wright in the building of the Lillooet-Clinton road. Considering that mules could only carry 250 to 400 pounds and needed frequent stopping places for watering, someone had come up with the splendid notion that camels would be a superior packing animal. Callbreath, acting as agent for the syndicate of Frank Laumeister, Adam Haffy (or Hefley), and Henry Ingram, bought 23 Bactrian camels in San Francisco for $300 each. The camels had been used as pack animals by the United States Army in Texas and in the desert country of lower California. These camels could, the syndicate was assured, carry 800 pounds each, go for days without food or water, and travel 30 or 40 miles a day. The partners estimated that they'd take in about $60,000 the first year, netting them a handsome profit in the region of $50,000 even when the cost of getting the camels to the Cariboo had been deducted. Unfortunately, Laumeister and his friends had not studied the habits of the camel closely enough; they were unaware that camels are highly odorous, extremely bad-tempered, and easily excited.

Frank Laumeister seems to have been the unfortunate who had charge of the actual operation. He accompanied them to Port Douglas on a barge towed by the *Flying Dutchman* sternwheeler. As they disembarked, the camels began to show their true colours. One bit and kicked a prospector's mule and, in the following days it became clear that these camels were liable at whim to bite and kick anything that moved, including oxen, horses, and men. They could, it is true, carry immense burdens, but on the road their stench was such as to make other animals shy and bolt. On one occasion as Judge Begbie was conducting a trial on horseback and in the open air on one of his periodic journeys through Cariboo, the camel train came by and his horse bolted, as did the horses of the other members of the court, carrying them all off into the bush. It is not recorded what happened to the prisoner.

For a time Laumeister tried to solve the problem by deodorizing his camels, a task which might make even Proctor and Gamble blench, but the scented water he used was ineffective. He also discovered that the camels' hoofs, while perfectly adapted for kicking, were not adapted to the jagged rocks of the Cariboo roads and trails. With a stubbornness, and an ingenuity, that does him credit, Laumeister fitted his camels with canvas and rawhide shoes, which did afford the animals some protection, but which soon wore out. By the end of the 1863 season the misnamed "Dromedary Express" was highly unpopular with everybody, including, one may deduce, Laumeister, Haffy and Ingram. Owners of other pack trains were grumbling loudly and talking of suing Laumeister for damages. In 1864 Laumeister abandoned the project and turned the animals loose, either on the flats near Cache Creek or in the San Jose Valley near Lac La Hache, it is not certain which, and there they eventually died. Before they were all gone, however, Mark S. Wade tells us [in *The Cariboo Road*, p. 81] that "the proprietors of the hotel and store at 150-Mile House tried an experiment. It was observed that though the camels failed in winter, the cold proving extremely trying to them, they became rolling fat in summer, and Adler and Barry of the '150' (they held it on rental only) decided to kill and dress one for its meat. This was done and it was exposed for sale but no one would buy it, and the venture fell through. Others of the camels were taken by Henry Ingram, one of the partners in their importation, to his ranch at Grand Prairie, about 40 miles distant from Kamloops, and in 1881 there were three females living. In the spring of 1892 there remained but one, so feeble that, falling down, it was unable to rise to its feet again and the owner mercifully had the helpless creature shot by an Indian named Nopia. Mrs. King, a daughter of the late Mr. Ingram, informs me that an attempt was made to tan the hide of this animal but it was not a success. Because of its thickness it was used as a floor rug."

Some of the camels wandered the territory for many years, bewildering and alarming those who occasionally glimpsed them.

One man, it is reported, shot one under the misapprehension that it was an outsized grizzly, and thereafter was called "Grizzly Morris." The camel shot by Nopia may not have been the last survivor, however, for there is a story that another one turned up unexpectedly at Grand Prairie some years later. It died in 1905.

Constable Sullivan caught up with the fleeing James Barry at the Suspension Bridge, 12 miles above Yale.

The Nugget Pin

from *The Cariboo Road*
by Mark S. Wade

An old manuscript discovered in a trunk in 1976 proves that
creative non-fiction was practised long before there was a fancy
name for it. Its author, Mark Sweeton Wade, might have called it
simply an entertaining way to spin a yarn. Medical doctor, police
magistrate and historian, Mark Wade was born in Durham,
England, in 1858 and received his medical training in California.
He set up his medical practice in central British Columbia at the
tail end of the gold rush, travelling by horseback to the bedsides
of the infirm, listening to their old-time stories of the Cariboo
Road as he patched and mended their hurts. A member of the
Royal Historical Society and the B.C. Historical Society, Wade
owned for a time the Inland Sentinel, *and used back issues of*
the newspaper to flesh out his manuscript, which was published
long after his death in 1929.

In the spring of 1866 there were many parties tramping on the Cariboo Road with the gold fields as their objective. One of these parties consisted of three individuals—Charles Morgan Blessing, Wellington Delaney Moses, and James Barry. Blessing was a Canadian from the Atlantic seaboard, a genial soul and physically a splendid specimen of manhood: he had come west with a party of axemen engaged for clearing the right of way for the Collins Overland Telegraph. Moses was a coloured barber, somewhat loquacious, and endowed with keen powers of observation and a well-developed natural shrewdness. The last of the trio, Barry, was an Irish-American, a man without means, anxious to reach Cariboo.

It was an oddly mixed trio. Barry had no money, and Blessing generously paid for his meals as well as his own at the wayside houses at which they stopped en route. The coloured barber paid his own way. He carried the tools of his trade along with him; they occupied but little space and did not add materially to the weight of his pack. So long as he kept his razors and scissors sharp his customers were not exacting. It was quite easy for Moses to earn his salt by barbering at the stopping places and small towns along the road. And thus they reached Quesnel.

At that town Wellington D. Moses found an abundance of clients and decided to remain there until he had scraped the last lip or chin. Blessing and Barry left him there and continued their journey of 60 miles to Barkerville.

"Don't wait for me, Mistuh Blessing! I'll see you in Barkerville in a few days," said Moses.

Notwithstanding the difference in colour, education, tastes and general attributes of the two men, Blessing and Moses had taken a genuine liking for one another. Blessing respected the sturdy independence of the coloured barber who would rather ply his trade to earn his meals than allow another to pay for them; and Moses admired the geniality and unbounded generosity of the big strapping Canadian.

Blessing had a fad, just as so many of us have, a harmless hobby. His was to have all his belongings that lent themselves to it marked with his initials. C.M.B. was stamped on his revolver; on his pocket knife and on his tin cup—that useful adjunct on a day's tramp. He wore good clothes, the usual outfit of the day, in good material: top boots, cashmere pantaloons and Hudson's Bay shirt. One ornament he particularly affected and took considerable pride in was a nugget scarf pin. The nugget had been mounted, just as it was mined, unspoiled by the jeweller, and, held in a certain position, was the perfect profile of a face. He wore it constantly and liked to have people take notice of it.

Every time Blessing produced his roll of bank notes to pay the current expenses of the day, Barry's eyes glittered with evil greed and his fingers itched to handle the money that was not his. His was an envious and covetous nature, and when he found himself the sole companion of his benefactor, he determined to possess himself of that ready cash. He dared not openly attack Blessing, for whose physical prowess he was no match. Besides, he was unarmed, while Blessing always carried a revolver and was adept in its use. Clearly, then, in order to take the money, he must first get the weapon in his own hands.

Day by day, as they plodded doggedly on, now drawing very near their goal, Barry formulated his plans. He must act quickly or the opportunity would be past. At length one day's tramp only lay between them and Barkerville. They reached a spot within a mile of Pine Grove and not more than 25 miles distant from the end of their long journey. There they decided to encamp for the night.

"Say, Blessing, let me have your gun for a minute," suggested Barry suddenly.

Without a word Blessing handed his companion the revolver and went on with the preparations of making camp. His back being towards Barry, he failed to see the evil gleam in the latter's eyes, and the quick steady aim. Barry pulled the trigger and Blessing pitched forward on his face with a big hole in the back of his head.

Moses found business quite brisk at Quesnel. He entertained his numerous clients with yarns of happenings at the "Coast," and incidents and gossip of the road. At the same time he picked up, along with the dollars he earned, scraps of local news which he treasured up among the material with which he would regale his customers at Barkerville. Day succeeded day and still the supply of clients was not exhausted. It was not until Blessing and Barry had been gone a full week that Moses packed up his kit and followed them along the road leading to the centre of Cariboo life and activity. The first few days following his arrival at Barkerville were occupied in finding a suitable location for his barbershop. After that he had time to look about him, but never for a moment did he forget his late fellow wayfarers; always he had an eye open for them, alert, eager again to exchange greetings with them and more particularly with Blessing. Not that he expected they would necessarily be in the town itself. They might be at Richfield, or Cameron Town, or Marysville, all camps along the creek, each within a mile of the other, or they might have rushed off to some new creek to locate claims. Then one day he encountered Barry, but a metamorphosed Barry, a well-dressed, prosperous-looking Barry, a man with money to spend in the indulgence of pleasure and whiskey.

"Hello, Barry!" exclaimed Moses, "what has become of our friend? I hoped to see him here."

"Oh, I don't know," replied Barry, indifferently, and as he did not seem disposed to pursue the subject any further, Moses forebore to question him but he thought it odd that Barry, who had so much cause to be grateful to Blessing, should show so scant interest in his present condition and whereabouts. He saw more of Barry after that and noticed that the former impoverished dependent seemed to have struck a streak of good fortune, and was a regular frequenter at the dance halls, where he was always effusively welcomed by the "hurdy gurdy" girls, a sure sign that he was a free spender of coin and dust.

The days passed into weeks, and one week rolled into another and still no sign of Blessing, nor could Moses learn anything of a man answering his description being in the vicinity. He attached no great importance to this, however, for men came and went by the score and no man knew whither they came nor who they were; each was too busy with himself and the ever-present desire for gold to worry much about his neighbour! Still, Blessing had taken to the coloured man, who treasured up in his memory a soft spot for his friend, and glad indeed would he have been to see again the pleasant smiling face and to feel the warm pressure of his friendly hand.

Among the many who were engaged in the transportation of supplies of every sort to the camps in Cariboo was Alex Burnett, whose shock of red hair stood sponsor for his more general appellation of "Red Alec." His pack animals were loaded for Barkerville and had almost reached it when the last night out, the men unloaded the packs for the final time that trip; then they would rest for a day before back trekking to Lillooet or Yale for another load. Pack animals wander a good deal, even though hobbled, and one of the first duties of a pack train crew in a morning is to gather them in. The morning after making this last camp, an Indian employed by Red Alec, in the course of hunting for the animals, noticed an overpoweringly offensive odour. His curiosity being aroused, he searched about to find the cause and soon located the body of a man, in an advanced stage of decomposition, among a clump of bushes. The face was disfigured by preying creatures of the wilds, but the clothing was intact. The Indian reported his discovery to Red Alec, who at once sent the man post haste to Barkerville to inform the authorities of the finding of the body. The news spread quickly all over the town and tongues were set wagging. "Who was the man, and how did he come to his death?" were questions asked on every hand. The barber, Moses, soon heard the news, and so did Barry.

The body was examined by the police, and there was found near by a tin cup with the initials C.M.B. stamped on the bottom; lying on the ground was a revolver and it, too, had the same initials marked upon it, as had also a knife found in the dead man's pocket.

"That is one of the men I came up with as far as Quesnel!" said the coloured barber, when these details reached him. To the police Moses described how Blessing had been dressed, and from the clothing and the articles above mentioned, he unhesitatingly identified the body as that of his erstwhile companion and friend, C.M. Blessing.

"There was another man with us, James Barry. The two of them left Quesnel together, and Barry is here in Barkerville," further declared Moses.

But so far as Barry's presence in Barkerville was concerned, Moses was wrong, for a search failed to reveal him. He was not to be found at any of his customary haunts, nor anywhere else in town, He had completely disappeared, since the day word had reached Barkerville of the finding of the body near Pine Grove.

"There is one thing missing—no, two things," said Moses. "Blessing had a fat roll of bank notes, and he wore a nugget scarf-pin that looks like a face."

Neither money nor nugget pin was to be found. The affair was the talk of the town and the road. Murder was suspected and discussed in bar rooms, in dance halls, in stores. The men spoke of it openly and loudly; the dance girls spoke of it in awed whispers.

"That's strange," confided one of the hurdy-gurdy girls to a friend, "Barry gave me a nugget pin that looks like a face!"

She produced the pin. There was no doubt about it; it was the very pin Blessing had been so vain of; there were not two pins like that in Cariboo. Suspicion fastened upon Barry. Where had he parted from Blessing, and how did he come to have in his possession the pin that he had bestowed upon a girl who had taken his fancy? But Barry was not there to answer these and many other questions that would have been asked him if Constable Sullivan could have laid his hands upon him. He was not in Barkerville, nor in any of the camps of Williams Creek.

Then new arrivals from points down the road brought the tidings that a man answering to the description given of Barry had been seen going down towards Yale on foot. Enquiry elicited the further fact that this man was seen only occasionally, and that he took shelter in the bush whenever travellers appeared, and that he did a good deal of his travelling at night. A few, however, wondered at seeing a man in his apparently prosperous condition hastening away from, instead of towards the land of gold at the season of the year when the human tide was set Cariboo-wards.

Sullivan required no further evidence to convince him that Barry was the man he wanted. Barry was the one man who could tell how Blessing had come to die, and who alone could also tell how he, who had been penniless upon the road, arrived at Barkerville with his pockets stuffed with ready money.

Determined to head Barry off, Sullivan took the first down stage. Barry would undoubtedly make for Yale and the Lower Fraser; he must eat to live and food was to be had along the Cariboo Road. Once at Yale he could board a steamer for New Westminster and soon get across the line into the United States. Sullivan made up his mind to prevent his reaching Yale unless he went along with him. As the stage travelled night and day the distance was speedily covered.

When the Suspension Bridge across the Fraser, 12 miles above Yale, was reached, Sullivan alighted. Being a toll bridge it was closed at night by a gate swung across the road. Within the great gate was a lesser one for the passage of foot passengers. Both were fastened at night and none could cross the bridge without the assistance of the toll-gate keeper. Sullivan told the keeper the main facts.

"Barry is headed this way," he said. "I feel sure he cannot have passed. I believe I am ahead of him."

"No man of that description," asserted the keeper, referring to Sullivan's description of the man wanted, "has crossed the bridge that I have seen."

"No; I'm sure of that; I must be ahead of him," agreed Sullivan. "He will come along any day now but he will not try to cross in daylight; he will wait until night. When he comes, do not open the gate. Make some excuse—say you have forgotten the keys, anything, and come and tell me."

And there at Suspension Bridge, Sullivan waited with the patience of a man sure of his game.

One night there came a summons from the gate; a foot passenger from up country and on his way to Yale wished to pass over the bridge. The keeper went to the gate and peered through the bars at the man on the other side. Quickly he made mental note of the solitary, fidgety traveller, of his clothing, his build, the details of his facial expression.

"All right!" he assured the pedestrian. "Just wait till I get the key!"

He hurried off to his cabin and gave the pre-arranged signal to Sullivan, who slipped around to the side of the gate while the keeper, humming a tune, hastened with jingling keys in hand to open the portal. Carefully he fitted the key in the lock, turned it and as Barry was preparing to step through, Sullivan suddenly pounced upon his victim and in a trice had him handcuffed.

"You are the man I want," he said grimly, as he fastened the shackles on the prisoner's wrists, behind his back. Barry was known as a desperate character and Sullivan had fully determined not to be caught napping.

"Here, what does this mean?" demanded Barry angrily. "What do you want me for?"

"I'll talk to you about that after a while," coolly answered Sullivan. "In the meantime we shall go down to Yale."

From Yale the constable and his charge travelled by stage to Barkerville, or rather Richfield—that being the seat of the government offices, one mile from the busier town. A vast crowd assembled to witness the arrival of the stage with its interesting passengers. Barry bore himself defiantly. He knew the chain of evidence lacked an important link and he trusted to the inability of the crown to fasten the guilt upon him.

At Richfield he was given a preliminary hearing, kept a silent tongue and was duly committed for trial at the assizes. The jail at Richfield had not been built for the purpose of holding desperate criminals. It served for the correction of the brawler, the petty thief, the disorderly drunk; but it was not intended to assure the safekeeping of men accused of murder, of men who would stop at nothing to gain their freedom. So Barry was sent down to New Westminster and there held until Judge Begbie made his next up-country circuit. When that came to pass, Barry was taken back to Richfield, in 1867, in company with two Indians charged with ... murder ... One of these Indians, the Nicomen, was sentenced to be hanged, as was Barry. In both cases the evidence was circumstantial, but both judge and jury were fully satisfied that Blessing had been killed by Barry.

When the time set for the execution drew nigh there was some difficulty in obtaining the services of a hangman. Then a happy thought occurred to the sheriff. He went to the Nicomen and suggested he should hang Barry.

"Nicomen, 'spose you hang Barry, you no hang. Hyas tyee [Great Chief, i.e., the governor] will forgive you and only keep you in jail," the Indian was told.

"No!" thundered the Nicomen, drawing himself up to his full

height, and beating his inflated chest with his fists. "No, me no hang Barry! Big Indian me, big brave!" His eyes flashed, the spirit of vanity possessed his soul. Not even to save his life would he soil his blood-stained hands with the placing of the fatal noose about Barry's neck.

It was rumoured that Barry had confessed his guilt to a priest, but he himself repudiated the statement and persisted in maintaining his innocence to the very last.

Cooey Lee recalled the days when paddlewheelers on the Fraser stopped at the Lee farm to load up firewood.

Neighbours

a new story by Sage Birchwater

Sage Birchwater has a knack for sounding the true heart of a community through its treatment of the outsider. In the first volume of Heart of the Cariboo–Chilcotin, *Birchwater introduced Chiwid, whose self-imposed exile from human civilization prompted random acts of kindness among citizens of the Chilcotin. He brings here a tale of communal generosity from the banks of the Fraser River, where a hard-working pioneer family, cast overnight as "outsiders" by the vagaries of war, were in danger of losing everything because they happened to be Chinese—in danger, that is, until a neighbour stepped forward with a helping hand.*

There's a story told around Marguerite, on the west side of the Fraser River between Williams Lake and Quesnel, about neighbours. Neighbours in the Biblical sense. Neighbours the way small, rural communities understand them.

It's a story of friendship and loyalty between two men and their families that had its beginnings when the Cariboo gold rush was still young. And it's a story that's still told today. It bears repeating.

The fever of the early gold strikes in the Cariboo and easy surface diggings had subsided by the 1880s when freighters William Leith Webster and Sing Chan Lee first met while working the Cariboo Road from Ashcroft to Barkerville. It was a month-long, round-trip journey hauling supplies to the goldfields, and a strong fellowship and camaraderie developed between the two men.

Mining operations in Barkerville had grown in size since the gold rush, but were fewer in number. Gold recovery required much capital investment and a workforce of paid labour to pry the metal loose from the bedrock beneath the surface. There was still a strong economy in the gold hills that required a steady stream of supplies. But the economy of the region was starting to diversify. As the mining opportunities petered out, the fledgling government of British Columbia offered land grants to encourage more settlement in the region.

British Columbia's transportation infrastructure developed quickly on the back of the gold rush. In the summer of 1862, boiler parts for the first Upper Fraser steamship were hauled by mules from Lillooet to Fort Alexandria. And there, on the east side of the river at Four Mile Creek where the banks of the Fraser slope gently to the water's edge, the SS *Enterprise* was constructed and launched in May of 1863.

Freighters hauled supplies with their teams and wagons from Ashcroft to the first navigable water at Soda Creek. From there paddlewheel steamers plied the Fraser north to Quesnel and Prince George and even up to Stuart Lake. The twice-weekly paddlewheeler service cut the cost of hauling supplies from Soda Creek to Quesnel in half, from five cents a pound to two and a half cents.

By 1865 the wagon road from Soda Creek to Quesnel was complete.

The start of the Canadian Pacific Railway in 1871 fueled the already insatiable demand for unskilled labour in British Columbia. Thousands of Chinese workers jumped at the chance to make their stake in the new land despite the cultural bias, disenfranchisement from voting and second-class status that awaited them there.

Sing Chan Lee was born in China in 1863 and came to British Columbia in 1877 at the age of 14. He dug ditches, mined the gravel bars along the Fraser and cut boards by hand with a whipsaw. Quickly he proved his worth.

He was astute at saving and careful with his spending, and eventually put enough by to purchase four teams of horses and two wagons and get into the freighting business.

Webster was older than Lee by 10 years. He had moved west from Ontario with his wife Margaret and small daughter Emily in 1887 and settled in Clinton. His son Bill was born there in 1889.

In 1891 Webster's uncle William Morrison invited him into a partnership on a 1,000-acre farm on the west side of the Fraser near Alexandria. It took Webster several winters of freighting to pay off his share of the partnership.

The friendship between Lee and Webster remained strong, and Lee took up land west of the Fraser as well, near Marguerite. Government records show that he formally pre-empted his property in 1910.

Skills Lee had learned while growing up proved useful to the two men. As a boy, he had worked on a boat freighting up and down the Yangtze River, and at Marguerite he built the first scow on that part of the river. It was 8 feet wide and 40 feet long, took 3 men to operate, and was big enough to transport the teams of horses both men needed for pulling their freight wagons along the Cariboo Road.

Lee was over 50 years old when he went back to China to be married. He returned to the Cariboo and was followed shortly afterwards by his bride. He made the long journey to Ashcroft with a horse and buggy to pick her up and brought her to the log cabin he had built on the ranch.

Their first child, Cooey, was born in 1916, followed in quick succession by Henry, Meng Foo, Chow, Danny, Willy, Maggie and Jennie.

The Webster and Lee families thrived in the pastoral community of the Fraser's west side. The fertile soil produced bumper crops of potatoes, grain, hay and vegetables. They raised cattle, sheep, pigs, horses and chickens, and cut cordwood to fuel the paddlewheelers. Both families operated stores.

In a 2003 interview Sing Lee's oldest son, Cooey Lee, then 87, described how it was back then. He said the paddlewheelers stopped regularly at the Lee farm to load up firewood to feed the steam-powered boilers. In the fall they would stop to take on loads of potatoes and other produce for markets in Quesnel and further up the river.

Cooey recalled one incident when he was a small boy watching the steamboat load up a ton of spuds from the farm and then get stuck on the gravel bar.

"They had to take a bunch of potatoes out. I sat and watched them trying to dig out the paddlewheeler."

He said it wasn't uncommon for the big riverboats to get grounded on the shifting gravel bars, especially when the water was low in the late fall when the river was starting to ice up.

"They had all kinds of trouble with the steamboats."

At the end of the steamboat era in the 1920s, he said the last of the paddlewheelers were left in the river, where they floundered.

"One got hung up on a bar and froze up where the Marguerite ferry is now," Cooey recalled. "It just lay there in the river for years. Then in 1942 they hauled it out and melted down all the metal and used it for the war."

With the demise of the steamships, cables were strung across the Fraser River and reaction ferries were installed; these used the force of the river current to propel them from bank to bank. These engineless ferry crossings were established at a number of locations along the Fraser: at Soda Creek, Marguerite, Alexandria and further downstream at Big Bar and Lytton.

But that era passed too. In 2003 the Marguerite ferry, the last of the reaction ferries on the Fraser River north of Big Bar, was taken out of service.

By the time Hitler invaded Poland in 1939 and Great Britain and Canada declared war on Germany, both William and Margaret Webster were dead. Sing Chan Lee was 76.

Then when the Japanese attacked Pearl Harbour in December 1941, triggering the Pacific theatre of the Second World War, the ground shifted for Asian-Canadians like the Lee family. Under the mandate of Prime Minister William Lyon Mackenzie King, despite Canada and China being allies, Canadians of Chinese and Japanese origin were told they could not own land. Overnight, Sing Lee's 29-year tenure on his ranch at Marguerite was declared null and void.

That's when William's son, Bill Webster, stepped forward and took over the title of Lee's property and promised to hold it for him until the war was over.

It was a commonsense gesture between neighbours. No big deal as far as Bill Webster was concerned. He had grown up around Sing Lee all his life. The two men had worked together, sweated on the freight wagons, forded the river together, and their children had grown up and gone to school together. The sense of community had grown up around them. The bond of friendship and loyalty of being neighbours was deeper than the insanity of a distant war.

Ironically Sing Lee didn't live long enough to see the fulfillment of Bill Webster's promise. He passed away at his ranch in 1944 at 81 years of age. But during those intervening years, the Lee family continued to live on the property.

"We ranched and farmed and had a store on the farm too," Cooey Lee recalled. "Chow and I worked together."

Cooey credited his sister for "raising hell" with the Canadian government after the war to speed up the process allowing them and other Asian families to own land again.

In the 1950s Cooey left the farm and began a career as a millwright and mechanic all over the Cariboo, while Chow remained on the property raising cattle and various crops. Eventually the title of the land was returned to him, and he continues to live there today with his descendents.

Another brother, Willie Lee, remained there also, and carved his niche as a long-time operator of the Marguerite ferry.

Cooey returned to the ranch to retire in a little cabin on the property his father had pre-empted beside the Fraser River in 1910, and died there in 2005.

But the story of how friendship and loyalty prevailed through generations still lives on in that rural community on the west side of the Fraser River. It's a story that will continue to be told, one that teaches the true meaning of being neighbours.

Early Life in the Chilcotin

from *The Life and Times of Texas Fosbery*,
a story related by Texas Fosbery to author Karen Piffko

*In this condensed excerpt, Fosbery recounts the homemade
fun of practical jokes and a miscellany of mishaps and quirky
events that peppered his growing-up years on a Big Creek ranch,
where he lived with his parents and brother Tony. Also raised
on ranches—first in Kamloops, then in Williams Lake—Karen
Piffko first met Fosbery when she was three years old. She
settled at Big Lake in 1976, and contributed to the* Williams
Lake Tribune *before writing this biography about Fosbery, who
by that time was known throughout the province as a heavy-
equipment operator, airplane pilot, cowboy, gold miner and all-
round Cariboo character.*

Bob Fosbery watches Tex and brother Tony harrowing the garden with their horse Mike in 1931.

Boom! Boom! The sound of the blasts from the double-barrelled shotgun filled the night air. The horses were bucking and bolting. The cowboys were grabbing leather. Some stayed in their saddles and some were thrown to the ground.

My dad, Percy Henry Vincent Fosbery, was slapping his thigh and laughing out loud as he watched the rodeo from the porch. He'd invited the local cowboys over to his place on Big Creek in the Cariboo for a Saturday night get-together. He knew that they'd have a few drinks under their belt before they arrived, and he decided to get the party started as they rode through the gate.

Earlier he had opened the gate, attached the shotgun to the gatepost, and run a string from the triggers. He tied the strings to the opposite gatepost and waited for the first horse to run through. The prank was a great success. No one was hurt, and as everyone laughed about it later, they were already making plans to top that one.

You might say that the Cariboo is in my blood. A series of events had brought first my dad to the Big Creek country, later my mother, and later still myself and my brother Tony.

Life was pretty primitive, and there were many hardships for everyone in those early years. We lived about a hundred miles from Williams Lake, the nearest town. We didn't go there very often because of the distance and the poor quality of the road. My dad owned a Star touring car at the time. My mother told me of one trip we made when I was six months old. We were going up the Chilko Ranch hill, which was dry and very sandy. The car was jumping and bouncing around as it struggled to the top. When it got there, my mother looked around to the back seat to see how I was doing. I wasn't there! The back door had flown open and I had slid out. They ran back down the hill and there I was, lying beside the track in the sand, apparently unhurt.

In 1928 my dad got rid of that car. He went up to Quesnel and bought a brand-new Model A for $500. He removed the lid of the rumble seat, built a box for it, and made a pickup. That's where Tony and I rode most of the time.

We also slept there when our parents went to dances at the Big Creek hall. We'd lie there looking up at the stars. One time my mother had given us each a nickel. We were playing with them and Tony swallowed his. He started to cry so bad that I went to find our parents. I wasn't very big, but I managed to get the door of the hall open. It was so loud in there. I was scared to death, but I went in among all those people. I finally found my mother and dad and they came out to the car. They told Tony that there was nothing they could do about it. They said that the next time he went to the bathroom he might be able to find his nickel.

Although things were tough sometimes, I'm glad that I was raised on the ranch. I've always loved the wide open spaces and the ranch animals, especially horses. My dad had five hay meadows where we put up the hay each summer and fed it out to the cows each winter. There was the Home Place, the Marston Place, Cooper Creek, Dolly Meadow, and Green Mountain Meadow (later known as Fosbery Meadow). We'd start at home and move from one meadow to the next. We were nomads!

My mother and dad cut the hay with horse-drawn mowers. They hired some of the Indians to actually put up the hay, using their own horses and slips and stacking poles. They were paid by the ton, so my dad would measure up the stack by throwing a long tape over it one way and then the other and cross-sectioning the volume. Two of the families who worked for my dad were the Jeffs and the Quilts.

Another fellow who contracted there was Laceese. One day he was pitching hay onto his slip. Tony and I were yapping away at him and I guess he got tired of listening to us. He stuck his pitchfork into the ground, pulled out his jackknife and said, "You come here an' I cut your nut. You come here an' I cut your nut."

Well, Tony and I took off on the run. I guess he was just fooling, because when we looked back across the meadow he was still laughing. We never bothered him again.

Every so often the Indians sent someone down to the Chilko Ranch Store with a pack horse to get supplies. They'd also get a big bag of sugar and some peaches to make homebrew. I remember hearing them hooting and hollering and having a great time down in their camp.

One day they didn't want to work because one of them was very sick. One fellow rode all the way to Stoney to bring back the medicine man. That night they got a big fire blazing in the camp. We sneaked quietly along a fence nearby and we watched and listened. The drums were beating and the medicine man was chanting and dancing around. It was exciting to see.

In the fall, when we were back at the Home Place, it would be time to round up the cattle from the summer range around Big Creek. My mother and dad sorted out the beef, which were to be sold, and kept back the cows and bulls.

When my mother rode out on the range, she'd often tie Tony and me onto a pack horse. She didn't have much choice as there weren't any babysitters nearby. She'd lead the horse until she found some cattle and then she'd tie it to a tree. Once she had the cows heading out, she'd come back and get us. I guess we cried and hollered a lot, but we did have our hands free so we could swat mosquitoes!

When our parents drove the cattle to Williams Lake to sell, it was a two-week journey because the cattle only travelled eight or nine miles a day. On these occasions they'd take Tony and me over to Charlie Bambrick's place. He and his wife were quite elderly, but they'd look after us while our parents were away.

I remember looking out across the creek one time, watching my dad and mother start out. I could just barely see them, but there was my mother, waving a white hanky at us. Imagine, going on a beef drive carrying a white hanky!

We sure had to do as we were told at the Bambricks' place. Mrs. Bambrick gave us way more oatmeal mush than we got at home, but we had to finish it all. We'd finally get it down, and right after that we had to sit on the pot. We had to produce something in that pot, too, even if we had to sit there all day! Between the mush and the pot, I never forgot Mrs. Bambrick.

Charlie would sit by the window sometimes, and I'd sit on his knee. He'd catch a yellow-jacket between his thumb and index finger and grind it up. He had skin like boot leather on his hands. Then he'd tell me to do it. I only did it once. We were always happy when our parents returned.

We'd stay at the Home Place awhile in the early winter, depending on how much hay there was to feed the cattle. We grew tame hay there, and it didn't always produce as well as the swamp hay. Sometimes we'd be at the Home Place until Christmas and sometimes we'd already be gone to one of the meadows by then.

My dad used a team and sleigh to carry our supplies from one meadow to the next. It was always so cold, sometimes down to 40 below. We'd bring the cats in a gunny sack and let the dog run alongside the sleigh. In the summer we'd even take the chickens in a box on the wagon, but we killed them off in the fall. My mother drove the cattle along the trail that had been broken by the team and sleigh.

We'd usually arrive at the meadow cabins after dark. My dad would get Tony and me and the potatoes inside as quickly as possible. We'd be crying from being so cold. My dad would put the potatoes in the middle of the floor and make us run around the pile so we'd warm up. In the meantime he'd light the fire and get snow to melt for water. He told me later that he had to give us a little "pop" on the backside with the bullwhip to get us moving. He'd have to go out and help my mother, and he didn't want us to sit down and freeze to death.

He'd light the gas lantern and go out to unhitch the team. Then he'd hook it up to a slip with a hayrack, they'd load it with hay, then take it out to feed the cattle. It was late when they got back. We'd have something to eat and go to bed. Tony and I slept on swamp hay on the floor, and Mother and Dad slept on a bed made of poles with a swamp hay mattress.

One winter at Dolly Meadow I had a wagon that my dad had brought along, even though the snow was too deep to really use it. One day I went out to play with it and it was gone. A few days later, on Christmas morning, we woke up and saw this beautiful Christmas tree—and my wagon with runners on it. I was so happy! Now I had a sleigh. Tony's present was up in the tree. It was a big green frog, probably made of inflated rubber.

Once when we were living in the Cooper Creek cabin, my dad brought home a dead coyote. There were lots of coyotes around because some calves had frozen to death, and the coyotes came to feed on them. My dad had shot several, but the one he brought back was a nice-looking one. It was frozen solid, so Tony and I put it on the sleigh, covered it with blankets and hauled it around for weeks. He was our pet dead coyote.

Another thing I remember about Cooper Creek was the owls. Dozens of owls sat in the trees around the cabin, hooting. My dad used to pack me outside at night to listen to them. I was so scared of their eerie sound.

My mother and dad were very strict, and Tony and I occasionally got in trouble with them. I still remember the three straps that hung in the living room at home. If we were bad, the only choice we had about our punishment was which strap we wanted used!

When I was six years old, I had to start school. I was pretty happy with my life, but when I learned that I would be riding my horse the two miles to the Big Creek School, I thought it was even better. Hazel, Duane and Veera Witte (now Veera Bonner) and Neville and Fay Blenkinsop were going there at that time.

Later on, my parents started talking about sending me to a boarding school in England. I didn't have anything to say about it. There were other discussions that summer, and the next thing I knew, we were going to leave the Chilcotin and move to the Okanagan.

Augusta's stories offered rare glimpses back to a time when her people lived close to the land—and the deep, bountiful waters of the Fraser River.

The Story of the Sturgeon

from *The Days of Augusta*
by Jean E. Speare

*Layers of history infuse Augusta Mary Tappage's oral story about
a successful sturgeon catch. It was over 30 years ago that historian
Jean E. Speare stood with this elderly Native daughter by the banks
of Deep Creek and recorded her tales. Even more historic is the
time frame of this story: it is set during the horse-and-wagon days
of the frontier west. And older still is the evidence of knowledge,
skills, traditions and beliefs carried forward through millennia by
the earliest people in the region—conveyed in such details as the
braided rope made only from spring willow, the way each part
of the sturgeon is carefully considered for practical use, and the
acknowledgement that this sturgeon's death was grieved.*

There was this one time I saw a sturgeon caught in the Fraser River. It was where Deep Creek empties into the river near Hargreaves Ranch. Yes, there is this big eddy there—deep too.

Deep Creek is this creek where I'm standing talking to you one day.

Well, this man, Captain Charlie—that one who caught the sturgeon—he must have got Billy Lyon to make him two hooks. They were joined together like this, back-to-back. Oh, they were big hooks, huge hooks. Made like a fish hook, exactly the same as a fish hook, but large!

Well, this old man, Captain Charlie, he was a pure Indian from Lillooet and he married a Soda Creek woman, I guess; is where he lived anyhow. Well, he must have known the sturgeon lived there in that eddy. He must have watched.

He got ready to catch the sturgeon, yes, Captain Charlie got ready. You would have to get ready to catch a sturgeon. He's not a little fish!

In my language—in Shuswap—the sturgeon and the whale are the same thing. It is just called by one name—*wholt*! It means the whale and the sturgeon. *Wholt*—just that. I can't tell you how to spell it—that Shuswap, that's hard!

I saw this sturgeon. Oh, it was nine feet at least. It was a monster, yes, I saw that one.

It was before I was married. I was single, staying down there with my father and mother. My father was going to water the horses. You see, we had a wagon and a team, and those horses would not drink river water. They wanted fresh water that comes from Deep Creek. So we had to take them down there.

And that's when we found out a sturgeon had been caught.

We passed him, Captain Charlie (he was riding horseback), and he said he had caught a sturgeon. He said he had to go to his house for something. He said, "I'll be back pretty soon." I guess he went for his son.

Well, we stayed around to help. He and his wife had a camp there at the mouth of Deep Creek by the big eddy. It was where they had the hook fixed and I guess they wouldn't leave that.

Well, this sturgeon, it had come up out of the eddy and it had taken the bait—a whole salmon—and it was hooked, and from the hooks, to keep the sturgeon from smelling human beings, they had a braided willow for several feet. They had peeled a willow and braided it—spring's the only time you can peel that willow. It's white when you peel it. When spring is here, it just comes right off, you know, the sap is run. It's their rope in the early days, long ago.

Well, it's what the old man had on these two hooks. It was braided about that big, like my wrist, and it was tied from the hooks to the main rope—the bought rope.

Well, Captain Charlie had all this coiled and staked by the river—staked with a long stick. So, if the sturgeon took the hook, the stick was missing, understand? That stick that was standing by the shore with the coiled rope around it, then if it wasn't there, well the sturgeon had the hook. The rest of the rope went up to a big tree, way up on shore, way up there, the rope did. Oh, it was a long rope, about from here to the gate—about two hundred feet? A long rope.

And the sturgeon bit the hooks, yes—swallowed them and it was right down here in the stomach. It was baited with a whole fresh salmon. That sturgeon had a big mouth. The head stood that high, I guess, as high as my table. Oh, it was a big thing that one I saw.

It swallowed the hook, and it was hooked against its insides in the rib part. You couldn't pull that hook out.

The sturgeon went as far as the rope would let it go. It was fighting the rope when we got there. It wasn't splashing the water. It was just going this way and that way.

And we started pulling on this rope. Captain Charlie, my father, we all held on and pulled at the same time. There were three of us close to the river and the grandson of this old man who had the hooks in, he was riding a horse and hanging on the rope and pulling with that horse.

It took us quite a while to pull this thing out. It fought. It was strong too, my God! It jerked this way and it jerked that way. It kept doing that and we kept pulling. When we thought it would start back this way, we'd pull again. Oh, we had to work hard to help to get it.

The horse was over there holding tight on that long rope. No one shouted. Everyone kept quiet. Didn't want to scare the sturgeon any more than he was. We'd let it have rope, you know, but we stood there on the shore to take it up again. It kept fighting the hook this way and that way. Finally it came toward the shore, little by little—getting tired, I guess. And I guess this hook was hurting too. It must have. Yes, it must have hurt. So finally, we landed it.

The old lady, Mrs. Captain Charlie, made lots of leaves, stripped the trees of leaves and spread them on the ground, spread them 'way out. Well, it was a big thing, you know.

So we finally landed it. And we put that sturgeon on top of the leaves to keep it clean. It died. It died from no water. Still he hammered it with an axe, the single-blade axe. Not the double-bitted, but the single-blade. Captain Charlie did this, yes. And he hit it three or four times to be sure it died. Well, when it kept still, we knew it was dead.

Then we flopped it on its back. We all helped. My father helped and my cousin helped—(she's dead, my father's dead, and all those fellows are dead; I'm the only one that's alive)—well, they flopped it onto its back and then they opened it up.

Yes, they opened it up and it had this—I can't tell you what they called it—it's a white thing. It looks like grease, you know, grease that comes from the butcher's, but it looked soft. It was white and it was big! And the way nature made it, it was full of little purple eggs—just full, anyway you turned the thing, it was just full. Where you cut it, it was just full of it.

I didn't cut it. It wasn't ours to cut. It was Captain Charlie's. We were just looking on—what happened and what it looks like.

Anyway, the old lady took it away. She put it on something clean. She said she was going to look at it to see what she would do with it. I don't know what she did with it, but it must have been useful.

But when we were looking at this sturgeon's stomach, we saw it had three more dead salmon inside. Yes, beside the one it swallowed for bait. That made four!

But I'll tell you, while he was butchering this fish here, while Captain Charlie was butchering this fish, we could hear the water in the eddy start to rumble and it started to roll—there in the eddy where he caught this fish. He told us to keep quiet. So we all stood up and we were looking to see what would come up from the river.

We were all scared too when it kept on rumbling and rumbling—loud, good and loud. And then we saw it! It was another sturgeon. And it brought its whole body out of the water like this, shooting water through its nostrils, like a whale. And the water curled up like this and fell back into the river and the sturgeon came up again and again.

And we were scared, yes. We were scared.

And soon it was quiet again. The eddy was quiet and still.

Old Captain Charlie, he says, "He's going away now." That's what he told us. He says, "He misses his mate and now he is going away. He has said goodbye."

I guess they had been living there in the eddy, those two sturgeon, right there in the big eddy where the river runs deep.

Cowboys cook breakfast beside Williams Lake.

First Williams Lake Rodeo

from *History and Events of the Early 1920s*
by Bill Riley and Laura Leake

In the first volume of Heart of the Cariboo–Chilcotin, *we saw
greenhorn Constable Bill Riley sent, without police training,
to thrust the long arm of the law into an unpoliced area of the
Cariboo–Chilcotin. He extended that arm to shake the rough
hands of railroad gangs and bootleggers in an effort to meet
them halfway. In the following story, Riley brings his law of
compromise to the very first Williams Lake Stampede, where a
job well done meant that no storefront windows were broken, no
barrooms were dismantled and no rodeo goers were murdered.
Lucky for Riley, there were only minor infractions, as Williams
Lake at that time did not even have a jail.*

Williams Lake was growing rapidly, and it wasn't long before it had everything that goes to make a town: three hotels, large general store, post office, smaller stores, barber shop, and bank. Everything except what I needed—a police station. There were times when I needed one badly, the nearest lock-up being at the 150 Mile House, 11 miles away.

In the fall of 1921, the town came of age, wanted to be on the map, and decided that the only way to do this was to hold a stampede or rodeo. A real good rodeo brought in ranchers, cowboys, Indians, prospectors, and every form of human life, as well as racehorses, quarter and bucking horses, and cash, for more than a hundred miles around. Also, there being no liquor store opened as yet, there were some bootleggers and quite a number of prostitutes scattered around the town. Because it was a railroad divisional point, most of the residents worked for the PGE, their homes spotted around, up to now, with no semblance of order until the place was organized much later. Everything had the appearance of a pig's breakfast.

The date had been set for this three-day melee, one couldn't call it anything else, and since I policed Williams Lake from Soda Creek, I didn't see it very often, being 30 miles away and not having a car. I was notified to be there and that constables Ashton of Quesnel and Gallagher of the 150 Mile House would be there to help me, but they didn't turn up until the end of the second day. What a job it was to do alone! Booze was flowing freely and drunks were everywhere, especially at night when everyone came in from the racetrack and rodeo grounds.

All I could do was to ride around, keep my mouth shut, and not interfere unless someone was being murdered, and it's a wonder there wasn't, with hundreds of men and women. I was treated with every respect, thank goodness, because about all I did was to keep them from the business section and breaking windows.

Most were in bootlegger joints or at the dance in a huge hall that had been thrown up for the occasion. It was thus that I first met my old friend Pat Newman, manager of 105 Mile House, Lord Egerton's ranch, an absolute stranger to me that wild night. I was watching a bootlegging joint where men would come and go, but this chap came out well loaded and rolled toward the stores. I asked him where he was going, and he told me to mind my own damn business. I told him who I was and suggested he go to bed. He got quite hostile at that. I was on the point of commandeering a Tin Lizzie car that was coming down the street and told him that I thought the 150 Mile House jail would be the best place for him. That snapped him out of it a bit; the bluff worked.

He said, "You know me—I'm Pat Newman of the 105." I told him that I had heard of him, and I then persuaded him to let me help him to the hotel. This I did, took off his shoes, and left him sound asleep, taking with me a sealed bottle of whiskey that he had on his hip, just in case he took a notion to drink more and start wandering again. However, when I went to see him that next morning to return it, he had gone. It was weeks later before I had a chance to square up with Pat. He was a surprised man when I eventually turned up at the 105, introduced myself, and asked him if he remembered the incident. He was very embarrassed and said he did.

I said, "Did you miss anything, Pat?" He sheepishly replied that he did, and when I produced a bottle of whiskey, he was more than surprised, pulled the cork, and between the two of us, it didn't last long. Pat was a wonderful friend from then on.

Later, when I was transferred to Clinton, the 105 Mile House was in my district. I stayed there quite often and got the Lord Egerton treatment.

At the stampede, I had been told to watch for suppliers of liquor to Indians, who were, in my opinion, really no worse than their white brothers. I would ride Murphy around about, just watching for anything unusual, when I spotted a car parked on the hillside and decided to check it. I had ridden up to it in the dark and put my flashlight on it when a man's voice said, "Get to hell out of here, Riley!" followed by a feminine giggle, so Riley, not wishing to disturb the peace, immediately retreated. I never did find out who the man was who could see well enough in the dark to recognize me.

I only had one complaint during the three days of the stampede. A PGE employee came to me after dark the evening of the second day and complained that a Negro prostitute had set up shop in a small house about a hundred yards from his home, and that cowboys were mistaking his place for the one the girl was in. His wife was being disturbed all through the night; he was on night shift and wasn't home to protect her. She had contacted him, so he went home to see what it was all about and, sure enough, the boys came. He met them with a shotgun and fired a couple of shots to emphasize the fact that this wasn't the place they were looking for. I had heard the shots, but such a thing was not unusual at a time like this; many were armed and just blasted away in their jubilation, against the law of course, but this was 1921 and cowboys were cowboys. But this was serious business when law-abiding citizens were being unduly disturbed. It was only for a day or two, when the girls would leave and return to the cities, but the black one would have to move.

I had no idea of just walking in on her to give her the bad news and then walking out, leaving a house of ill repute, so I asked this chap to go with me and wait, out of sight, near the door, which I left open, so he could hear the conversation. Here again, I was without any uniform. I thought to myself that she would think she had another customer, wanting to change his luck. My knock on the door was answered by a very good-looking dark girl who smiled expectantly and invited me in. She asked me if I would like a drink when I showed her the police badge under my coat. This was apparently not the first time one had been flashed on her, and she asked what the trouble was.

I explained to her that I wasn't interfering with any of the girls in town unless I had complaints. I told her what was happening to her neighbor and that I would give her two hours to move.

"Where to?" she asked. "The hotels are full, and I couldn't get a room anywhere." I said I had no idea where she could get accommodation at this time, but that she would have to move, just the same.

There I left her and joined my friend outside, asking him if he was satisfied. He thanked me and went home, and I went about my business. An hour or so later, a taxi driver (taxi drivers had come from goodness knows where for this little bonanza) came to me and asked if I had chased the girl out of the cabin, that she had come to him to drive her to Ashcroft, and he had told her it would cost her $200. She had to give that a second thought; in those days a dollar was worth a dollar, not forty cents. However, these taxi boys were a resourceful lot, and this one suggested that she could have his room at the Chinese hotel for $50 a night and he would flop in his cab or hole up with someone else, but he would have to have my permission.

I told him I couldn't care less. I didn't want to make it tough on the girl, and so all was well again. The lady got her room, the cab driver flopped some place, and Riley wished he was home in bed.

Well, Williams Lake's first rodeo finished with a bang, and since has been an annual affair, increasing in size and popularity year by year until now it is one of the biggest in the province.

Joe Fleiger's grey managed a jump of 33 feet in the Mountain Race;
Fleiger won the race three times in a row.

Those Cariboo Stampedes!

from *Pioneer Days in British Columbia, Volume One,*
edited by Art Downs
by Bill and Joyce Graham

*Stampedes were an established tradition throughout the Cariboo
before the Williams Lake Stampede was conceived. They were
an inevitable culmination of western frontier culture, with its
expertise in handling animals, its passion for gambling and
competitive feats of bravado, and its sheer love of fun. If the fun
got a little dangerous, that only added spice to the dish. As an
announcer, Bill Graham witnessed first-hand those wild and
woolly early years of Cariboo stampedes, the likes of which will
never be seen again. He co-wrote this story with his wife Joyce.*

Over 50 years ago the Williams Lake Stampede was born, a slam-bang affair that has grown into the largest of its kind in B.C., although old-timers grumble that it mellowed in the process.

Stampedes have always come natural to the Cariboo in general and Williams Lake in particular. Way back in the 1860s during the Cariboo gold rush, a race was held on the Pinchbeck farm where the modern town of Williams Lake is now, with the purse over $100,000. After a while the Pinchbeck boys made a racetrack in a wheat field up on the hill, and for a long time people raced there. Then it was decided to run the horses around the edge of a natural amphitheatre on the flats. Since Indians are born bettors, they soon brought their wiry little ponies and matched them against the whites'. Then cowboys came with wild horses and had bucking contests, calves were brought in from the ranches and roped and tied, and first thing a genuine Western-style rodeo had taken hold.

During my first years in Williams Lake I was too busy scratching a living to bother about the Stampede, but by 1922 I was rolling and became the announcer. I had a big black horse called Darky, and on him cavorted in front of the grandstand, telling folks what was going to happen and feeling very pleased.

There were visitors from everywhere, and no place to stay since this was long before the days of motels. They set up tents and teepees on the hill and around the Stampede grounds, by the lake and even up Williams Creek. There were ranchers, cowboys, bankers, dudes, Indians, kids by the dozen and dogs by the score. Transportation methods ranged from saddle horses to wagons, Model Ts to democrats. Colour we had aplenty, and since the Stampede was held early in July with weather hot and conditions dusty, participants were a thirsty bunch and later even a little tipsy.

We had all the usual racing, bucking, calf-roping and steer-riding. There weren't any Brahma bulls, but we didn't need them. Some of the experts brought in trained bulls that would buck till they ditched their riders, then trot off mild as milch cows towards the corral gate.

Our local stock was different. They were mostly real outlaws that would pitch their riders and then turn and gore them; so we put in a handyman called Mutch as clown, with something to flap if the brute got vicious. There were top riders like Roy Inscoe of the Gang Ranch, Joe Elkins, and Joe Boytanna, who brought a black trick horse he'd caught as a wild stallion and gentled and trained himself. That pony could do everything but swear! He would even buck to order, and stop when Joe told him to.

Mostly it was only men who raced, but I wanted to be different and tried to organize a Squaws' Race. I announced this race, but when nothing happened I went over to the Indian Camp and tried to get some women to enter. But all they did was shake their heads and tee-hee at me. Finally one of the husbands told me: "They say make horse run man's work, Beel. They want stay here, watch."

I was preparing to announce that the race could not take place when our schoolteacher, Miss Mellish, and Bessie Peters from the Government Office said they would ride. So we dolled them up in long skirts and bright blouses, painted their faces and got them horses. Miss Mellish had long dark hair that she let down, and it streamed behind her while she was racing. Bessie was fair, but she made herself a wig from a horse's tail and it hung down around her shoulders like a squaw's hair would. I went out and announced who was riding, and the crowd near had hysterics cheering them on. I got on Darky and galloped along beside them, while Joe Boytanna rode around inside the circle, putting on a whooping and hat-waving ceremony of his own. I don't know yet who won; but everybody whooped and hollered and had a helluva good time. In the evening there was a dance, and the next morning everybody folded up their tents and went home.

The next year they were all back. I was announcing again, and the big event was the Mountain Race, the worst piece of damn foolishness anybody ever thought up. It was banned later because it was too dangerous. The riders had to go to the top of a hill near the stampede grounds and gallop their horses down a slippery hillside, all stones and loose gravel, till they came to the road. Then down another hill along past the chutes to the racetrack, then around the track to the grandstand.

The first part of the course was so steep all the horses could do was jump and scramble and slither—someone measured the jump Joe Fleiger's grey took and it was 33 feet from where he took off to where he landed. Joe had trained this grey horse special for this race. The other riders, 10 of them, were Indians who had been at the booze and thought they could ride anywhere. When the race started they all came sliding and slithering, whooping and hollering down the first hill, horses struggling desperately to keep their footing. Joe's horse got down okay but practically all the others fell. One tumbled head over heels onto the road with its rider after it. When they reached the grandstand there were only 5 left, with Joe Fleiger's grey leading by about 500 feet.

Big Tomah was one of those who started. When the race began he gave his horse a kick and did not even try to rein it. The poor brute jumped goodness knows how far before landing, then stumbled and slithered down the slope into a tree and killed itself. Big Tomah was thrown and skidded past the tree, his head scraping the rough bark and almost scalping him.

Prosper Bates, telling me about it afterwards in his slow, soft drawl, said: "You know, Beel. that Big Tomah, she's damn good rider ... and that horse, she's damn good horse! That horse, hims jump so hard she's fall down, bang into tree, get killed dead. And Big Tomah, she's fall off, tree pull off all hims hair, pretty near make all hims brains fall out!"

The next year, Harry Curtis put up a board dance pavilion with roof, rounded up an orchestra of a piano-player and some local horn players and with a $2 admission charge hoped to make a killing. My job this time was to help Benny Franklin give a barbecue for the Indians. He'd lived among them for a long time and had friends all over the Chilcotin. But he was now getting old and wanted to put on one more party before he died.

So when the Stampede got underway, a bunch of us went with him and helped dig a barbecue pit 10 feet long by 8 feet wide and about 3 feet deep. Then I fetched my team and we hauled rocks and firewood and piled them into the hole—first a layer of firewood, then a layer of rocks, then another layer of firewood, and so on.

Benny Franklin was not a drinker, but most of his friends were. By the time the fire was lit and the pit ready for the meat, most everyone around was also lit. The blacksmith, Sam Marwick, had made Benny a huge carving knife by taking the blade of a scythe and stubbing it to the end of a long stick. We gave this impressive weapon to Benny, and some of the boys rode off to get the meat. Benny, meanwhile, had hopped onto a rock and was waving his knife around his head, calling to everybody to join his feast. All the Indians crowded in, laughing and chattering and getting ready for the big feed.

By this time the party was getting so wild most of the whites pulled back and watched from a distance. I had to stay because I was the Indian policeman, but I took time off while the meat was cooking to see what was happening with the Stampede. I got there in time for the Wild Horse Race, and saw one of my mares break away from the enclosure and go bucking and kicking through the Indian encampment. The rider clung like he'd been nailed there, while the pick-up men worked their way between tents, washing lines, wagons, screeching squaws and scuttling children to catch her and take him off.

When I got back to the barbecue, Benny had decided the meat was cooked and was slashing off great chunks of half-raw meat with his scythe-blade knife and throwing it into the crowd. You never saw anything like it! Squaws, kids, and bucks snatching the meat and chewing it, or carrying chunks off to finish cooking it at their own fire. Benny's hair was flying, his wrinkled old face was beaming with happiness, and he kept calling: "Come on, Annie! Come on, Charlie! Have another steak, Joe. There's lots more, and it's all free!"

And the Indians stuffed till their bellies bulged. The fire was crackling and smoking, and the smell was something you just couldn't believe unless you were there to sniff it. Scorched cow hair and burned meat, dusty Indians and sweaty clothes made a potent blend. Most of the whites decided the safest place was at the main Stampede and left, but I was worried about Benny and stayed. He was an old man and awfully excited. When the last of the crowd stopped whooping and waving their bottles at him and catching the lumps of meat, he dropped his knife and looked around uncertainly. His party was over, and he did not know what to do. There was music coming from the fancy board dance pavilion and he started out to go get his violin and play like he always did. But I caught him and took him home to bed. He was laughing and crying and talking, all at once. I had quite a time quieting him down. "Keep still and go to sleep, you old fool," I kept telling him, "can't you ever remember you're getting to be an old man?"

By the time the next Stampede rolled around old Benny was dead and I was living in Vancouver, so I don't know what went on. But the Williams Lake Stampede got bigger and bigger, until now it ranks as the largest in the province.

They even revived the Mountain Race, but had to drop it when the new Cariboo Highway cut through the course. I heard that on one occasion a policeman was sent up on horseback to keep an eye in things, but when the race started his horse got so excited it jumped off with the rest. The poor policeman fell off and got banged up like Big Tomah so many years before. Whether a tree nearby "pull off all hims hair" I never heard. But if old Benny and the rest of the boys had been around, they would have considered the mishap as part of the show, and next year would have wanted it included in the program.

Pete Colin

a new story by Hilary Place

Hilary Place was featured in the first volume of Heart of the Cariboo–Chilcotin *with a new story and an old favourite, both about memorable characters of the region. Here is another brand-new story by Place about a man of Dog Creek who wove a strange kind of spell with square-dance calls and chewing tobacco—a spell that forever stamped its magic in the impressionable folds of a country boy's memory.*

The newly opened Dog Creek School was the setting of a lively, memorable hoedown.

Pierre Colin was one of the originals at Dog Creek. I believe he owned the property, later called the River Ranch, that was owned and operated when I was a kid by my dad's brother, Frank Place, and his wife. Pierre Colin had a family that I don't know much about, except for his son Pete.

Pete was a character, there was no doubt about that. He was a tall man and thin. He wore a moustache that drooped down at the corners and gave him a bit of a mysterious look. He had a gentle way about him that was contradicted by his looks but was, nevertheless, his real nature.

He married one of Placida Valenzuella's daughters, a quiet, shy woman, and they started what turned out to be a very large family. Pete's dad, old Pierre, had sold his interest in the River Ranch, and Pete took up property farther up Dog Creek, first at what was known as Pete's Lower Place and later, by Gustafson Lake, Pete's Upper Place. They lived there quietly and kept to themselves.

In 1926, when the Dog Creek School was established, Pete moved his family down to Dog Creek so his children could attend. On the occasion of the school's opening, I remember Pete played a very important part. A dance was to be held in the old store warehouse, and everyone had gathered there to celebrate and to meet the new teacher, Miss Pansy Kathleen Price. We were all staying in the old cabin called "Casey," and I remember walking over to the store building with a lantern showing the way. As a kid I was always half-scared of walking with a coal-oil lantern. The shadows half-scared me this time too, but the excitement of the occasion offset it.

The old store warehouse had been cleaned out, and the only thing in the room that wasn't breathing was a great old iron heater with a top-opening lid and a small draft opening low on the front. It was cherry red and smoking a bit when we arrived. We kids soon found ourselves huddled along one side of the hall, and the dancers were kicking up dust on the floor. Somebody asked for a quadrille, and Pete was chosen as the caller. He took up his position by the heater stove and the fiddle player started to play.

"Allemande left and grand right and left," Pete hollered and away they went.

He had fortified himself with a big plug of Prince of Wales chewing tobacco and, in one incredible sweep of his hand, Pete lifted the lid on the heater-stove draft and aimed his spit at the opening with deadly accuracy and in time to the music. I was fascinated.

"Down the centre and cut off two, make a curtsy to you know who."

Things were getting hot now. Pete was really in the groove, the fiddle player was really dusting the bow, and Pete was hitting that opening in the draft on the heater with the aplomb of a real expert, dead centre.

There was some magic in this whole incredible scene. The flickering, pale lights of the coal-oil lamps, the roar of the fire when Pete opened the draft, the clatter of the dancers' feet on the floor, the authority of the caller's voice. It is a moment that is indelibly imprinted on my memory. It was the first dance that I ever saw and it touched me in a way that I never forgot.

Not long after this, Pete pulled his kids out of school and headed back to his Upper Place, 30 miles from the school. Along with everyone else, Pete and his family went broke during the Depression of 1929.

A Land Primeval

from *Wilderness Welfare: An epic of frontier life*
by Earl S. Baity

Raised in the Cariboo, Earl S. Baity worked at jobs that kept him close to the land, like gold panning, trapping and hunting—the familiar activities of men he grew up admiring. Baity lived for a time in the city with his young wife, but city life was hard during the Depression and nature called him back to the life he was born to. In this excerpt, his account of returning to the Cariboo to live off the land instead of a welfare cheque, Baity is on a solitary expedition to set up a trapline in the gloomy heart of a forest that covers the northern mountain slopes. He realizes how his relationship with nature has been altered by his economic dependence on its resources. Still, he maintains a sense of reverence for the aloof, primordial landscape that seems forever suspended in a time before humans walked there.

Wild and timelessly primeval, the country around Mountain Creek
seemed newly emerged from the mists of creation.

The Mountain Creek cabin was still new and bright, because I had built it just the previous spring while trapping beaver. The pack rats, those loathsome, destructive, stinking pests that are such a scourge to all trappers, hadn't yet found it.

It was a pretty spot there in a wild way. The open expanse of Mountain Creek was gradually giving way to the deep woods, and that was about the last of the meadow country. Heavy timber pressed in from both sides. The meadow that still remained was about to succumb to a thick growth of black birch brush, and many of the more adventurous pines had left the safety of the forest and ventured out onto the meadow and taken up aggressive position.

The cabin sat at the edge of the woods under the spreading branches of two of those bold pines. It was a nice little cabin, with the roof extending out beyond the end wall to form a sort of dirt-floored porch. The door and one small window were in that end. I had peeled the pine logs and they shone golden in the evening sun. The roof was steep and the stovepipe above it was just crooked enough to give it a storybook-illustration effect. As I rode out of the woods that afternoon and again got a glimpse of the cabin, it reminded me anew of a fairytale house.

I had planned on returning to Landslide that evening, but fortune decided otherwise.

I gave the horses an hour for grazing on the meadow while I made tea and ate lunch. I left the grub in the panniers just the way it had arrived. It would be a big job to put it all away properly, and I didn't want to take the time then. The flour, rolled oats and sugar would have to be hung from the ridge pole with a wire so that the mice couldn't get at them. Other perishables, such as tea, coffee, beans and rice would be put in cans. Things that would gather mould—bacon, salt pork, lard, butter and dried fruit—I would put in the safe on the back of the cabin. But that would all have to wait until tomorrow.

I caught the horses and started back down the trail. I hadn't gone more than a mile, however, when a young bull moose came out of a spruce swamp and stopped on the trail in front of me. I wanted meat but would rather have got caught up with my work first. However, even when game is plentiful, a hunter can't afford to be too particular. Game can be pretty capricious in its habits at times. Also, if I shot this one while I had the horses along, it would save me packing it in on my back. I got off the horse, pulled the .303 British from the saddle scabbard, took a bead behind his shoulder and pulled the trigger. He slumped to the ground. I tied the horses to trees and, before cutting his throat, stood looking down on him. He was a magnificent animal with his long, trim legs, massive neck and gold-coloured rack. Stilled in death, he still looked majestic. To a sportsman hunter, he would have been a prize indeed, but my satisfaction came from knowing that this was a winter's supply of meat. And where those few minutes should have been charged with thrilling excitement, the kill had been just a straight-out business proposition. I wondered why. What was this thing doing to me that I couldn't now get any more response than that from shooting a three-year old bull moose? I decided that maybe my meat had come too easily and let it go at that.

It wasn't until later that I realized the truth. I wasn't up there for sport. I was there on a strictly cash basis. All I was interested in was something that wore a dollar sign. I was trying to commercialize the woods and the woods had their own way of evening the score.

I was glad of the meat, nevertheless. I skinned the moose out and packed him to the cabin. I cut one quarter up for immediate use and put it in the safe. Two quarters I hung in trees and covered with canvas to freeze. The fourth one would go to Landslide.

By the time I had all that done it was too late to go back to Landslide, so I picketed the horses on the meadow and prepared to spend the night there. I tended to all the grub, then made a bannock and fried a big pan of moose liver. It was well after dark by then, so I settled down for the night.

The evenings are long in those lonely cabins and a fellow has to try to keep interested in something. I had never been bothered by loneliness before but could see that this time it was going to be different. Other winters I had always been able to entertain myself by reading, by writing on wrapping paper poems and short stories—which I invariably burned in disgust—and by whittling. Thinking of using those diversions that night seemed rather like expecting a child to play with toys it had outgrown. The long hours of that first evening were finally spent in quiet reverie. Had I chosen the only way? The hard way? The line of least resistance? Well, I had chosen to trap.

The six weeks passed quickly enough at that. I was very busy and that helped. Above the Mountain Creek cabin, I had a four-day circle line with two more cabins and an open camp. There were about three hundred traps on that line. It is a big job to set up that many traps, pack some grub to each camp, and cut up even a small supply of wood at each one.

The work was so familiar and had at one time been so much a part of my life that soon I was back into the same old pattern of living. Aside from that newly acquired loneliness, and constantly wondering how Freda was, I found I was following a groove made smooth by familiarity.

It is a strange country up there on the north slope of that circle of mountains where the many creeks that go to make up Mountain Creek have their origin. It is not only wild, but timelessly primeval. You feel it, feel the newness of it as if it were only recently brought up out of the mists of creation. The dense growth of heavy timber never allows the sun's rays to reach the ground, and the forest floor is forever in shade and semi-darkness. The vegetation is mostly strange species that you don't see anywhere else. It is weak and anemic-looking, as if still in the early stages of evolution. I have seen fungi and slimy-looking toadstools in there that only a naturalist could identify. As you walk through the damp, deep moss and peer into the gloom around you, it would be easy to let yourself imagine—as did the Indian wanderers of another era—some prehistoric monster suddenly taking shape before one's very eyes. Even the small creeks that work their way through those spruce valleys don't run, they soundlessly and darkly ooze along. Trying to keep a channel open in that fast-growing moss and rotting vegetation has proven to be such a losing game that they are content to seep and sink through the obstructions from one dark pool to another.

There is a strange absence of bird life throughout the whole region. The songs of birds are something you don't hear, even in midsummer, and that adds to the sense of the prehistoric about the place, as if the birds were yet to evolve, as if birdsong were for a future age.

With the character of Mountain Creek so radically changed, it willfully gave up its individuality just above the cabin. So many were the small creeks that came straying in from all directions there, that Mountain Creek just ceased to be. The largest and longest of those creeks, my dad and I called Indian Creek. It seemed to be up to us to name the creeks and lakes through that country, because, as far as we knew, there had never been another white man in there ahead of us.

Years ago there had been one Indian, Old Paul, who had run a line of marten and fisher deadfalls up that one creek (hence our name Indian Creek). Other than that, neither one of us ever saw as much as an axe mark in the whole country that wasn't our own.

My trapline followed the creek right to its source, which was a myriad of small swamps and boggy springs in the midst of the heavy timber. That was on the summit, and the water that drained the other way eventually reached Narcosli Creek far to the south. The line crossed the summit, left the swamps and springs behind and followed another little creek down some distance. The country dropped off faster on the slope, and the creek soon acquired steep sides to its valley and had fall enough that the water could race and run.

On that creek I had another cabin. The timber there was still big and thick-standing, but the spruce and balsams had begrudgingly made room for a few pines, which stood tall and stately as if trying to show the other trees that they had no intentions of being second-raters in someone else's forest.

My father and I had built the cabin out of those big pines some four years before. We had used big logs because there were no smaller ones available. They made such a solid cabin that being in it felt almost like being within fortress walls.

But nature, as if resentful of any intrusion into that museum of its early creation, at once put its forces to work to destroy it. Bacteria, prolific in the damp air and semi-darkness of the forest, immediately made an all-out attack on the logs. They became green and acrid-smelling, and slimy with mold and mildew. Mushroom-like fungi attached themselves to the logs, and slimy toadstools grew up through the floor on spindly, crooked stems. Any food that was left there over a summer grew mold and spoiled. The air was so dank and musty-smelling that even the bush rats forsook the cabin.

We always referred to the place as Old Moldy, and the dub was an apt one. On the first trip in there each fall, to get rid of the stench of decay, I always had to scrape the walls, leave the door and window open with a tremendous fire in the stove, and scrub all the dishes, table and cupboard with strong soap and boiling water. After that it would be somewhere near fit for human habitation.

From Old Moldy, the line swung northeast and followed the north slope of the summit around to Three Lakes. After about five miles, the big timber suddenly broke off in a distinct, jagged line where a fire in some bygone time had been stopped, probably rained out.

From there across Bear Den Mountain to Three Lakes, the country became a jungle of second-growth balsam, pine and spruce woven in among the windfalls of big, half-rotted trees that had lost their lives in the big fire and had fallen to the ground, eventually to become food for the heedless next generation.

This strip of jungle was the worst offender on that whole line. In early winter you were continually climbing up one side of some windfall and sliding down the other. Then as the winter's snow started piling in, each sapling would collect a big gob, hold it in its branches just waiting to dump it down the neck of the first unfortunate wayfarer to come along—which would be me.

But as more and more snow piled in, the mischievousness of the trees always turned out to be their own downfall. In greediness, each tree would collect more load than it could bear. Its head would be pressed inexorably to the ground with its body bent in a high arch until the whole jungle would be just a tangle of bent saplings. Then as more and more snow piled up on it the whole thing would become a solid wall of snow reinforced with the saplings. Pack-laden, I have stood looking at places like that with a sinking heart, wondering how in the world I was ever going to get through.

As a safety measure for such times, when a fellow was lucky to make a mile an hour, I had an emergency camp on the western slope of Bear Den. It was just a canvas lean-to with a place for a fire in front. I always kept a little grub there and a couple of blankets and a good double-bitted axe for cutting wood. It didn't exactly offer the ultimate in comfort, but to pull in there about dark, tired, hungry, and generally wet, it could look like a welcome haven-a place that offered some slight addition to scant creature comfort.

Three Lakes, which were merely small ponds of about 15 acres apiece created by beaver dams in the creek, were set in a spread of country that might well have been sitting on the edge of the barren lands. When a branch of the fire swept through there it must have been a holocaust. Evidently every living thing had been burned up clean. There were no windfalls, no snags, not even any soil left on the lava bedrock; in its place was an inch or two of crumbled, burnt clay and ashes. The second growth of pine and spruce that had eventually tried to make a comeback were still small and stunted-looking. Everything was new, as if the country had just recently crawled out from under the foot of the glacier. The tundra-like appearance of the swamps dotted with scraggly, small spruce, the spacious aisles between the squatty pines and spruce on the flats and benches all added to the illusion of the Arctic, and in winter when swirling snow was whipped along the open areas on the high pass, and across the swamps in the teeth of a howling blizzard, the illusion could be complete. It was bleak enough.

But the light from the sun and the summer winds reached the cabin, sitting just back from the edge of the lower lake, and it didn't mold up as did Old Moldy. It was light and warm and cozy in there; and after I got the rats chased out in the fall, it didn't smell too offensive.

From there the line continued north, crossed over a mountain and dropped down into another valley that was more or less a replica of Three Lakes Valley, only more spacious. There were only two lakes in it, and they were much larger. The creek that ran out of that valley my dad called Dirty Creek, because it was "such a dirty mess to get through."

But once you were through that dirty mess, the creek swung back and joined Mountain Creek just above the valley cabin. Getting back there always felt like entering another part of the world, one that had kept pace with evolution.

So up in there was where I had spent a good portion of my time for the last six winters. I hadn't trapped on the same line continuously, however. At one time I had run a line southwest from Old Moldy to Fish Lake. It took three days to go in there, but it didn't prove profitable. I learned that I could do better by concentrating all my traps and efforts on a shorter line. Besides, I never seemed to like staying up in that country too long at a time. I liked it in there, and when I was away, it was forever calling me back; but after a week or 10 days, I was always glad to get out of the deep gloom for awhile. Could be I was afraid I might degenerate into something primitive myself.

Besides, the lower end of Mountain Creek was always good for a little extra revenue from fox, coyote and mink. By running a line down there I could contact Dad occasionally. Of late years, he had trapped over the summit from Landslide on the Blue Ridge Mountain. One of his cabins in there, which he called his Blue Ridge Mountain Home, was within half a day's travel of Landslide. By having a line down there, we could rendezvous, either at Landslide or at his cabin, and check up on how the other fellow was doing.

I suppose there are various reasons why I kept at trapping until I was married. One of them was that I had got started at it so young that it seemed that trapping was the only real occupation there was. Anything else was like substitute action—something to play at occasionally for a change. I had pretty well been raised on a diet of trapping and amongst trappers. All the men who had seemed to me to be heroes when I was a boy had either been trappers or were following some occupation akin to trapping. Obviously, too, I enjoyed the feeling of freedom and independence it gave me. I didn't necessarily relish the hardships and dangers connected with it, but responded with satisfaction to the feeling of self-reliance I would experience after winning a battle with some of the many adversaries the country provided.

Beyond all this, I liked the money. Lynx, marten, coyote, beaver and mink were plentiful in those days and I could come out in the spring with a nice little stake. Knowing that I could go back the next winter and make another gave me a feeling of security that bordered on prosperity.

Geoff was awakened in the night by "a great racket in the brush."

Jolly Great Rabbit

from *Campfire Sketches of the Cariboo*
by Fred W. Ludditt

*Sons of England who were an embarrassment to their upper-class
families or too low in the birth order to inherit property were
sent to the colonies to make what they could of themselves.
Dubbed "remittance men" for the regular allowance they
received from home, these young men of the silver spoon were
generally ill equipped to deal with the rough conditions of frontier
living. Some became mud pups on ranches or turned a clumsy
but earnest hand to any activity in which they could prove their
salt. Others, dandified beyond all redemption, never quite made
the transition. In the following selection, historian Fred Ludditt
recalls one amusing character, Geoff Smith, who gave it the old
college try. Ludditt was born in Birmingham but grew up in
Saskatchewan, where his father was a stonemason. He developed
an appetite for Cariboo history while working in the many phases
of the mining industry around Barkerville and the Fraser River.
He was a driving force behind resurrecting Barkerville as a
museum town of gold-rush days.*

Quesnel in those years had a population of perhaps eight or nine hundred people. Some of these were the descendants of pioneers who had come seeking their fortunes in the Cariboo gold rush in the early 1860s, and who had remained to open up this new land, and to prosper. Others were newcomers, some moved there by the Depression, some well off, others not so. It was a varied population.

Geoff Smith, an acquaintance of ours, was a graduate of Oxford University. His father was the editor-in-chief of a prominent London daily. Thinking of Geoff recalls to mind some amusing incidents. Every month he received a substantial allowance from his people in England, which made him a wealthy man by any standards. Sadly this did not often last long, but was soon dissipated among his many friends. On one occasion when I met him and he was feeling rather low I remarked on this, thinking how wretched a man of his stature must feel to awaken in the morning and find himself broke. "Broke be blowed," said he. "I'm just financially embarrassed at the moment. I shall write to Motha and she'll advance me a few bob."

Geoff was a tall, well-proportioned young man in his late 20s. He wore heavy-lensed glasses that gave to his countenance an air of seriousness. In fact, he was a serious chap. There was a kindliness and innocence about him that must have been at constant discord with this "barbarous" frontier. How often he must have compared his rough-and-tumble surroundings with his sheltered and refined life at home in London.

Ben and I met Geoff on the street one day as we were getting together some supplies to take on a prospecting trip up the Quesnel River. When he learned of our plans he said, "How I should like to be going on such a venture!"

"Well, why not come along?" Ben said.

"By Jove, that's an excellent idea. When are you leaving?"

"We plan to leave about 8:30 tomorrow."

"What shall I need?" asked Geoff.

"Just bring your bedroll and some grub," said Ben.

"What's grub?" asked Geoff.

Well, anyway. "We'll meet you at the corner of S.N. Williams at 8:30 in the morning," said Ben.

Next morning we were there at the appointed time and awaiting Geoff's appearance. At nine o'clock we were just about to set off without him, thinking that he had changed his mind, when we saw him making his way up the street. At first we couldn't make out why he was bent half double and walking in a very ungainly manner. As he drew near we observed his pack. It consisted of one long roll of blanket, bulging in the middle and tied at each end with a rope that extended under one arm, across his chest, over his shoulder and down to the other end. The main burden, the bulge in the middle, was riding so low on his back that it was almost impossible to balance it properly. In one hand he was carrying a billycan with a lid covering that threatened at any moment to drop off.

"What in the world have you got there?" asked Ben.

"Just my bedroll and supplies," answered Geoff.

"You won't get through the woods very far with a pack tied up that way."

"Oh, I don't know," said Geoff, slightly miffed. "Bandoleer-style, you know, bandoleer-style."

However, we were able to persuade him to let us make a neater pack of it. This we did without, unfortunately, examining the contents. So we started out, Geoff still carrying his billycan, which had been purchased at Cowan's Hardware especially for the trip.

Our destination was about 16 miles up the old road to the river. We had travelled perhaps a couple of miles when Constable Vickers of the provincial police overtook us. He was driving a Chev touring car and, on learning where we were headed, offered us a lift. This took us to within about three miles of the river.

The trail to the river, abandoned for years, was overgrown with willows and often blocked by windfalls. In places there were steep grades and sharp cutbanks, making it rough enough for anyone. Poor

Geoff was often far behind. Besides, he found it difficult to keep his footing, and when we looked back it was generally to see him picking himself up and searching for his billycan or the lid off it, which in the fall would drop and roll out of reach.

"I should jolly well trip over my own shadow," he said once in exasperation as we sat for a while giving him a chance to rest.

We reached the river in mid-afternoon and immediately began to set up camp. For a while Geoff sat about seeming at a loss as to what should be done. Ben, noting this, suggested that he take an axe and gather firewood. We had put up the fly tent, arranged our bedding and supplies, made a fire and had supper cooking on it, when Geoff returned, carrying a small armful of wood and the axe in the other hand.

"Where on earth have you been?" asked Ben.

"I should jolly well get lost walking around a blooming pool table," said he. "I shouldn't have been back yet had I not seen your smoke."

He then set about arranging his own bed and unpacking his gear. What was our amazement to discover that his pack was made up mostly of about a dozen or more heavy magazines and some notepaper and pencils; and that all he had in the way of supplies was a loaf of bread and a can of bully beef. (In the next few days he made copious notes on all about us.)

We had an ideal campsite on a grassy bench and the river made a pleasant shishing sound as it slipped past our tent. Often in the evenings we looked across the water to the wooded slopes and could count as many as 16 deer and fawn, the latter bouncing and jumping about much as lambs might do in a field. To us, and more so to Geoff, this was a pleasure almost unbelievable. There he would sit making additional notes, as he commented on the beauty of it all.

We prospected for a day or so, even setting up an old rocker that we found nearby, but there wasn't enough gold in our cleanup to warrant remaining. So we tested the bars farther up the river, and came to one that was much more promising.

When Ben remarked that we would pack up in the morning and go to the new site, Geoff exclaimed, "Move! Why should we leave this lovely site?"

"There's no use staying. We're not making any money here," said Ben.

"Well," was Geoff's comment, "I shouldn't think it matters so long as we are working."

We spent a week on the river, during which time Geoff learned a lot about camp life. He became quite adept at handling the various chores and procedures. In the evenings he became the storyteller, giving us vivid accounts of his life in London and his trips to the continent.

At the end of the week we decided to return to Quesnel, and Geoff found it considerably easier now to travel in the woods. Besides this, his pack was lighter, he having rid it of most of the magazines, and the "supplies." When we had reached a spot not far from my first camp with Leo Martin, he expressed a desire to remain out one night on his own. He wanted to prove to himself that he could do it. So we set up the fly tent for him and left him there to make his own fire and cook supper.

Next morning we returned to help him carry in the gear. "How did you make out, Geoff? No problems, eh?"

"Well, I slept not too badly, first with one eye open and then with the other. I was awakened during the night with a great racket in the brush."

"That could have been a pack rat," said Ben.

"Pack rat be blowed! It was a jolly great rabbit galloping up the hillside," said Geoff.

So ended our little "expedition" with Geoff.

With countless tales of their prowess on the ice, the Alkali Lake Hockey Team was the pride of the Cariboo in the '20s and early '30s.

Alkali Lake Hockey Team

a new story by Hilary Place

In his book Dog Creek: A Place in the Cariboo, *Hilary Place wrote briefly of the Alkali Lake Hockey Team. He describes their preparations for games:*

> On Friday the Alkali boys would be getting ready to travel.
> The old green-and-white uniforms ... had been checked over
> and patched and mended with loving care by the wives and
> sweethearts of the players. Players packed up their gloves, shin
> pads, and short pants, the sum total of their equipment, which
> was usually handmade from buckskin and willow sticks, along
> with deer hair for extra padding. Their skates were sharpened
> by hand file and stones. Some had been sharpened so many
> times that there was precious little metal left.

Place's new story about the Alkali Lake Hockey Team has all the makings of a first-rate movie. A man is hired to take the boys north to the big city to face off for the championship. He loads the team onto the back of his pickup, where they huddle for hours in minus-forty temperatures. They arrive stiff, frozen, hungry and tired after a dangerous blowout delays them. With no time to rest or eat, they thaw themselves enough to lace their skates and hit the ice. The rest is Cariboo history. One shining player, a natural all-star in every sense, gave his best despite being very sick. He would not live to play another game. (The 2006 CBC miniseries and companion volume Hockey: A People's History *included a look at the Alkali team, and an excerpt about it from Place's* Dog Creek.*)*

Ray Curtis was a very powerful man. He was undoubtedly the strongest man in the Cariboo when the woods up there were full of strong men. He kept a large family by doing hard work and doing it well. When I was about 10 or 12 years old, Ray spent the winter feeding cattle and working for Ray Pigeon. We were playing some scrum hockey and one time, while in full flight, I ran into Ray. It was similar to hitting a brick wall. When I had gotten myself straightened out, he skated over and said, "Did you hurt yourself?"

Everybody in the Cariboo had a Ray Curtis story and they all saluted his honesty and his strength. The local surveyor would hire Ray as a packer and tell how if the new car Ray bought every year wouldn't make it over some stump that was blocking the way, Ray would just reach down and lift the car over it.

There were some who disparaged Ray's intellect. One time Ray was telling me about how the surveyor worked. Ray said, "We did that by triangulation," then cocked his eye at me as much as to say, "You didn't think I knew about that, did you?" Ray was no dummy, believe me. All you had to do was get into a horse-trading deal with him to find that out.

Ray told me a story about the Alkali Lake Hockey Team over his kitchen table at his home in Williams Lake shortly before he died. The team in the '20s and early '30s was the pride of the Cariboo. There were countless tales of their prowess on the ice and, in particular, of their clean and enjoyable play. Most people remember a sensational game or play made by the team, but there was another quality that was not spoken of by most. That was the hardship and intolerance in which they played. This story is illustrative of the treatment they got, and their fortitude ...

Ray was living in Williams Lake and on this occasion was cutting and hauling firewood for people living in the town. He was called to the phone that was in the telegraph office close by Mackenzie's store.

Mr. Barbour, the operator of the telegraph service, had sent the word out that Ray was wanted on the phone and, in due course, Ray was found and turned up for the call. It was David Johnson on the other end of the wire and he had a problem. David was the captain of the hockey team at Alkali Lake, and his problem was that they needed transportation to get to Prince George to play a final series of games for the Cariboo championship.

Ray agreed to a price and took on the job of getting the team to Prince George for the game. He fired up his old two-ton truck and went out to Alkali Lake to pick up the team. Two of the players got into the cab with Ray, and the rest got in the back with the wood chips and the bark. No cover, no seats, no heat. The thermometer was hanging around 30 degrees Fahrenheit below zero. This type of transportation was even worse than Tiger Williams' iron lung for being primitive. There were no cars on the reserve at that time, except for one that belonged to Henry Squinahan, and it was broken down.

When the team was all on board Ray's truck, they took off for Prince George, some 150 miles away. When they got to Williams Lake the lights on the old truck wouldn't work, so Ray wired them up directly to the battery so they did work, all the time, unless you pulled the wire off the battery. With this minor repair they continued on the way to Prince George. They were about 10 miles from Quesnel and doing just fine when a front tire blew out. They skidded across the road and, with some fancy maneuvering by Ray, managed to stay right side up. The tire was a goner. There was nothing for it but to hitchhike to Quesnel and get a new tire. Finally a car came along and Ray got a ride to Quesnel. His problems were not over. There was no tire available in that size in the whole town. What they did have was a wheel that was a size smaller than the old one with a tire on it, so Ray settled for that and hitched a ride back to the truck with it. It was soon mounted and away they went. Ray said the smaller wheel pulled hard to the right, but he was able to hold it if they didn't go too fast. North of Quesnel the lights were hooked up and there was clear and cold sailing to Prince George. The game was scheduled for eight o'clock Saturday night, and they arrived in Prince George at seven-thirty. They were all hungry, having had nothing since breakfast, but there was no time for eating. "Besides," Joe Clemine said with a laugh, "we all play better when we're hungry." It was like heaven to get into the change room, where there was an airtight heater puffing and smoking, cherry red with heat.

The game started on time, and in the first period the Prince George team bounded ahead. But in the second and third, the Alkali boys simply outran them and won the game handily. Ray said that one of the players, a fellow by the name of Gaby Jack, was simply outstanding. He hadn't been feeling too well going to the game and had been given a front seat in the truck. Ray said he looked pale and shivered a lot from the cold. Gaby never said much, but always stood in the background and sort of hid.

On the ice he was magnificent. He was one of those players who made the game seem easy. His skating was effortless, and he turned either way with grace and ease. He handled his stick like it was made of glass, barely touching the puck to put it into position for a shot. And then the sweeping wrist shot accurately placed the puck in the net. Everything about his play was deceptive. He looked like he was going slow, yet nobody could catch him. He looked vulnerable to hits, but he just seemed to be missed; his shot looked weak, yet it would find the back of the net.

He was a very, very good player and he was sick. Actually, he was dying from TB, and a few weeks later he was dead.

Accommodation was a poor-quality hotel run by an eastern European who didn't like Indians, so they got the worst and coldest rooms and were allotted two to the bed. Breakfast was greasy bacon and eggs. And there was the final game at two o'clock. Alkali won that one, too, and the championship of the Cariboo. They then turned to the trip home, tired and sweaty, and eight hours of travel in the back of a two-ton truck in the cold.

Ray said the trip home was uneventful. He even got a tire that fit the front wheel in Prince George, and he took the small one back to the garage he got it from in Quesnel. The man said that he wouldn't charge them for the use of it because they had beaten Prince George, which was what he wanted.

"It was a tough trip," Ray said, "and we didn't get invited to the league championship dinner either."

Danger Dodges Us as the Ice Breaks Up

from *Tenderfoot Trail: Greenhorns in the Cariboo*
by Olive Spencer Loggins

In the first volume of Heart of the Cariboo–Chilcotin, *we read in Olive Spencer Loggins' story "Danger Comes Calling" (also from* Tenderfoot Trail*) how she and her husband, newly settled on an isolated homestead near Deka Lake, B.C., had to defend themselves and their baby against a pair of marauding outlaws bent on taking their food supplies, guns and if need be, their lives. In this excerpt from the same book, the danger lurking is not in human form, but in the thawing ice that in winter served as a reliable road. Tension mounts as mother and father travel that road in the dead of night to deal with an emergency, leaving their child unattended.*

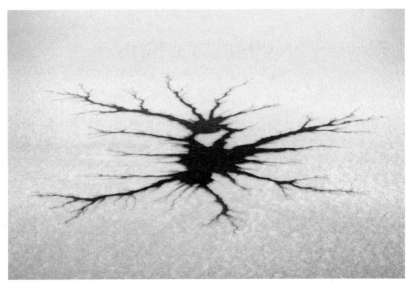

"The ice suddenly split beneath the runners of the sleigh and huge jagged fissures shot out in all directions."

Arthur saddled Speed early and rode off across Dragonfly Lake where dark areas were beginning to appear, which Ed Martin had told us marked a deterioration of the firm ice surface, so that before long it could not be used to travel upon. "I'll make good time getting to Jenners' place, but it may take some time to lead the cow back, so don't look for me too early this evening," said my husband before starting the trip.

I watched him ride away across Dragonfly towards the south end from where a trail led through thick woods to Hathaway Lake. As the day wore on a heavy March snowstorm developed and soon I could scarcely see more than a few feet away from the cabin. Everything became muted under a heavy fall of snow, but later I heard the sound of horses approaching. I looked out to see that two riders were dismounting and as they came to the cabin door I recognized one of them as Danny Hatch, the father of the small boy whom he had brought to me for help at Deka Lake.

Danny held out to me a large hindquarter of deer meat. "Is it for me?" I asked doubtfully. I knew that the Indians had been without meat just as we had during the long winter. "How did you know where to find me?" I asked the young man.

"This first game of the season, Indian want to pay debt! I go to Deka Lake house first. Little white mother him gone! Squaw with bitter tongue say where you live. Danny bring meat to Dragonfly. This Lily's man," he said, indicating his friend.

I suppressed a chuckle at the native description of the unfriendly Mrs. Charlton. Apparently their dislike of each other was mutual. "Will you come in and have hot coffee before you ride on? I'm very grateful to you for bringing me this meat." The visitors accepted my offer of coffee but left soon, saying they hoped to reach Canim Lake before it grew dark. They had had a successful first hunt and wanted to take meat to their tribe.

When my husband returned that night after his long ride, I would be able to set a delicious roast of venison before him. I divided the generous piece of meat and hung part of it in my small root cellar, safe from pack rats, and contentedly planned the evening meal that was to be such a welcome change from baked macaroni. Not that macaroni hadn't served us well, but one could get terribly tired of that old standby. I even thought up an eggless, milkless dessert as well. I began to anticipate a lovely celebration.

The afternoon brought an end to the snowstorm, and the brilliant sunshine that followed made a white wonderland of the woods around Dragonfly Lake. It also accentuated the airholes in the lake, black watery patches showing in many places now. Arthur's plan to bring back the cow today had been a sensible one.

I had figured that my husband should be home by seven at the latest. But eight o'clock came and he was not back, I finally ate my dinner alone. The tasty roast was beginning to dry up and I was disappointed, but set Arthur's plate in the warming oven to try and keep things hot for when he got home. Roland had his evening bath and his meal and was put to bed. I tried in vain to read; my thoughts kept straying. Several times I stepped out onto the porch and peered towards the lake, but it was now a large indefinite area of blackness. I could see or hear nothing except the plaintive yapping of hungry coyotes far off. Suddenly, quite close to the cabin, the lonely howl of a wolf sounded and was answered by another howl further down the shores of the lake. Wolves! These would be the large black predators known as the Siberian or Russian wolf, and a formidable foe.

I went indoors and really did some worrying. If the wolves were in a pack, they would not hesitate to attack a man. Arthur would be leading the cow and would not be progressing very fast. If there were only telephones in this country! But they were still several years into the future. Perhaps my husband had stopped overnight at the Hodges' ranch if he had seen that it had become too dark to continue the trip. With a telephone he could have contacted me and set my mind at rest. Pioneer women in this forbidding north country had often waited alone in some lonely cabin for husband or sons, and how often their men had never returned, victims of some mischance that had overtaken them in this tough, relentless land.

At midnight my vigil was still on. I couldn't dream of getting into bed and sleeping, I was far too tense. Waiting and listening! The night seemed endless, broken only by the baby needing his 2 a.m. meal. I had never been able to get him to forgo this feeding in the wee small hours, although the best hospitals recommend it. Suddenly my heart leaped; I heard Arthur give a command to Speed and approach the door. They were home at last! But my joy was shortlived.

Arthur sat down with a dejected slump of his shoulders and started to eat his dinner and drink the hot coffee I offered him. "I'm afraid our luck has run out, dear. That darned cow got as far as the lower end of Sulphurous Lake and simply refused to come across the ice. I just couldn't budge her an inch. I finally had to tie her up to a tree beside the lake and I've come back to try with the team and sleigh. I'll need your help, too. Our best plan will be to get the cow onto the sleigh and haul her home. We must get back right away, I heard that wolves are running in packs, so that fool cow would be just like a sitting duck if the wolves spot her there!"

"But what about Roland? I can't leave him here alone! I guess I'd better wrap him up warmly and put his little box in the sleigh, don't you agree, Arthur?"

"No, I don't agree! This is no place for a five-month-old baby. We'll have that cow in the sleigh if we can get her in. Our child will be much safer here. I hope we won't be away for very long." My husband went to the barn to harness the team and I fussed around like an old hen, putting the fire in the stove completely out and blowing out the coal-oil lamps. I knew that I'd worry about my son, he had never been left alone in his life, but now circumstances demanded that I leave him here in this isolated cabin while I went out at three o'clock in the morning to try and help bring back a balky cow over the weakening surface of the lake ice. I never could have anticipated having to make such a choice. The north country was a hard taskmaster.

I joined my husband on the seat of the sleigh. He had tied Speed on behind just in case, he told me, we might need the saddle horse, too. The melancholy howl of the wolves sounded again, quite nearby. The frightening ululations echoed from hill to hill around the lake. Arthur told me he had stopped for lunch with the Hodges. Anne Hodges had told him that the wolves had been seen on Sulphurous Lake in groups of seven or eight.

The waning moon made the scene as bright as day, and it also revealed to my startled eyes the number and extent of the airholes. They looked larger and far more dangerous than viewing them from the safety of the shore. "Good heavens, Arthur!" I exclaimed nervously, "do you think it's wise to bring the team and sleigh out on this rotting surface? It looks awfully risky to me!"

My husband was exhorting the team to the best pace they were capable of. "Giddap, Molly. Shake the lead out of your feet, Daisy!" Turning to me he said, "I had no alternative really. We need that cow, and when I paid Jack Jenner, it took the last of our cash. Knowing these wolves are around, I feel we must take the chance. I'm sure she wouldn't be there in the morning."

Often the large hoofs of the team seemed to barely miss a huge hole where the water spread out on the top of the ice, but my husband guided the horses with a sure hand and we were soon on the short portage between Dragonfly and Hathaway Lake. This lake being longer required more time to traverse, but finally we reached Sulphurous Lake and here the holes seemed even larger and more numerous. I admit that my imagination works overtime in cases like these and once I barely repressed a frightened scream. "Relax, dear! You're too tensed up, everything is going fine! Before long we'll be down to the place where I've tied the cow," my husband said, reassuringly. He seemed to have nerves of steel.

We passed the Hodges' house all in darkness. It was about three-thirty and intensely cold, although I felt hot with excitement. Arthur was gazing intently down the lake and I stared too. Did I really see five black forms rapidly crossing the ice, or was that, too, a figment of my imagination? But my husband said, grimly, "Yes, you really see wolves, I'm afraid we'll be just a few moments too late. Shout! Yell! Make all the noise you can. Giddap, Molly, Daisy!" He brought the whip down smartly on the horses' rumps. Startled by such unaccustomed severity, the team put their backs into it and we sped down the final piece of lake ice as if the devil were after us, instead of in front, in the form of five huge and hungry Siberian wolves.

Yelling like banshees, we converged upon the spot where the cow loomed, a black blur near the lake edge. Almost at the same time the wolves completed their run across the lake from its western shore. The noisy arrival of the team and drivers deterred them temporarily, as they slunk into the cover of shrubs at the shore. My husband jumped off the sleigh seat and reached behind into the box and brought out his rifle. He took random aim and fired in the general direction the wolves had run. Apparently he found a target because a high howl filled the night, followed by a violent thrashing in the brush and then such a savage snarling and the heart-stopping noise of crunching fangs on bones! One of the wolves had been shot and was now being attacked by his companions. I shuddered as I turned my attention back to the cow.

She regarded us with suspicion. Now what did we think we were going to try to make her do? Arthur placed the gun in the sleigh box and removed from it a large door which he set at the back of the sleigh. He untied the cow and led her to the makeshift ramp and tried to lead her up this, but the heavy animal pulled back on the rope and braced herself for a struggle. It was a ridiculous sight, no doubt, a man and woman shoving and pulling at that stubborn creature, but we were desperate and kept trying for an hour. What a mistrustful bovine! In the brush the yellow glow of the wolves' eyes reminded us that they were just waiting for a chance to rush upon us. Finally, exasperated, my mate gave up. "It's no use," he said, replacing the barn door on the sleigh. "Do you think you could ride herd upon this cow, if I tied her to the back of the sleigh, sort of keep her walking straight alongside? It seems to be about the only means to budge her."

I looked at Speed, remembering that he was just recently saddle-broken. I specifically recalled the many devious ways he had devised to unseat his rider. Nevertheless, with a do or die attitude, I told my husband that I was willing to try this plan. So he untied Speed and put the cow in back of the sleigh. I mounted the horse and Arthur took the reins, and the team, glad to be in motion again, started back up the lake.

For a short time all went well, I even forgot to search for large airholes. I felt leery of Speed, however, and in the uncanny way of animals he sensed my fear. In spite of having been warned not to display fear of animals since I had come into the wilderness, the feeling was there and I couldn't hide it. Perhaps the tense way in which I grasped the neck rein informed my mount, because soon he began to shove closely against the side of the sleigh, so that my leg was being jammed against it. Or else he shoved against the flank of the cow, which was worse. Up until now she had been going along with the idea, but Speed's ornery actions put a stop to that and the cow started to pull back on her rope.

Arthur shouted back over his shoulder asking what was the trouble. I told him and suggested that we change places. I had driven the team a few times and, anyway, I wouldn't mind giving up riding Speed, who appeared to be a completely one-man nag. So we made the change and things went along as before Speed started his shenanigans, except that I tensely peered ahead and gasped at every large airhole as we came up to it. "Stop worrying, the horses don't want to walk into a hole any more than you do!" said Arthur, sympathetic to my fear although not comprehending it.

How wonderful it must be to have so much faith in the horses; I wished that some of this confidence would rub off on me and I admired my mate even more than I ever had before, but I went on fighting to keep my heart where it belonged and not up in my throat! We covered Sulphurous Lake, Hathaway, and made the portage over to our own lake, Dragonfly, without any mishaps and I began to feel that my fears had been unfounded.

Only three miles to go. I relaxed and that made everything so much worse when what I feared actually did happen. About halfway across Dragonfly there was a tremendous cr-r-ack! The ice suddenly split right beneath the runners of the sleigh and huge jagged fissures shot out in all directions. The team drew to a standstill, casting terrified glances back towards us. Did the ice actually heave and tilt beneath us? It certainly seemed to. Here, just a mile from safety, would we all plunge to our deaths in the icy waters? I prayed wildly and stifled my screams and heard Arthur yelling urgently at me, "Keep the team going! Don't let them stop or we'll all be killed! Giddap, Molly, Daisy, giddap there!"

In her terror, all her original fears about travelling on ice having been confirmed, that nerve-ridden cow had slumped forward on her knees and was bawling to the skies! Arthur rode his horse forward, pulling the cow to her feet. The team responded gallantly as I applied the whip; they realized the danger as much as we did, and stepping carefully, they started away from the dangerous spot and the ever-widening area of dark water. Gingerly the horses drew the sleigh onto safer ice. Arthur had managed to calm the cow enough so that she plodded behind and we covered the remaining distance to the safety of the shore. I said a heartfelt prayer when we finally climbed off the ice to the bank. I can't remember ever being so happy to feel solid ground beneath my feet! With a relieved sigh I jumped from the sleigh and dashed towards the cabin while Arthur drove the weary horses and frightened cow to the welcome shelter of the barn.

I ran into the cabin to find that the baby was still peacefully sleeping, although the cabin had grown very cold. I hastily lit the fire in the range and prepared coffee and a hot breakfast for my husband. He never needed sustenance more, I'm positive. When he came indoors the first thing he did was to hold me tightly in his arms. "I'd never have managed to get that cow home unless you had been there to help," he declared gratefully.

"I don't think I was of much help," I replied, "we seem to be learning to pioneer the hard way, though I doubt if there ever was an easy way. I guess it's all in the day's work as Jack Jenner would say. But I hope it's not all going to be as tough as this night has been. Still we proved we can stand on our own feet, and I think we earned a promotion from the tenderfoot status!"

Our real help came from God, who surely and safely guided us out of danger that night, and before we slept we both acknowledged our debt to the Creator of all things on earth.

"Old Annie seemed as much a creature of the past as the present."

When Annie spoke, her fingers were always busy, making birchbark baskets like the one shown here.

Lady of the Lakes

from *He Saw With Other Eyes: Stories from the Cariboo*
by Todd Lee

To a young Todd Lee and his brother Eldon, Annie Basil was like a nature spirit, appearing with the change of the seasons, and disappearing as naturally and mysteriously as she had come. She was old, but timeless, her years bridging past and present. They knew her well enough as a devout woman who attended church regularly on the reserve. They knew her better when she camped at Squawks Lake, for it was there that she captivated the two lads with her nature lore and adventure stories of Indian wars and gold while her busy hands picked berries or fashioned bark into beautifully crafted baskets.

My favourite place for solitary recharging was the Knife Creek Range, where I had spent my boyhood. There I walked old trails and relived the times when my brother and I had roamed the woods during carefree summer days. It was here that I came in late afternoon one September day.

The road that led from the 141 Mile House to Squawks Lake was not one that invited faint-hearted travellers. The mudholes were deep and the rocks were high and sharp. It didn't stop me, however; I knew the location of all the hazardous spots. Parking my car below the lakes, I wandered along a trail above Knife Creek until I came to a beaver dam. Eldon and I had fished and swum here as boys, and later set mink and muskrat traps in season. I sat down on a fallen tree trunk and opened memory lane. And then I remembered her—Old Annie—Old Annie Basil. In moments the passage of 20 years was erased and I was a 10-year-old, eager to learn about the world around me.

Annie came, I recall, with the regularity of the seasons, year after year.

It might be in that interlude of early spring when winter had given up its harsh grip and nature worked its miracle of renewal. It might be when summer haze lay heavy on forested slopes and sunbeams filtered through the pines of the blueberry swamp to ripen plump fruit for the delight of bird, beast and man. It might be during the first crisp days of Indian summer when gold and scarlet from poplar and sumac joined in the task of laying a rich carpet on the forest floor; when fat young partridges dusted along the roadsides, and proud antlered bucks roamed the alder thickets.

At one of these special times she would come, hobbling along the road, one dusky hand holding a gnarled walking stick and the other grasping the lead rope that made her one with the ancient grey nag that carried her camping equipment.

We called her Old Annie—everyone did, and though she bore the surname of Basil I never heard that name used. Annie was her Christian name and old she certainly was. How old, no one seemed to know. "When Annie was a little girl, white men came to this country," she told us, her eyes twinkling as she worked away at a basket in front of her camp. My brother and I never tired of listening to her stories or of watching her hands, which always seemed to be busy. The tales she told us did much to recreate in our minds a picture of the glorious past of her people.

Although Old Annie was a very sociable person and loved to sit and visit by the hour, she was also a solitary wanderer who travelled alone with no other company than her faithful pack horse. When she tied her horse to our gate post and stopped for a visit, we put up a tent for her and urged her to stay. She always stayed, a few days or a week—time worried her not. She had about her an atmosphere of timelessness that gave a quiet rebuke to the hurry and bustle of the world about her. One morning she would be gone, moving back into the wilderness to find the solitude of nature that gave her delight and peace.

Sometimes Eldon and I found her sitting motionless beside a beaver pond, a fishline dangling from the end of a long pine pole, patience and contentment written in every line of her face. Intent on her fishing, she wasn't interested in idle chatter, but would always nod and smile. We would go on about our business with no thought of disturbing her.

Sometimes we would find Annie's campsites after she had gone. They were left ready for her return, a small supply of dry wood piled near the neat circle of stones, and usually the polished sticks with which she kindled her fire.

Old Annie seemed as much a creature of the past as of the present. She could discuss current events with intelligence and wit, and she loved to talk about the daily life of the reserve and to share humorous incidents from the lives of those around her. When on the reserve, she was faithful in attending the Mission Church and dressed to suit the occasion, a far cry from the ragged clothes that were a part of her nomadic wanderings. From Red Cross nurses she had learned the skills of a practical nurse and midwife, and had brought into the world some prominent citizens, now reaching senior-citizen status themselves.

More true to Annie's image, however, was the quiet figure relaxed by her tent, hands busy with basket and beadwork, but thoughts a half century or more in the past as she spun a web of adventure for two small boys who hung on every word. And what stories they were ... Hardships and danger, Indian wars and buried gold ... Each tale seemed to bear its own stamp of authenticity and in the telling, Annie appeared scarcely conscious of the present, but living again in days long gone by.

Old Annie spoke the dialect of her people fluently, we knew, but with us she always used English in the soft, drawling sing-song inflection of her race. There were two exceptions to this: for things that particularly pleased her, she would use the Salish adjective "Hie-yu," nodding her head vigorously and otherwise showing every evidence of pleasure. On the other hand, for something that displeased her, she would use the explosive "Hai-lo!" following it with disapproving clicks of her tongue.

Sometimes Annie would take us into the woods to share with us her vast store of woodlore. On one such trip she paused by a clump of wild lily plants, then, using a sharp stick, she probed in the ground. Presently she produced several small bulbs which she handed to us to taste.

"Hie-yu, good," she exclaimed, smacking her lips, then grinned broadly at the wry expressions on our faces as we spat out the bitter root. "You cook him," she explained, "then he just like a potato."

Another time Annie showed us a bush laden with bright red berries. She picked a handful and squeezed the juice into her mouth, inviting us to do the same. Again we were amazed at the horrible soapy taste of the fruit. Annie laughed openly at our discomfort. "You have to learn to like him—Indian boys think hooshem berry juice just like soda pop!"

Perhaps the most fascinating of Old Annie's activities was her skill in making birchbark baskets. Starting with a piece of unblemished bark, she would carve and fold until she had fashioned it into a square vessel with slightly rounded corners. Next she prepared thongs, not of thread or sinews, but of long fibres stripped from a length of green spruce root. Some of these she dyed scarlet with the juice of hooshem berries, others a bright blue from huckleberries. Black came from the coals of her campfire and yellow from the golden plumes of the dandelion or snapdragon. With the point of her skinning knife serving as an awl, she made rows of tiny perforations along the edge of each seam, then her fingers fairly flew as she wove the multi-coloured roots in and out, in and out, until there was a bright border up each corner and completely around the top. The finished product was a surprisingly attractive and useful basket. I still have one of them on display.

There came a spring when we waited in vain for Annie to make her usual visit. Later we learned that her relatives, afraid that something might happen to her in the bush, would not let her go away again on her own.

Annie was not to be so easily dissuaded; when the blueberry season arrived, Annie arrived also. She moved more slowly, it is true, but then her old pack horse had reached the age when he was not difficult to pace.

"I run away!" Annie reported gleefully. "Andrew think he keep me home, but I fool him. I tell him, 'Annie just go down to the store at the 150 Mile' ... then I go quick down the road." She chuckled with delight, hugely enjoying the thought of how she had outwitted her guardians.

Annie did not go to the Lakes, however, but was content to accept the hospitality of our tent and spend the days near our ranch. Most of the time she sat in the sun by her camp, content to listen to our small-boy chatter. When she readied her pack to return to the reserve she was reluctant to leave, turning again and again to repeat her goodbyes. It was as though she could sense that she would never come that way again. Finally she walked away, the old horse hobbling along behind her, the two of them tired emissaries from another day.

I saw Old Annie once more the following spring when we made an infrequent trip to the reserve. She was sitting in front of her tiny log cabin, seemingly watching the goings and comings of her neighbours, but in reality almost blind. Her shrunken figure was wrapped in successive layers of sweaters and shawls. At my greeting a smile of recognition flitted across her face, but when she spoke, her face took on the passiveness of resignation.

"I go no more to the Lakes," she said sadly. "My old horse, he is dead. Now Annie die, too."

Old Annie lived on, however, for several more years. I went away to university in Seattle and for a time lost track of familiar people and places. One day I read an item from the hometown newspaper describing a fire on the reserve. An elderly woman had perished in the blaze. Even before I read the name, I sensed that it was my boyhood friend, Old Annie Basil.

My thoughts were broken by the swish of wings as a covey of ducks swooped in to a landing on the beaver pond. With a start I came back to the present, but the memories persisted. How much my life had changed in 20 years! There were the university years, marriage and a young family, my return to the Cariboo as a minister; but how little had changed here. A few feet from where I stood the grass grew up through a circle of stones where once there had been a campfire. I was certain that it was one that Annie had left long ago, tidy and ready for her return.

Twilight came and with its coming the beaver came out to trace silvery paths on the surface of the pond. A trout leaped high to catch a drifting fly and landed with a plop and a dash of spray. High overhead a nighthawk chirped in its circling flight. I could almost see Annie there, her face a picture of contentment as she surveyed *her* fishing grounds. Was it only imagination conjured by the heady scents of the summer evening? Or was it Old Annie's voice echoing softly through the shadowy pines in praise of God's creation: "Hie-yu, good!"

George Harrison and I Start the OK

from *Cariboo Cowboy*
by Harry Marriott

What can you do if you're a poor Cariboo cowboy and you feel the stirrings of an ambition to own your own ranch? If you're Harry Marriott, you comb your hair and go down to Vancouver and find a rich man to partner up with. In the first volume of Heart of the Cariboo–Chilcotin, *we saw Marriott working for the Gang Ranch, where he learned the cowboy trade. In the following excerpt, Marriott relates in his cheerful, understated and utterly endearing way the ups and downs, ins and outs of being a new ranch owner.*

Buying the old Haller place and turning it into the OK Ranch opened up a new era for Harry Marriott.

The early fall of 1933 I had heard that a ranch, down the creek from Big Bar Lake about 14 miles, was for sale at a very reasonable price. It was an old-time spot, having been once owned by old Joe Haller, who was one of the earliest white men to come to the Big Bar country. I had known of this layout for many years, as it was only seven miles away from the old Crow's Bar pasture where I had put in my first few years for the Gang Ranch. It had some hay and lot of good bunch-grass pasture, and the mail stage to the Gang Ranch ran right by the door every week. At this time there was a telephone line running from Clinton to the Gang Ranch along the road—which surely was a real godsend in the matter of getting in touch with the outside world.

My heart was always tied up with a longing to have a good-sized ranch, a pretty good herd of cattle, a pile of good haystacks and grass for the cows. It seemed to me to be a sort of empire-building complex that I had in those days. I have heard it described as the cattleman's itch, which amounted to the same thing—always wanting to get bigger and better.

I guess the whole thing in a nutshell is Old Man Ambition everlastingly driving at a fellow to get ahead and get more—just like a squirrel piling up pine cones. Well, it would sure be a poor-looking world if we all set back and didn't take a chance on getting ahead somehow. If I ever hear of a fellow who has no ambition or get-up in his makeup, I just figure he will never set the world on fire at anything and is on the same level as a useless drone in a beehive.

I did quite a bit of meditating as to how and where I could get hold of this property. I finally put on my blue suit, shined up my shoes and combed my hair and went down to Vancouver to find Mr. George S. Harrison who, I was told, was a man of quite a bit of money and might finance me.

After three days of discussion, in which I laid all my cards on the table for him to look at, Mr. Harrison came back to the lake with me. We went down and looked the old Haller place over, and after some more lengthy pow-wows, we agreed to form a small company. We piled up all the different little places—land, cattle, buildings, etc.— into what we called The OK Ranching Co. Ltd., the name being taken from my brand "OK" on the left ribs. It had been my brand for many years.

This opened up a new era in ranching for me. Mr. Harrison and I became lifelong friends over many years until he died and passed over the High Mountain a few years ago. I respected and admired him, just the same as I would have done to my father. He was always the business and financial brains of the OK Ranching Co. Ltd., and on many, many occasions, he played Santa Claus to our hard-working and struggling little company.

It was a good combination, with Mr. Harrison possessing, to his fingertips, the principles and outlines of good business, and a seldom-failing knowledge of human nature. Always an optimist, and always interested in all things going on around him.

I figured I was the practical man—the dependable, long-hour, hard-working type that I had been, of necessity, trained to follow. I was never afraid to face an issue, or scared to make a decision. I drove myself hard, and tried to get reasonable value and loyalty from anyone who was working for us. Anytime I had a little brainwave come over me that I thought would be good for the company, I always submitted it to Mr. Harrison for his judgment. Our little company had its first start-off on October 8, 1933. Peg and I and Ronnie, who was eight years old, all moved down from the lake to the old Haller place, which became the headquarters layout of the OK Ranching Co.

My first chore was to look around and see if I could buy up "she stuff" to raise up the cattle herd on our OK setup, so I stepped on my [horse] Sunny Jim and rode down to the ferry on the Fraser at Big Bar. I rode for about four miles south, on a real jackrabbit trail, till I got to the Chisholm brothers' ranch, which is on the west side of the Fraser River.

These two brothers, Willie and Kenny, were a great pair of boys. I had known them for years. You could not find a better or more even family if you were to ride to Hell and back. They were great horsemen and number one men at packing a horse with a pack that would not loosen up or turn sideways. These boys just naturally had to be good at the pack horse game because their ranch had no road into it, and any supplies they got had to come over the trail on a pack horse or not at all. Their saddle horses had to be pretty sure-footed, because those narrow sidehill and steep gulch trails along that river were no place for a bumblefoot.

I stayed three days with the boys, and I proposed to buy 60 head of their breeding stock, cows and heifers. After considerable quiet consideration on their part, they agreed to sell them to me. We cut out the bunch and started for the Big Bar ferry, driving them down the trail. They were kind of oily to handle. You could always get a real wild and woolly run out of them if they took a notion. We got them down to the ferry and crossed them over the river and I paid Bill Chisholm. The next day I drove them on up the Big Bar Creek to the OK and a couple of days later saw them branded with the OK on the left ribs— the brand standing out on them like an old-fashioned privy in a fog. These Chisholm cows were all more or less mountain-raised stock, none of them real fat, but they had a real good frame on them and when bred to good white-faced bulls, they left us some good calves.

I also made a trip to Williams Lake stockyards that fall, and brought back around 20 to 30 good yearling steers that I shipped down from there to the Chasm on the PGE and drove them home to the OK in two long days.

I had two real good men with me at the OK Ranch that winter, with times still pretty tough, at $25 a month and their board. One was a pretty tough old customer named Bill Bunnage, who even today is a real mainstay of the OK Ranch. The other fellow was a good local boy named Ernie Love, who was a good hard worker. Bill Bunnage, with whom I had joined our army years before in World War I, was a man of many parts. In his time Bill had been a sailor, a soldier, a wild horseman, a freighter on the Cariboo Road, a ferryman on the Big Bar ferry, a mail-stage driver, a cowboy, and a ranch hand.

When it came to rough and tumble scraps, there were very few men around the Big Bar and Clinton country who would undertake to give Bill a physical trimming, as Bill was a rough tornado in action and knew all the stunts that go with no-rules fighting. Being plumb full of Irish grit, he always figured a way out of any situation that came along. Uncle Bill, as we called him—some of the boys had him nicknamed "Colonel Bill"—had a great pride in always doing his best, and a great loyalty to the OK Ranch, which is one quality in a human being that you can't buy.

Bill really loved to tell about the many hair-raising exploits he'd been into. Sometimes I wondered if he wasn't perhaps a little careless with the handling of the truth, but I know that he was sure a tough old customer, and no one could match his stories. In all the years I have known Uncle Bill, I have only heard him outdone once. It was at breakfast table one morning at the OK in the late '30s. I had a few men working on the ranch, one of them named Frank Dinger, who had been raised in the Utah country in the States, before drifting north to our British Columbia. Frank was a good all-round handyman on a ranch and could turn out pretty near anything in the ranch blacksmith shop.

My friend Bill was holding forth and telling us all how good a freight team skinner he was on the Cariboo Road in earlier days, how he had driven teams strung out two-by-two ahead of each other. In fact, they were strung out so far ahead that Uncle Bill had to have a loud megaphone on the wagon seat beside him so that his lead team would hear him calling to them. This Frank Dinger boy, who was a silent sort of fellow, very casually remarked that when he was just a boy on the plains of Kansas, he drove so many teams of oxen strung out two-by-two they damn near stretched as far as the human eye could see. The last team on the wagon tongue, in which he was sitting, driving, were slithering and staggering and weaving up and down and were up to their eyelids in bullshit. Uncle Bill looked at Frank Dinger and just gave a slight cough at that one. Dinger never moved a muscle in his poker face, and I allowed that, it would seem like, to me, that he must have been driving a fair to middlin' long team of oxen.

In the winter of 1933 we had to take a lot of our cattle up to Pine Crest to feed, which was now 28 miles from the OK headquarters, so Uncle Bill loaded up his sleigh with grub and blankets and drove the team ahead of the cattle, who strung along out behind in the sleigh tracks. After the haystacks were fed out at Pine Crest, we brought the cattle down to Big Bar Lake and continued to feed them there.

Towards the first week of March the snow got pretty soft and melting on the mountain about a couple of miles above the OK headquarters, and a lot of waving grass showed up in the last four inches of snow, so I turned out about 30 head of coming-two-year-old steers up in a real good pasture field, figuring they could get all the grass they needed without any hay feeding. They were all in fair shape, and I hoped to ship them in early August before the prices started to drop, which meant that I'd probably get at least $15 a head more for them, as against keeping them till October, when the big run of beef cattle comes on to the market.

One afternoon I sent Ernie Love up on the mountain to take a ride around those steers and see if they were all right and had a couple of blocks of salt to lick. Ernie came back, in an hour or so, riding on the run to tell me he was sure some of those steers were sick. A few minutes later he and I were riding to beat hell up to look at them. I saw some of these steers in very evident distress—their hair stood out, their eyes were glaring and bugged out, and every little while one would fall down, and stagger up again with all four feet braced outwards. A lot of them would pass out a long thin string of very strong-smelling manure. Ernie and I gathered up the steers and brought them all down to the ranch and I cut out 20 of them who certainly were very sick and kept them in the yard back of the barn.

These steers acted to me like they had eaten something poisonous, but I sure couldn't figure out what it could be. I got a few bottles of glycerine and drenched them, hoping that it would smooth out their stomachs, ease their pain, but one by one, out of the 20 affected, 16 died.

This was a rough jolt. I was sure worrying to beat hell, as I knew we needed the cheque for the steers in August, and now that they were dead there would be no pay from them. I wired Mr. Harrison in Vancouver, telling him the story and asking him to please contact the Dominion Veterinary Department in Vancouver, and to please send a vet up at once, as we were in real trouble. The department sent up an elderly vet called Dr. Jernyrs, who reached the OK away late at night.

The next morning, right after breakfast, he cut one of the dead steers open and informed me that the steers died of hemorrhagic septicemia, which was more or less known as cattle stomach flu. He told me to get some vaccine at once, and inoculate all the cattle on the ranch.

I disagreed entirely with this diagnosis. I had had previous experience at the Canoe Creek Ranch and the Gang Ranch with this cattle stomach flu before, but I felt that I could not put myself up as knowing more than a government veterinary doctor, and so I sent a wire to Calgary for enough vaccine to inoculate around 190 head. I got a message through to the postmaster at Clinton asking him, by every means, to see that the vaccine was sent out by the mail stage that was due three days later, as we sure needed it. It did not arrive, and two or three days later after a lot of desperate phone calls to Clinton, I got word that the vaccine had arrived at the Clinton post office. I made up my mind that I was going to get that vaccine and inoculate all the cattle on the ranch, following the vet's instructions.

I telephoned a great friend of mine, Mr. James Robertson, who, with his brother Raymond, was the owner of the famous Robertson Brothers' store in Clinton. I arranged for him to pick up the vaccine from the post office, and I'd be at his house to get it sometime that night.

I got Peg to get me a couple of cups of coffee and some sandwiches. Then I went out and saddled up a little bay mare. I called her Babe. She sure was a dandy little mare to ride, as she had a fast running walk, which was just what I wanted to go over the miles. I told Peg I'd be back by morning, and not to worry. At half-past three in the afternoon I stepped up on Babe and started for Clinton, 38 long miles through the snow, and a lot of high mountain country to ride over. You climb to nearly 5,000 feet on the road from the OK on Big Bar Creek and dip down again at Kelly Lake, but lucky for me the road was broken all the way.

I knew that I had to watch the strength and the ginger in this little mare because I had the return ride to make, and I'd told Peg I'd be back come early morning. If you ever tell anyone in our country you'll be there on a certain day and don't come, you have everyone wondering what's happened, if you are hurt or something, and they'll maybe start looking for you. If you just say you'll be back as soon as you can, then people don't expect you to come along until you're good and ready and nobody worries.

I kept up a steady even gait all the way, the snow was fairly well packed down in the sleigh tracks, and along about ten o'clock that night I arrived in Clinton. My little mare was tired some, but not too tired. I put her in the big livery barn on the upper end of the town, and fed her some hay and grain. After having downed some hot coffee and ham and eggs in the restaurant, which was just about closing up for the day, I walked up to Jim Robertson's house and got my vaccine.

I rested my little mare for an hour and a half, then put the vaccine package right underneath my undershirt next to my hide, figuring that would keep the vaccine from freezing. I said "so long" to my friend Jim and his missus, walked up to the barn, stepped up on my little mare and started to ride home on the 38-mile trip.

I decided that I would ride by the lake road instead of taking the Kelly Lake road over the mountain. I knew the road was broken, and I knew that Uncle Bill was at Big Bar Lake feeding some of our cattle there. So I rode on, mile after mile through the darkness with only a few stars shining, hoping all the time that my saddle mare would not play out. As the morning hours came along I could feel the cold settling down in the night air and my mare's feet rang out more clearly as they plugged along the frozen sleigh track. Along about three that morning I rode into Big Bar Lake, put my mare in the barn, and went into the house to wake Uncle Bill up. I told him the story of the dead steers, and he shook his head and said, "That'll sure raise old blue Morman Jesus with you, Harry." I said, "Yes, it sure will, Uncle. There's no money in dead cattle."

Bill had a brown horse called Blaze in the barn at the lake, so I traded horses with him, leaving little Babe at the lake. I pushed along the last 14 miles of the trip, riding into the OK at around half-past five in the morning, having made the round trip of 76 miles in 14 hours. Boy-oh-boy, they were long, long hours in the snow, cold and darkness.

I walked up to the house, and Peg already had the cookstove going and hot coffee waiting for me. As soon as I had eaten, Ernie and I and two other local boys corralled the cattle and I inoculated them for septicemia with a hypodermic needle. I was so dog-tired and weary that night that I fell asleep at the supper table. However, still being reasonably young (in my early 40s), I was none the worse for the trip after a good night's rest. It was a tough, wearing experience, as it was normally a two-day ride. Yet it had to be done. Anyone living in these isolated parts of our wide-open Cariboo had to school himself to meet any kind of an emergency. It was well to follow the philosophy and the grit of the old mountain men who, when rough stuff hit them, which was often and regular at times, pinned their ears back, set their faces, buttoned their lips and took what came without complaint or hollering blue ruin. I always felt kind of glad in my own mind, that I belonged to that hardy and resourceful bunch—the kind that never hollers "whoa" until the wagon is upside down.

I was feeling kind of worried and discouraged over the loss of those fine young steers, as I had had hopes of getting around $40 a head for them as beef in August. I said to young Ernie one day out in the barn, "Ernie, I don't know what I'm going to do for money to pay you and Bill now I've lost those steers." The damn good lad just looked at me for a few seconds and then said, "Well, Harry, don't worry about me, I'll wait for mine." That brightened up the picture quite a bit, and I got to thinking the sun would get to shining on both sides of the fence after a while maybe.

Pan Meets a Girl

from *Grass Beyond the Mountains: Discovering the Last Great Cattle Frontier on the North American Continent* by Richmond P. Hobson Jr.

Rich Hobson's admiration is palpable in this story, as he marks the arrival of each heavily laden horse in his pack train, just returned from a supply run to Bella Coola. Before roads, pack trains were the transport trucks of the frontier, hauling people, food, furniture, building materials, farming equipment, whatever was needed for survival and settlement. Unlike most transport trucks, every pack horse had its unique personality, as complex as any human. Hobson pays tribute to their individual characters in addition to their impressive burdens as he greets each horse like an old friend. Panhandle Phillips, Hobson's two-legged friend and business partner, returns with the pack train, ready to help Hobson build a frontier cattle company on the uncharted territory they'd laid claim to. But unlike the horses, Pan's usually blithe, derisive, and wisecracking personality has changed in inexplicable ways. For one thing, Pan suddenly wants to know how to spell.

Pan's voice sounded "like a horse rasp on hard steel."

Rich Hobson, riding tall on a horse called Rhino.

Pan and Alfred Bryant broke through with the machinery pack train the day before Tommy and I planned to strike towards Anahim on a searching party.

I was stirring a moose-meat and rice mulligan in an iron pot on the campfire, when I heard a continuous series of yells coming closer through the spruce jungle across the creek. It was now the middle of August. The sun had dropped into the bullpines behind camp, leaving a yellowish twilight, the smell of pine—and deep silence.

Stuyve had been acting mighty strange, pawing the ground, whinnying, trying to get out of our newly finished horse pasture. For some time I had been conscious of a faint staccato sound breaking the stillness. Now I knew what it was. I pulled the pot out of the fire, grabbed up my battered old Brownie, swapped ends, and splashed waist deep across the creek into the spruce.

I stopped to get my wind on the edge of a long brushy opening. I could hear the noise of horses' hoofs on the hard ground, and the raspy ripping sounds that tired-voiced men make at tired-out horses—and then a pack-laden cayuse came into view, and behind him another one—and still another—until a long snakelike line of slow-moving horses, carrying on their backs strange and awkward loads, strung out across the opening.

The feat of manoeuvring this heavy and ungainly tonnage with our inadequate string of horses through the unmapped muskegs and jungles that cling to the southern slopes of the Algaks and Itchas, and finally across the tangle of peaks and glaciers of the summit to the Blackwater, was a stupendous one.

Now two riders appeared cut of the bush behind the pack horses. I could hear Panhandle's voice. It sounded like a horse rasp on hard steel.

I raised the camera—looked through the lens.

Big black Piledriver is in the lead. He stumbles every few steps.

Look at his pack—a great bulk of rake teeth, mower knives, parts of a hayrake.

Two hundred pounds is a heavy load for any horse to pack in this kind of country. Piledriver is toting nearly three hundred.

His long Roman nose turns in my direction. I click the shutter. He pauses a moment, looks at me curiously, then, pulling himself together, he moves on by.

I wind the film. Another horse.

"Buck!" I yell. "You ornery old buckskin bastard."

The game old horse follows close behind Piledriver.

"What a load," I say out loud. "A whole damn rake frame and the wheels."

Old Buck flicks one eyelid at me as he passes, then he pretends not to see me. I snap the lens.

A big chunky black horse steps easily on Buck's heels. He is Nigger, Pete McCormick's much-written-about pack horse who climbed Mystery Glacier on the famous first ascent of Mount Waddington, the highest mountain in British Columbia.

I draw in my breath as the big, sure-footed black reaches my side. Two cast-iron, heavy-duty mower wheels and parts of the frame—more than 350 pounds—are lashed down on his back.

More horses, more big packs follow. A picture of their back trail flashes across my mind. Three hundred miles of bush and timber and rock and mud. Torturous miles over narrow passes and mountain summits, with back-bending loads, sore backs and sore feet, scorching heat and sweat, silent shivering nights on mountains near the sky.

There's Little Roanie. He moves jerkily ahead—dead tired. His eyes have a blank look. On one side of his back leans an iron stove. Roanie shuffles by me. I click the camera.

Next comes a big rack of windows. Almost hidden beneath this load is Old Scabby White. I pretty near bust down and cry. Old Scabby isn't confused by my step in his direction. His load isn't too heavy, but it's bulky and looks like a terrific tonnage. Scabby kind of shrinks back under his burden and pretends he's moving a terrible weight. He glances sideways at me, then looks straight ahead. Beyond me he turns halfway around, groans and proceeds on his way.

A long faltering whinny floats up from one of the horses in the drag. It's a special kind of a whinny, sounds like a donkey stuck in a mudhole. Only one horse can make that noise. Nimpo! From the horse pasture across the creek comes Stuyve's high nasal answer to his pal. And now Old Buck's voice breaks the sound of thudding hoofs.

These horses are coming home—these conquerors of the rocky trails—these unsung heroes of the silent lonely lands. These cayuses whose strong backs and brave hearts have made possible the opening of a new frontier. Horses who carry within their flesh and hold within their souls the untold deeds and the unrewarded greatnesses of their ancestors, the ghost horses from frontiers of the past.

Here comes Nimpo in the drag. The little black cayuse with the crooked blaze sprawled across his dished face is thin, and he's awful tired.

Here he is now. Look at his pack. High on one side he is toting the unbelievable bulk and weight of a Massey Harris oil-bath mower frame—weight approximately 350 pounds. On his other side, to balance this terrific weight, is slung a 100-pound anvil that hangs down even with the bottom of his belly.

As he stumbled towards me across the opening, his head swaying from side to side, there was nothing except the great pack he was toting, and a certain glint in his eye to indicate that some day this nondescript little black range horse was to become a legend on this last cattle frontier—that his fame would reach across Canada—and that his indomitable will, his heart that couldn't be broken, and his feats of endurance in the face of great odds, would earn for him the title of "The Horse That Wouldn't Die."

And there—grinning down at me—were Pan and Alfred.

I barked at them, "Mulligan's burned—the rice has died—you're late for dinner!"

After we had unpacked the leg-weary, trail-worn horses, Pan, who was as trail-worn as the cayuses, dragged himself around the new horse pasture. He was pleased with the high horse-proof enclosure, and after a light supper lay down on his new bunk to test it out. He fell asleep almost instantly. I pulled his boots off and let him lie.

Alfred managed to crawl out of his dusty clothes before trying out his bunk, and before he started to snore, said, "Boys, we've got a real good one on Pan this time. I'll tell you about it in the morning—but whoever wakes up first, ask Pan how he likes the Bella Coola girls—or was there just one girl he saw? Kid him about the Blackwater being a real nice sociable place to bring a wife to."

Tommy and I were up early. We dug around with a great deal of pleasure through the packloads until we found a 100-pound sack of flour, a 4-pound tin of baking powder and a can of dried eggs. We uncovered a slab of Swift's premium bacon and a can of strawberry jam. Tommy picked up his hackamore and started for the wrangle pasture and I went happily to the cookfire with the delicacies.

Alfred and Pan were still dead to the world when I went to the bunkhouse, picked up my fishing rod and headed for the creek. I made a clumsy cast into the big pool in front of the cabin, and the Royal Coachman fly lit heavily on the water. There was a swirl as a shiny body flashed to the surface from the black rocky bottom.

The Coachman vanished. I jerked, and felt the hook set in a heavy body. My reel screamed—line ran off. I slipped on the bank, fell, got wet to the waist, came up out of the water cursing.

My line was tangled on a snag, but I finally landed him—a rainbow trout weighing about five pounds. He was fat.

Back at the fire I cut the trout through the middle into two-inch pinkish red steaks, and dropped them into the sizzling pan of bacon grease.

I had been the camp cook so long that I had acquired all the annoying habits of one. The only difference between me and the average cook was that I sported a large appetite, an appetite that never seemed to be appeased. When I had the grub to cook with, and I don't mean rice and moose meat, I ventured forth into new and untried fields. Some of my Blackwater mulligans made history, and the fame of my specially constructed hotcakes travelled beyond the Canadian National Railroad.

During the summer of 1936, after a particularly rough encounter with two big hotcakes, Ole Nucloe and Tommy Holte nailed the third one to the doorframe on the bunkhouse. It was still strongly in evidence several years later, having weathered all kinds of storms, thaws and freezes.

The last time I saw that old cake, he was staring down at me unmoved, hard as the Rock of Gibraltar. Recently Andy Christenson told me that Pan had shot a number of holes in the old boy with his six-shooter, but that it had withstood the lead, and still looks down from the doorway of the Blackwater bunkhouse.

Now, with my mouth drooling from each corner, I brandished a hotcake turner in one hand, and a homemade wooden spoon in the other. I was overdoing myself in the preparation of a super-meal.

When all was ready, I walked hurriedly into the cabin and rolled the Top Hand out onto the floor. I returned quickly to the fire and our rough-hewn log table. I heard Pan mutter that he had picked up a splinter on the lousy floor, and then heard another thud, a groan, and Alfred asking what had happened.

It was a sunny pine-scented day. Pan and Alfred charged nude out of the bunkhouse and plopped into the creek. Their loud, cold yells echoed away in the spruce across the water, and then, with towels wrapped around their middles, the packer and the Top Hand advanced upon the breakfast table.

Tommy came around the corner of the bunkhouse saying that the horses hadn't moved far from camp, but that there were some sore backs and big swellings, and two horses were lame.

"That's good," said Pan, as he sat down on a log stool and reached for the hotcakes. "They told us in Bella Coola that whatever horses packed that Massey frame and McCormick rake would have to be put out of their misery before we got over the Itcha Mountains. We'll go over the whole bunch of 'em after we eat; but it won't pay to do no worryin' about those cayuses now. Look what that bald-headed old cook has produced for us."

While he talked, the Top Hand had filled his wide tin plate to the brim with golden brown hotcakes, fat trout steaks, bacon and a load of strawberry jam. He sniffed into his coffee cup. Tommy made for the table in a hurry as he saw the grub disappearing at such an alarming rate.

While Pan and Tommy talked, Alfred had concentrated on his meal. I stumbled about between the log stools scraping out pans, pushing bowls and pots around the table.

Finally Alfred gurgled happily into his coffee cup, reached for the coffee pot, filled his cup again, stirred in sugar and canned milk. Then he shoved himself contentedly back from the table and spoke to me.

"You know, Rich, this spot here on the Blackwater is mighty beautiful—but there's something lacking."

I took it up quickly.

"All it lacks is the soft touch of a woman."

"That's it," said Alfred. "This place would be just about complete if one of us boys would break down and marry the right little woman."

The Top Hand coughed up a fishbone that had hung up in his throat.

"Too many bones in these trout," he said.

"Eat your breakfast," said Tommy. "We're talkin' about women—not fishbones."

Pan snorted loudly. He carefully gulped down a mouthful of coffee and setting down his cup, pointed his finger at Tommy.

"Now, Tommy—just what do ya know about women?"

He looked sternly at the kid.

"Have you ever seen any women except your own mother, and the three other Anahim ladies?"

"Sure I have," said Tommy. "I seen lots of 'em—and I've talked to 'em too. I've been to Williams Lake."

"That's right, Tommy—you've been to Williams Lake," Pan said seriously. "I'd forgot about that."

I could see that Pan was swinging the conversation away from Alfred's and my lead. He was turning the talk to Tommy, and he would have us sidetracked before we knew it. I thought this over. Why was the Top Hand steering away from Bella Coola woman talk?

This wasn't in keeping with Pan's usual habit of making the boys envious of his good luck and his happy times on a trip.

I said to Alfred, "Say, Bronco, you fellows haven't told us anything about your trip. Tommy and I want to hear all about those pretty Bella Coola girls, and about all your parties down there. What kind of a figure did the Top Hand cut on his first appearance?"

Pan broke in.

"Boys, we better cut the talk and get after those horses. There's got to be a lot of doctorin' done."

He pushed up from the table, retucked the towel about his middle, and strode seriously for the cabin. I watched Pan walk to the bunkhouse. Tommy got to his feet and followed the Top Hand. I turned to Alfred, "What's eating Pan? I never saw him act like this."

Alfred looked knowingly at me and said, "Pan didn't go on any parties while we were in Bella Coola; he wouldn't even take a drink— said the stuff dulled a man's brain. I finally left him altogether. He spent his time taking the prettiest and smartest little girl in the village out riding. You met her when we took the pack train down last winter."

Alfred paused a minute and carefully relit his cigarette.

"Well, I'll be damned," I said. "You mean that beautiful little Shorty?"

"That's the one," replied Alfred. He drained his cup. "I think Pan has fallen like a ton of bricks. Maybe it's too bad for him. She's a smart girl—been outside to school, and she doesn't spend much time at her family's home in Bella Coola—been away a lot in the city—you know the kind, Rich—wears swell clothes and looks real slick in them, talks about books and music and things that folks in the outside world talk about. She's about as different from that horse-minded snorting old Pan as a red rose is from a cactus bush."

We used two 45-foot straight-grained spruce trees as our hay stacker. These two limber poles were joined together at the top with a chain. Guide wires held the A-frame up in place, and a set of centre-breaking slings were constructed. With this rigging and several blocks and pulleys, we sweated up the first stack of hay in the country beyond the Itchas. Alfred helped us up with the first stack, and then struck for Anahim and his own hay problems.

Something on that trip to Bella Coola had changed Pan. He wasn't the easygoing, smart-cracking, practical-joking character of old. He seldom laughed, and only once did he pull off his "nothin' to it" remark. That was when I asked him about finances.

"Why, hell, man," said Pan without snorting, "there was nothin' to that. It was just like I told ya. Those saddlers of mine was worth money. Stanley Blum and Ashley Williams just drove the bunch up to the Diamond G. Dude Ranch. It was just what they were lookin' for—well-broke, snappy-lookin' mounts for their dude wranglers and dudes. I had to wait a week in Bella Coola before Stanley cleared me for a thousand dollars."

"I was just wondering why the trip took you so long," I said lightly. "How did you spend your time? Roping those Bella Coola farmers' calves?"

The Top Hand gazed off towards the mountains. He looked sick.

"Well, friend—I guess it done those horses some good, restin' theirselves before that tough trip back. Those 10 days in Bella Coola didn't hurt 'em a bit—and then there was that machinery to take down—every nut and bolt of it, to lighten up the main parts. I was busy enough all right."

Pan stood up from the table and went out of the cabin.

"Somethin's wrong with Pan," observed Tommy. "He must be worryin' about gettin' his hay up in good shape before it rains."

One evening we were topping out our third stack of hay. I had been complaining to Pan about working after the moon was up, and the Top Hand was grunting something at me when my slip team, Big George and Baldy, threw up their heads and whinnied.

"Look," exclaimed Pan, "here comes a cowboy ridin' a pinto pony."

I glanced up and saw through the twilight a flashy-looking black and white pinto dancing across the meadow. Tommy drove his team to the stack, yelled "whoa," and hooked the stacker snatch blocks to his load of hay. He unhooked his horses and turned to Pan.

"That's Dad. He finally musta got the nerve up to ride that Redstone pinto wild hoss of his."

"I'll be damned," said Pan. "Seein' a white man in this country jolts a man up."

Andy Holte let out a yell as he approached us. Riding in close, he held up his side-winding pinto as he lashed out hard at Pan for using the teams at night.

"Sure as hell," rasped the Teamster, pointing his finger at the bunch of us, "you've fog-heaved every last one of them cayuses."

Big George took a kick at Andy's pinto. It had been biting him on the rump.

"See there," grated Andy. "That petrified-boned, lumber-footed, pinch-backed swamper is fog-heaved and he's stretched. You've killed off your horses, boys," he hollered. "Where's the cookhouse? Me and my Morgan ground-gainer here have got to tie on the feed bag. Unhook—you horse killers."

Pan snorted for the first time in days.

"Who ever saw a pinto Morgan? What the hell ya talkin' about, Andy? There's a thousand carloads of them little painted ponies down in the deserts—and they call 'em broomtails in that country."

Andy let out a high whining wail—snatched off his golf cap, and the big leggy pinto sprung high in the air.

"Wowie," yelled Andy.

Straight up and straight down went the pinto. At each jump Andy let out a wild piercing yell and lashed his legs forward in unison with the horse's pitches. Finally the pinto raised his head and looked about him. Andy reined him over to the haystack.

"Them little U.S. pinto desert rats," he rasped at Pan. "Did ya ever see one of 'em lope 50 miles over the mountains and pinnacles in a day and then start shakin' the hump out of his back?"

"Come on, Andy," I called, as I swung my team and slip about and headed them across the meadow towards the bunkhouse. "It must be near ten-thirty. Leave that damn slave-driver and his yes-man back there. We're going home to eat."

Andy trotted up alongside of my slip and we moved across the opening. The Teamster turned in his saddle and yelled at Pan, "I've packed in your mail—and there's a nice sweet-looking little letter for ya from Bella Coola."

Pan and Tommy must have gone into action then, for Tommy's hay slip, with Pan at the ribbons, caught up to us before we reached the wrangle pasture.

Back at the bunkhouse Pan moved fast. He lit the lantern, shook the pile of mail out of Andy's gunny sack, and scattering it hurriedly about my bunk, snatched up the letter he was looking for, and without a word of explanation, dashed out the door, where he crashed head on into the Teamster, who dropped his golf cap in the sudden confusion.

Andy looked bewilderedly after the disappearing Top Hand, and stooping over, picked up his headpiece.

"He's fog-heaved and he's brain-fevered hisself," exclaimed Andy, shaking his head. "Night life in the swamp bottoms will do it to man as well as horse."

Andy sat down on a bunk and I went to work on the supper.

"How's it going back here in these muskegs?" he asked. "Figured I'd better check up on you boys, and it's a lucky thing I did."

"How you making out, Andy? Which way did you come in?"

"Over the mountain on Pan's pack trail. There's a high slanting glacier above a rock slide on top. Don't know how those boys ever got that machinery train over it."

The Teamster fumbled for makings, and I pointed to an opened tin of tobacco. Andy helped himself.

Tommy stepped through the open door.

"I'm hungry," he said, sniffing at venison steaks that sizzled on the griddle. He threw his Stetson at Andy, who neatly ducked it.

"How's haying going?" he asked his father.

Andy looked sheepish.

"Well, I'll tell ya something, Tommy. I'm not supposed to be here, so don't ever tell your mother you saw me."

I started to laugh, but Tommy looked serious. Andy waved his arm carelessly.

"I busted my mower knife up on a rock. Had to get a new batch of sections, so I saddled up and rode out to get some."

There was a moment's silence. Andy glanced furtively at Tommy and then stared hard at a crack in the floor. Tommy looked incredulously at his father.

"Rode out?" he said. "Out here 80 miles to Blackwater for mower sections?"

Andy looked apologetic.

"Well, I rode to Anahim for the knives and got the word that gold is going up to $36 an ounce—and there's prospectors in the country."

The Teamster took off his golf cap and scratched above his ear. He looked shrewdly at me.

"I figured I'd look over that Box Canyon on the mountain before those prospectors got in there first—so I brought you boys' mail along. I've found a placer proposition, and hard rock as well. That crik up there is filled with gold."

"How did you find that out?" I asked.

"I used my cap for a gold pan, shook out some sand along the crik." The Teamster showed his cap to me. "See the black sand in there?" he asked. "It's still stickin' inside the band."

Andy now spoke in a high-pitched voice.

"It's a placer gold proposition sure as we're livin'—anybody can see that. There's copper, silver and zinc in that mineralized belt too, but I'm more interested in the gold end of the proposition, even though the copper and silver will pay the operatin' costs of the whole thing."

Pan came through the doorway. He slapped the Teamster a resounding blow on the back, and yelled at me to snap out of it and get the dinner on the table. I noticed immediately that his personality had reverted to its old state with the reading of his letter.

After cleaning up our supper, Pan asked if any of us had writing paper and envelopes.

"This here jumbo pad," said Pan, "ain't very stylish to write a business letter on."

"There's some brown wrapping paper over in the corner," I said. Pan looked sheepish.

"No—not that kind of paper."

Tommy looked admiringly at the Top Hand. "I wish I was good enough to write a real businessman's letter," he said.

Pan snorted, and started upsetting bags and coal-oil boxes in a vain effort to find writing paper.

I got up, put everything back in place, and told him to stop trying to be so high tone.

"Use the jumbo pad," I snapped at him. "It's paper, isn't it?—and good enough for any man to write on. If the receiver of that letter judges you by the paper you write on, that person is no good anyway—and you've found him out. You can mark that guy down as a small-minded ignorant son of a b."

"You betcha life," chimed in Andy. "You're lucky to have any paper at all."

Pan was visibly impressed by Andy's and my sound logic. He carried the big schoolboy pad to his bunk, sat down, said, "Maybe you boys are right."

Then he ducked his head to his work. I thought over his last remark. This kind of a statement from Pan was out of character.

While Pan was writing, I turned to the Teamster, who was carving on one of the bedposts with his jackknife.

"I'm leavin' my brand here," explained Andy without looking up.

"That's a good place for it," I said.

Pan spoke from his pad, "Say, Rich—I guess I am not a very good hand at writing."

"Your English is improving," I answered. "You're getting so you can talk like a professor."

The Top Hand looked embarrassed,

"Say, Rich—how do ya spell 'forever'? Is it one word or two words?"

I looked at him closely.

"Two words," I said.

The Top Hand was now obviously confused; he glanced in the direction of Andy, who seemed to be deeply engrossed in his job of carving up my bed.

The Top Hand wrote something down on the pad, and then looked back up at me. He cleared his throat.

"Are you plumb sure that 'forever' is spelled with two words? I've got to get this thing right. You know how it is, Rich—when you're writin' a real business letter—well—ya just got to get the thing spelt right."

I was staring hard at the Top Hand.

"One word," I said.

When Andy rode south into the Jack pines the following day, he carried in his pocket Pan's "business letter."

Moleese

from *Three Against the Wilderness*
by Eric Collier

Moleese may have been a hunchback, but he was no slouch.
He was Eric Collier's man of choice to assist him with a project
near and dear to his heart. In the first volume of Heart of the
Cariboo–Chilcotin, *we featured a selection from Collier's classic*
book about frontier living, showing Eric and his wife Lillian as
newcomers to Meldrum Creek. Collier saw that the land around
their new homestead was sick for lack of beavers, who had long
regulated the natural water supply. Beaver had been trapped out.
Collier, a new father, resolved to repair the beaver dams so the
land could heal and renew itself. It is now five years later and the
little family has settled in and learned to live within the rhythms
of their remote environment. With Moleese's help, it is time for
Collier to fulfill a promise.

Meldrum Creek after the dams were repaired.

Moleese was a hunchback. He wasn't born a hunchback, but according to Indian history, his back was broken at four years of age, when a horse fell and rolled on him. Nature, not surgical skill, eventually, after a fashion, reknit the broken backbone, and Moleese was able to ride again. But Nature could not possibly hide the evidence of her handiwork: the hunch would still be there when Moleese set out for his last happy hunting ground. Besides being a hunchback, there was this about Moleese: he was the first man I'd hired. For despite his deformed back, it was Moleese who helped me tame and harness the floods that spewed down Meldrum Creek.

In early spring of 1935 a major flood threat lay over the Fraser River drainage system. Five feet of packed snow covered the three- and four-thousand-foot levels, nine to ten feet at six thousand feet, and still more above that. Whether there was to be cataclysmic disaster or not all depended upon when and how the snow melted. In normal springs, all snow at the lower levels had run off to the river at least three weeks before the snow at higher levels started to move. But if because of an unseasonably late spring the runoff at lower and higher levels coincided, then the Fraser River, where it spreads out and moves slowly through the reclaimed lands about its mouth, could not possibly digest the flow within its banks, and unless the manmade dikes about it were stout enough to contain the surplus, thousands of acres of farmland must again, momentarily anyway, go back to that river from which they had been filched in the first place.

Depth of snow was not the only factor contributing to the threat. The prolonged cold of last December and January presented still another, in the form of ice. Unless there is sufficient volume and depth of water moving along any watercourse, at a temperature of 50 below zero, the flow becomes momentarily dammed by the action of the frost, and then the water backs up and forms a miniature icefield. Eventually the law of gravity exerts itself, and the water cuts another channel through the ice and starts moving downgrade again, but only to find itself once more shut off by frost a little farther downstream. By spring, such miniature icefields are present at frequent intervals along the whole watershed, each awaiting a moment when the sun and the wind would melt them. Then, every such icefield melting and feeding the watershed when its banks are already filled to their carrying capacity contributes just that much more water to a drainage system that neither needs nor can properly digest it.

But in the spring of 1935 the province was spared major flooding. By early May the snow at the lower levels had melted and run off to the Pacific Ocean. The freshets from the mountains did not get underway until early June, and by that time the Fraser River could contain them. The dikes barricading the farmlands were never in serious threat of being breached, and contented farm folk tilled their reclaimed acres behind them, watching the broad sweep of the river pass innocently by. Not for half a century or more had those reclaimed lands been inundated, and in the meantime the dikes had been raised and strengthened, and thousands of acres of hay, grain, vegetables, and other crops were being cultivated behind them. Never again would the Fraser breach those dikes, at least so everyone thought.

To us this sudden extravagance of water was as a gift from Heaven. The snows that had so seriously upset our hopes where the winter trapping was concerned now gave us fleeting opportunity to proceed with the building of many more dams. Several winters might come and go before such opportunity came our way again.

In early May every gulley and fold ribbing the watershed was bursting its britches, spewing the melting snows into Meldrum Creek. There was no need now for us to worry about the ranchers and their irrigation ditches. The creek channel held more water than all the agriculture at its mouth could use. It rushed down the land in a muddy, turgid tide, through many a broken beaver dam, out of the ditched mouth of many a shrunken lake, tarrying nowhere, fired by a frantic urge to keep its tryst with the river in the briefest possible time.

Apart from the few dams we had built, there was nothing to check the flow and hold and conserve all this excess water. But if neither agriculture, river, nor ocean had use for it there were others on the creek who did: ourselves. For five years now we had been almost praying for a chance of this sort to come our way, and now it had come, bringing with it opportunity to close the gates upon the larger marshes, soak their blotting paper, and fill their saucers until they overflowed.

In the five years that had gone by since we came to the creek to live, we hadn't fared too badly. The cabin now had a board floor it. The second-hand mowing machine and rake were there in the makeshift shed. We had been able to replace the blocks of wood that were our original chairs for more elegant furniture. And besides these indexes of accumulating wealth, we had managed to amass a bankroll totalling almost $300. So, comforted by thoughts such as these and convinced that if we now smote while the iron was hot, and allowed none of the water to go to waste, we would soon be able to start trapping large numbers of muskrats. I took a deep breath and arrived at a momentous decision: I would become an employer of labour.

In the opening up of a frontier or the taming of a wilderness, woman has often played equal part with man. Without Lillian at my side sharing the common life through good fortune or bad, giving to that life the many things that only a woman can give, I know that my hopes and aspirations to do with the waters of Meldrum Creek would never have been fulfilled.

But enough is enough. Though Lillian had helped me with every dam hitherto built, I could now hire an Indian for two dollars a day and board, and we had money enough to pay such a wage for maybe six weeks. Working from seven in the morning until six at night, I reckoned two men could move a pile of dirt in six weeks and rebuild several dams.

When I broached the matter with Lillian she stamped a heel angrily down on the floor and scolded, "Six weeks wages and board to an Indian means parting with around $80 in cash. With that much money," and her eyes darted around the cabin, "we could buy a little more furniture, or that set of matched dinner dishes I've been wanting so long."

"Why the dinnerware? I asked mildly, grinning. "We've been

eating off enamel plates and drinking out of enamel cups for a good many years now and don't seem to be any the worse off for it."

"You just don't understand," said Lillian flatly.

"Sure I understand." Then in a more serious tone, I said, "It's not right that you should be shovelling dirt now that we've money enough to pay someone else to do it. And then again there's another problem we'll soon have to tackle."

"Problem?" Lillian frowned. "What sort of a problem?"

"Veasy's education," I replied quietly, then waited for that to sink in.

Veasy would be six years old on the 28th of next July. The very thought of sending him away to school and boarding him with others was more than either Lillian or I cared to contemplate. We were miles from any school. The environment of the wilderness had made the three of us as a single unity, the one dependant upon the other. From one month's end to another we seldom saw anyone else. At five years of age Veasy could set a snare and catch a rabbit as professionally as I could, for the woods themselves had been a school of sorts to him. And the process of setting the snare demanded a certain amount of patience, a concentration of thought and effort, which is why I taught him how to set them in the first place. The job sharpened his mind, gave him something constructive to think about, and so taught him how to make use of his brain.

He was already trailing along at my heels now and then when I went out in the woods to hunt, and often his keen eyes spotted a deer before I saw it myself. "Look, Daddy, deer!" And then I'd see the deer myself, lying very still, head and neck flush with the ground as deer often will lie and watch the hunter pass by.

Already the simple everyday chores of the woods were leaving their mark on his character. He never asked Lillian or me to do anything for him that he could possibly do himself. Lillian no longer had to fill the woodbox at night if I wasn't home in time to do it for her. Though he could only pack a few sticks of wood at a time, Veasy took care of the woodbox. If when playing by the lake he came running to the cabin with the news that he'd just seen a timber wolf or moose travelling the shoreline then we knew that it was a moose or timber wolf he'd seen.

He never lied, perhaps because he'd never known occasion when a lie was needed to cover up the truth.

Mostly at his own initiative, he was already spelling out simple words in a book, and making sense of them too. If so far he couldn't write or print the words, I judged that he was only a short step from being able to do so. I'd given considerable thought to the matter of somehow giving him a fair education, and arrived at the conclusion that between Lillian and me, we'd try to do the job at home and see what came of our efforts.

In England, I had gone from governess to kindergarten, kindergarten to grammar school. Along with other subjects I'd delved into Latin and chemistry, algebra and trigonometry and like matters usually taught in correct establishments of learning. But since my thoughts were so often leagues away from the book on my desk, no sooner had my mind mastered a verb or equation than the process of its mastering was promptly forgotten.

But Lillian never had been blessed with such opportunity for education. At 11 years of age she'd been shipped away to Soda Creek, 40 miles from Riske Creek, to board with relatives, and walked 3 miles each morning to a 1-roomed log schoolhouse attended by 9 other pupils. At 14 she quit school, but in the 3 years at Soda Creek she had learned to read very well, write fairly well, to add and subtract, multiply and divide. And every lesson she learned was one she never forgot. So what with all that I'd forgotten, and all that she remembered, I saw no good reason why we should send Veasy away to school and so break up the unit.

"We'll sit down right now," I said to Lillian, "and send away for pencils, scribblers, and textbooks. And from now on you can do far more good keeping him anchored to his lessons than helping me build dams. Then, remembering the set of matched dinnerware, I promised, "Come next March I aim to trap around 400 muskrats and I know that I can do it. Out of the proceeds of the fur I'm going to buy you the fanciest set of dinner dishes there is in the catalogue."

Moleese was no darker than any other Chilcotin Indian, no fairer either. As was the case with so many of the Indians, a white man had to guess at his age and claim top marks if he came within 10 years of guessing right.

Moleese and his woman Cecelia occasionally came to the headwaters of Meldrum Creek in early spring to catch the squawfish moving upstream to spawn. Though the white man might turn up his nose at such bony fare, the true Chilcotin Indian, in the spring of the year, when moose and deer were thin and tough, considered them a delicacy, bones and all.

In that early spring of 1935 Moleese and Cecelia again had an appetite for squawfish and came to the creek to net them. They pitched their tent a mile upstream from the cabin, and the ring of their horse bells told me of their presence. That evening I paid them a visit.

The layout of the camp was as familiar to me as the smell that pervaded the atmosphere around it. The tent, pitched under a pine tree, was small, maybe 8 feet by 10. The canvas, once white, was now a dirty gray. It bore evidence of continual patching, but no doubt it shed rain after a fashion. The customary campfire smouldered in front of the flaps, and behind it was another fire, mostly smoke, burning beneath a rack of peeled pine poles. On the rack rested scores of squawfish, split and opened down the belly, flesh to the smoke. It was the smell of the curing fish that permeated the atmosphere. Cecelia was behind the tent too, methodically and stoically scraping hair from the hide of a recently killed deer. Deer hides were everywhere, though all but the one Cecelia laboured at had obviously been skinned from kills of long ago.

Moleese grinned at me as I approached, and, twisting his distorted back, heeled down by the fire on a deerskin. The two saddles chucked carelessly under a tree had deerskin blankets beneath them too, as was the case with the two packsaddles a few feet away. I was quite certain that if I peeked into the tent there would be a deerskin flattened out— serving as a sheet to the mattress of boughs it covered. Just as there'd be a deerskin spread on the dusty floor of the tent on which food was served when it was too cold or wet to eat outside. I thought, "Take away their deer and what have they left?"

Bidding Moleese a gruff "hello," I too heeled back by the campfire, as if absorbed in its flames. It was fatal to appear in a hurry when doing business with an Indian.

Then after at least two minutes of silence:

"You catch lots fish?" I inquired to open up proceedings.

"You betcha." Moleese patted his belly. "He damn good too."

"How long before your belly get all the fish he want?" I asked.

Moleese picked his teeth. "Two-three days, and then me and my woman don't want to eat fish for a long time."

It was time to come to the point. "You want catch job for maybe five or six weeks?" I said it casually as if I didn't care whether he replied yes or no.

The grin dropped from Moleese's face. His eyes took on a hard, crafty look. "What kind of job?" he asked suspiciously.

"Shovel job. You damn good man with a shovel. All you have to do is fill barrow with dirt."

"Goddamn hard work," complained Moleese. "That kind of work make my back sick."

That I didn't believe. In 1927 Moleese had dug a ditch for the trader at Riske Creek 200 yards long and 6 feet deep, and in quick time too. My back wasn't broken when I was four years old, but I doubt that I could have dug it in less time.

After 15 minutes of barren silence Moleese said cautiously, "How much you pay me?"

Knowing there would have to be a great deal of skirmishing before a wage was settled upon I offered: "Dollar and a half a day and grub."

Moleese scowled. "Too cheap. Two dollars and fifty cents more better."

Not if I had my way. "One dollar and seventy-five cents." Moleese waggled his head. "Two dollars and twenty-five cents more better."

I said, "Just fill shovel with dirt and then fill barrow. Easy job that." And: "One dollar and ninety cents," I came up to.

But it wasn't quite enough.

"Two dollars more better."

"Okay, you win. Two dollars a day it is." Though I intended to pay that much anyway, I scowled as we clinched the deal, letting on that an Indian's shrewd bargaining had bested that of a white man. And Moleese registered his satisfaction the way things turned out with a gaping grin. "When we start work?" he asked.

Moleese was worth every cent of his hire. Sparing of words as so many Indians are, breath that might have been frittered away in small talk was given to loading the barrow. The work proceeded swiftly and efficiently. Six miles downcreek from the cabin were two of the largest marshes on the watershed, one containing some two hundred acres, the other slightly less. In two weeks the gates in the two dams were closed and slowly the water in front of the first began spreading out over the marsh and creeping higher up the face of the dam. How very different now were aquatic conditions on the watershed than those that had existed when Lillian and I hesitantly began work on our very first dam. Then the creek was so anemic it seemed that only a miracle could succeed in restoring its health and vigour. Perhaps miracles had happened, and the winter of the heavy snows was one. Anyway, now we had water to work with, plenty of water, and not a drop of it was permitted to make its escape to the river. Our recently constructed dams upon these two larger marshes stopped it in its tracks, forcing it to drop its plunder of precious topsoil that was being carried toward the river, and dump it on the marshes, where soon it would enrich the bottoms of the lakes, thus making sure all forms of life that moved into them to breed and multiply would always have plenty of food. So, with the help of the hunchback Indian Moleese, the freshets of 1935 were harnessed and put to use.

In the meantime, and for five hours every day excepting Saturdays and Sundays, the cabin became a classroom. The pencils, scribblers, and textbooks travelled from Riske Creek to Meldrum Lake on the back of a pack horse. Promptly at 9:30 A.M. Veasy sat down at the table and applied his mind to the work Lillian set before him. Promptly at 11:30 he shoved away from the table and ran outdoors to stretch his legs and his lungs. Sharp at 1 P.M. he was again seated at the table, there to remain until 3:30 when Lillian sang out, "School's out for today."

One morning around 10 A.M., shortly after "school" had opened, I walked into the cabin to scrounge a cup of coffee. Veasy glanced up at me as I entered and then without a word, his eyes went back to his books. I poked Lillian playfully in the ribs and told her, "You missed your true vocation in life. You should have been a school marm." Lillian replied with a quick laugh, "I could teach you a thing or two," and she meant it.

Save for the patch of land we'd cleared for the vegetable garden, the three- or four-acre flat around the cabin was a jungle of aspen and willow. A few hundred feet upstream from the flat was the beaver meadow that so far had supplied us with winter feed for the horses. The remnant of the beaver dam was 460 feet long, and shaped something like a horseshoe, as beaver dams often are. Either end of the dam tied into a steepish bank that would, I judged, provide an ample source of easy-shovelling dirt and gravel.

If for the moment we hadn't the vaguest idea as to how or when a pair or two of beavers could be brought back to the creek, never for a moment did we waver from the firm conviction that someday, and in our time too, they would come back. I had already made a few inquiries as to how one went about the purchasing of live beavers, but with negative results. So thoroughly had the watersheds of British Columbia been ransacked of their beavers that in 1920 the B.C. Game Department prohibited any further trapping of beavers throughout most of the province. With a situation like this existent, what hope had we of ever getting a pair of beavers to begin the restocking of Meldrum Creek? If the question was without answer at the moment, we knew that somehow that pair would be found. And furthermore, we believed with all our hearts that someday the meadow that now supplied us our hay would again be occupied by beavers.

With one eye on the tangle of brush and the other on the beaver meadow, I decided that the aspens and willows must go, the tough sod be plowed, and the flat seeded down to a permanent crop of hay. But any time spent in clearing and plowing the flat would be wasted unless water could be brought to the land to irrigate it.

With the use of a somewhat crude triangle and plumb bob I surveyed the right of way for a ditch that would carry water from the dam to the projected hayfield. In order to raise the water high enough on the meadow so that it would flow of its own free will into the mouth of the ditch, the dam itself had to be raised almost four feet above its present level. I don't rightly recollect how many spruce trees were cut down for their branches, or how many hundreds of wheelbarrow loads of dirt and gravel were wheeled away from the pit and dumped on the boughs before at last the job was finished, and the entire length of the dam raised four feet. But finally, with the help not only of Moleese, but also that of Lillian and Veasy when the schoolday ended, we were able to lay down our axes and shovels and watch the water spread out of our hay meadow.

Then came the digging of the ditch, and it took most of a week. By that time the dam had filled and I was able to test the accuracy of our survey work. There was nothing wrong about that survey; the water flowed serenely along the ditch, and if some seeped away through the gravel, a sufficient amount reached the end of the ditch to ensure that as long as the dam held, our hay crop would not wilt for lack of irrigation.

Clearing the brush from the flat was the hardest task of all, for every aspen and willow had first to be chopped off well above the ground and the tops cut into lengths and packed away and windrowed up in piles ready for burning. Then with the help of our work team and cable and blocks, the stumps were lifted from the ground and hauled off too. Then all hands pitched in to grub out the network of roots with only one mattock and bare hands for tools. With most of the roots removed, the ground was not too hard to plow, and when the very last furrow was turned I hitched the team to the wagon, journeyed out to Riske Creek and obtained temporary use of a set of spring-toothed harrows from the trader. By late June all was done. Except, that is, paying Moleese his wages.

One had to be careful about this when dealing with an Indian who was as primitive as he was independent. You didn't hand him a check or a roll of bills as you would a white man, and say, "I'll not need you any longer." At least not if you wanted his respect. But between us, Lillian and I had all this figured out several days before the moment of parting. On the night of the payoff, we'd ask Moleese and Cecelia down for supper and treat them like royalty if they came.

Moleese wore a clean, unpatched pair of denim overalls and an equally plain, though badly faded, black silk shirt with the head of a horse embroidered in pink thread upon the flap of its breast pocket. Obviously the decoration hadn't been there when the shirt was purchased at a trading post. Cecelia's gnarled fingers were no doubt responsible for the artistic design. His face and hands were clean too, and his black coarse hair plastered straight back over his forehead. That was unusual; as a rule it was as disheveled as a magpie's nest. Cecelia was dressed for the occasion in a snow white cotton blouse and print calico skirt. The raven-wing, braided ropes of hair that trailed almost to the thin buckskin belt about her waist were at least partly corralled by a huge yellow handkerchief. Cecelia was obviously several years older than Moleese. You could tell that by the miniature gulleys that lined her face. Cecelia's face somehow reminded me of an eroded patch of dusty ground that has long lost hope of growing anything bright and beautiful.

Lillian had opened two jars of her precious willow grouse, canned the previous fall, and made a dandy stew of them, complete with feather-light dumplings. For dessert she had a deep blueberry pie. The berries, too, had been preserved the previous summer.

As Lillian and Cecelia were cleaning up the dishes, I handed Moleese a cigar—in mid-May the trader had given me a pack of five for a birthday present—and lit one myself. Then I spent two tedious hours teaching Moleese how to print his name with the stub of one of Veasy's pencils. He learned surprisingly fast, and at the end of the lesson could sign his name in rude but readable fashion. Then with a simple "Thanks, Moleese," I paid him off.

The two Indians stepped out through the cabin door. There was yet light in the sky. Moleese hesitated. He scowled, as if he was thinking of something he couldn't put into words. The scowl evaporated, and he grinned from ear to ear. "Goddam, you one damn' good white man" was his parting. Coming from an Indian that was a compliment indeed!

Give 'im air! It's not Alan on this bucking bronc, but this photo gives us an inkling of his ordeal.

Rodeo

from *The Ranch on the Cariboo*
by Alan Fry

It's a rare boy who can resist testing his mettle in some risky business that, if he had any sense, he would know to stay clear of, at least until he's older. Often it's an activity he sees experienced men tackling, and he jumps in with both feet, unaware that the men have taken years to gain that comfortable state of being less sorry than safe. In the first volume of Heart of the Cariboo– Chilcotin, *Alan Fry proved his young mettle as he helped his father through some rough weather on the family ranch. In this excerpt, Fry, a little older but not yet wise enough, tests himself in a larger arena, and learns a thing or two about underaged bronc riding, and just how sorry a boy can be.*

The community at Lac la Hache held a rodeo on the 24th of May. I found a ride with a friend to my old home and soon was walking out the Eagle Lake road to Gussy's turnoff to fetch my saddle and see my friends.

Lester was there, greeting me royally. I told him what I was about. He looked at me solemnly, shaking his head.

"No brains, huh?"

"Nope. None at all."

"That's the stuff, boy!" He was on my side, I could see that, and Mrs. Haller shook her head in dismay as we went to the barn to fetch my rigging. Gussy, a great believer in everybody making his own mistakes, had no comment.

I wanted to stay at Whitehorse [Lake] that night and of course I knew it was my privilege to do so, but I had to be at the rodeo grounds early enough to enter and Gussy couldn't be sure he'd be there as soon as that. Therefore I walked out carrying my saddle and before long had a lift from a stranger going by in a pickup truck.

The saddle bronc ride under the rules at that time lasted eight seconds. Your time began when the chute gate opened, spilling you and your squealing bronc into the open arena.

When he took the air in a great bucking leap, you reached for his mane with your dull-rowelled bronc spurs. As he hit the ground you raked him back to the flank, then reached for his mane again, and look out if you were late doing it. If your feet were back of the cinch on the up, you'd probably find the ground on the down. Keeping in time was important.

One hand gripping the halter shank, the other stayed clear of the rigging on pain of disqualification. For eight hard seconds you rode him thus, then the pickup men moved in on trained horses from both sides, one to take the halter shank, the other to take you clean out of the saddle, slip you onto the back of his own rig, and drop you safely to ground on the other side. Great sport that. Ruins horses and kills men. I was all for it.

I put the night in at my mother's house and after a light lunch the next day at noon, made my way to the rodeo grounds. Already a crowd of spectators had gathered, cars lining the arena, two deep in places. I could have done without the crowd. The gut-twisting scariness of what I was doing suddenly moved in on me. I thought I might be sick.

I ducked under the fence, carrying my saddle across to the chutes. Leaving it there, I went to a table set up at one side of the arena where entries were being taken.

I strode up to the table, my mouth as dry as the dust underfoot, $20 clutched in a sweaty fist for the entry fee, three weeks' poker winnings in a game of 10-cent limit with my schoolmates.

Rex Williams sat at the table, a shoebox of money before him, taking the entries. He looked up, squinting into the sun. "Where you going, dressed up like a cowboy?"

I gulped, searching around for my voice. "Put me down," I said, "for the saddle broncs."

"How old are you, Alan?"

"I been 16 for a month."

He shook his head, took my money, gave me a flag with a number on it to pin to my shirt, and wrote my name down.

The saddle bronc contest makes the main event, taking up the first couple of hours of an afternoon show. Then the bareback riding, steer riding, calf roping, and what have you are run off. The pattern is much the same for two- or three-day shows.

I hunkered down near the chute, by the arena fence, out of the way, to watch the broncs boil out, their riders fighting to stay in the saddle. I hoped to be up before long, and I might as well see a few others take their licks in the meantime. A fist-sized knot churned around in my insides.

A couple of riders came out, performing passing well. Then there was a delay at the chutes over something, accompanied by a great lot of cursing and hollering to "look out."

The crash of splintering wood sent the crowd in front of the chute scattering for safety. I jumped up in time to see a big horse all but clear the releasing gate, hooves flailing against the timbers, his great neck arched in a fury of effort.

He came down in the chute and two alert saddlers grabbed his head, haltering him in a deft split second. They both jumped clear as he reared again, but the man on the far side had the halter shank. He soon wrapped twice on a timber, forcing the brute's head against the chute, holding him still at last.

"My Gawd!" the other exclaimed. "You think we'll ever saddle him?"

"You betcha. Where's the rigging? Where's the cowboy?"

I'd seen his number and picked up my saddle. "Over here. Both of us." I spat in the dust and passed up my rigging, mustering a weak grin. They mustered the biggest belly laugh I think I've ever heard.

I wasted no time. The saddle once cinched, I climbed up on the chute. The big horse was under me then, every muscle tense, legs braced, 1,400 pounds of untamed dynamite waiting for a chance to explode. I shivered, in spite of the heat and the sweat, and spat again, but the taste of fear stuck to my mouth like lye.

The gateman readied himself. The chap on the other side, holding the shank, gave me a nod. I lowered myself into the saddle, fixing my feet in the stirrups.

Quickly, when I reached for it, the shank man passed the rope. I measured it, tucked the loose end under my arm, clamped my arm down on it, leaned back a little.

"You ready, young fella?" It was the gateman, a little anxiously.

"Give 'im air," I said, remembering I'd wanted to say that.

The gate swung open. The arena waited like a yawning pit of destruction. The bronc wasted a moment in indecision. Then in a bellow of fury, he threw himself in the air and plunged down his head, tearing at the shank.

My legs weren't mine. They held in their own clutch of fear to the battering saddle, yanking me everywhere in inescapable jolts. Come out reaching ...

I tried to catch track of the jumps, vaguely knowing the pain of coming to ground had happened twice already and this was three and I hadn't hit his shoulders yet, never would now.

Four, and the saddle was getting farther away from centre. Five. The saddle? No, me. There were two hands on the shank. Disqualified. How? I didn't ... But I must have, of course.

I came to ground rolling and stood up unsteadily, immersed in a vast weariness. There was a big noise and I wondered what was wrong around me. Then I realized it was the crowd. and I was ashamed for pulling leather. But maybe they didn't know about that.

I walked back to the chute slowly, nothing much to hurry about. In a way I didn't want to go there where so many men stood about, men who'd seen what I'd done, who must know now how scared I'd been, so scared I'd tasted it, foul in my mouth.

A big man, stranger to me, came forward, grabbing my arm. He was grinning through a layer of dust and perspiration.

"How ya feel, kid?"

"Okay." Then: "I made kind of a mess of that."

"So what? You think there's many would do better? You drew a tough horse."

"Did he look bad?"

"Damn bad. You better go take it easy."

I saw Gussy in front of the arena fence, off the end of the chute, and made my way over to him to sit down. He said nothing as I joined him.

After a bit I volunteered: "I need some practice."

Gussy thought awhile. "Yes," he said at last, "you do. But this is a poor place to get it. And you'd be a whole lot better off if you was to forget the whole idea."

In the realm of advice, that was a long speech from Gussy. We sat thereafter in silence.

There was another rodeo at Williams Lake a few weeks hence, so I wasted no time gathering funds one way or another to be sure I had an entry fee. A two-day event, it gave a man two rides, but he paid proportionately more for them.

Alfie Eagle, after whom one of our meadows had been called and who now lived a quieter life than when he was the champion bronc stomper of British Columbia, was chute judge and general sergeant-at-arms in the busy area of the arena immediately in front of the gates.

My horse in, I passed up my saddle. Alfie, who had watched me grow up my few short years, spared a moment to stand by me while I watched the saddlers.

"How do you feel?"

"Scared."

"So's anybody here if they're normal. You'll be all right once you're on. Try to get in time with him. And come out with your feet in the mane."

The saddlers done, I climbed the gate, dropped into the saddle, fitted my feet into the stirrups. Alfie reached through and straightened my chaps to be sure there were no wrinkles under my leg, instructing the saddler to do the same on the other side.

I measured the shank, tucked the end.

"You ready?"

I nodded.

The gate opened. The horse stood there, suspicious of the arena, trembling and white-eyed. I struck him on the off shoulder with the spur.

He bolted out the gate on the dead run into the arena. Oh, hell, what luck! I threw my feet up to strike his shoulders, raking back to the flanks.

My feet back, he exploded straight in the air. In a futile second I fought to get in time, spurs ahead on the up, back on the down. I couldn't. Another jolt tore me sideways. I felt the hard impact of the ground against my back.

Perfectly conscious, I couldn't move. But the thought that ran through my mind had nothing to do with the paralysis. I need more practice than I can get this way, I swear. I've gotta get hold of a couple of broncs and a piece of soft meadow somewhere, get used to that damn ...

Then voices gathered and a man asked me a few questions, did some gentle probing, rolled me onto a stretcher.

It was cool in the tent and a pleasant, middle-aged woman sat with me, asking if there was anything I wanted. She raised my head just enough that I could drink some cold juice, then I rested some more.

"You're young," she said, looking worried, as though she'd just realized it. It was a statement of fact I was growing used to hearing.

"A lot younger'n you think, at that." I grinned at her to show her everything was all right. "C'mon. Give me a hand. I'm okay now. I'm gonna get up and walk outa here."

I had been cautiously aware of the feeling coming back into my legs and back. There was one devil of a sore spot in the small of my back, right on the spine itself. I knew enough anatomy to conclude that the impact had temporarily suspended the transmission of command in the main line.

"Do you think you should?"

"Positive." I rose up slowly, and hesitantly she helped. Once sitting, I sat awhile, then dropped my legs over the edge of the cot, to which I'd been transferred from the stretcher. I paused again at that stage.

"Another drink of juice?"

"I'd love it." I drank another glassful. Then I thanked her for her kindness, stood up and walked out to go fetch my saddle, which by now would have been brought back to the vicinity of the chutes, then find a shady spot out of the way where I could watch the remainder of the day's events.

I didn't ride the second day, Alfie saw to that. He turned my horse out when it came in the chutes and I knew better than to protest, to dispute his judgement. My short venture into rodeo riding had fizzled out in ignominy. I was indeed a sad boy.

The gals from the Rat Trap Saloon entertained the condemned men. Left to right: Barb Poirier, Ralph Chetwynd, "Willie" Blair, Einar Gunderson, Marj Margetts, Edie Baker (the lady known as Lou), W.A.C. Bennett and Thelma Rife.

The Day We Hanged W.A.C. Bennett

from *History and Happenings in the Cariboo–Chilcotin: Pioneer Memories*
by Irene Stangoe

In the first volume of Heart of the Cariboo–Chilcotin, *we included a selection by Irene Stangoe from* Looking Back at the Cariboo–Chilcotin, *her second published collection of Cariboo yarns, about her and husband Clive's experiences taking over the* Williams Lake Tribune *as possibly the youngest publishers in the province's history. In the following story from her third collection, Irene describes how the townsfolk of Williams Lake ambushed a train loaded with dignitaries, and kidnapped and hung not only the premier of British Columbia, but a few of his lackeys, too.*

In August 1956, when the link between North Vancouver and Squamish was finally completed, a special train loaded with dignitaries travelled from the coast to Prince George to celebrate the great occasion. The train was scheduled to stop at Williams Lake for only two hours, but it was a two-hour stop that Premier W.A.C. Bennett, railways minister Ralph Chetwynd and PGE manager Einar Gunderson would never forget.

The shenanigans started at the public beach on South Lakeside. Seven holdup men touched off 24 railroad torpedoes, and the special train ground to a halt. Three of the masked desperadoes (Tom Madison, Bert Roberts and Bill Sharpe) jumped aboard, brandished their revolvers and apprehended the three VIPs, who were then hustled into a BX stagecoach. With Claude Huston at the reins, they endured a bone-rattling three-mile ride in to the depot.

There the accused were marched up to a makeshift gallows, outsize nooses affixed around their necks, and the charges read by Sheriff Frank "Woody" Woodward. "I charge you PGE riding varmints with disturbing the peace in our once quiet town, cluttering up our railway track with trains and engines, also making it unsafe for cows or cowboys to sleep on the right-of-way."

They were found guilty, naturally, but Cariboo folk are basically a kindly lot and they decided to let the condemned men rest their feet awhile in the Rat Trap Saloon before they were hanged.

The nearby Central Service Garage had been transformed into an old-time barroom, complete with sawdust floor. The big hit of the day was the dancing girls, headed by queen of the dive Edie Baker as the "lady known as Lou." Without doubt they were the most photographed women in North America that day as dozens of news cameras, reporters and visitors flocked into the saloon.

Bartender Tom Hawker was all togged out in striped shirt and handlebar moustache, and the bill of fare listed such drinks as the "PGE

Slowball" and "Cariboo Calamity." Big WANTED posters covered the walls. Under Bennett's picture it read: "Wanted—Whispering Ac(e) Bennett, half alive or half dead. Reward for either half 5,000,000 Socred dollars (17½ cents Canadian)."

Chetwynd's poster took several jibes at his balding pate. Listed as "Curly 'Please Go Easy' Chetwynd," he was charged with breach of the easy way of Cariboo life by bringing in a railway, and of rustling Socred cows. Reward—two passes to the 1928 Stampede.

"Run Again" Gunderson was also charged with conduct contrary to the Cariboo way: "In making a business pay, not equipping trains with barrooms." The reward for him was one mounted head of rare Socred Cow.

Everybody had a wonderful time; in fact the visitors were so taken with the entertainment that the Rat Trap Saloon almost lost Lou and bartender Hawker. When everybody flocked back to the train at departure time, the two were hustled on board and only managed to escape near the cemetery by pulling the emergency cord. They walked back to town.

And this all happened at eight o'clock in the morning! The train was scheduled to stop at Williams Lake the previous afternoon, but a rock slide north of Horseshoe Bay held it up for 22 hours. This didn't surprise the local enthusiasts, who were used to the vagaries of the PGE, and the show organized by the local Board of Trade went on as scheduled.

No wonder Williams Lake had a reputation for hospitality and western-type celebrations that was unmatched by any other town.

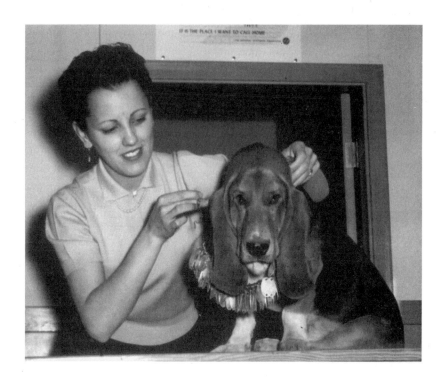

Town clerk Noreen Carson drapes Homer with a necklace of dog tags to publicize the deadline for 1961 dog licences. Homer's sorrowful mug was a fixture in Williams Lake.

The Tail End

from *History and Happenings in the Cariboo–Chilcotin:
Pioneer Memories*
by Irene Stangoe

*In this second story by Irene, she introduces us to her basset
hound, Homer Stangoe, a well-known, well-loved character in
Williams Lake.*

This is not really history, just a "look back" at a dog who carved a little niche for himself in the memories of many Williams Lake residents who were here in the late 1950s and early '60s.

His name was Homer Stangoe and for a time, he was the only basset hound in Williams Lake—a sloppy ponderous beast with huge floppy ears who endeared himself to everyone and was welcome everywhere. Well, almost everywhere.

For years he ambled his sad, sorrowful way into homes, stores, schools, beer parlours, and even churches; traffic stopped so he could cross the street, and he regularly hitchhiked rides home. No social event was complete without his doleful appearance, and Tribune customers regularly had to step over his ungainly form as he lay sprawled on the front step or in the office.

Perhaps the most hilarious episode in Homer's checkered career was the time he followed his family to the United Church. At that time, services were held in MacKinnon Hall until the church proper could be built. The stage was effectively hidden by red velvet curtains, and the altar with its candles, flowers, and an open Bible was exactly level with the stage. It was a setting for disaster.

I was playing for the services that fateful morning when my young daughter Elaine appeared beside me, urgently whispering, "Mom, Homer's on the altar!"

I turned with disbelieving eyes to see Homer, his tremendous front paws firmly planted on the altar, staring mournfully with bloodshot eyes at the congregation.

I was immobilized with horror, but my good friend Cathie Kerley quietly stepped into the breach and managed to coax Homer back through the velvet curtains, off the stage, then out an open basement door, all the time hoping he wouldn't give voice to deep baying howls of disapproval. I managed to get my trembling fingers on the keys and was quietly awaiting the minister's arrival when Elaine appeared once more.

"Don't look now, Mom, but Homer's on the altar again." Indeed, he was. Finding another basement door open, he had plodded back upstairs and shuffled onto the altar to sniff the flowers, knocking the candles over in the process. By this time the congregation was in stitches.

Somehow I managed to pry myself off the piano bench and with Elaine's help coaxed our reluctant dog off the stage. As we pushed him down the steps, there was Todd Lee, our minister, coming up. "What will we do?" I wailed. He smiled gently and said, "Perhaps he would like to take the service for me." We got Homer out the second open basement door, and finally the service got underway.

Then there was the hopeful chap who wanted him for breeding purposes. "Where's Homer going?" asked all the neighbourhood kids as our reluctant hound was pushed into the car. Caught off guard, Clive replied, "Oh, cougar hunting." The idea of our pudgy, lethargic hound chasing cougars could make most people slightly hysterical, but the kids were suitably impressed and talked of Homer's hunting prowess for a long time. No little basset hounds ever appeared, however. You see, Homer was *very* reluctant.

Even his illnesses were unusual. I'd never known a dog to have tonsillitis until Homer came down with it—not once but three times— in 1963. At first, veterinarian Dr. John Roberts managed to control it with shots of penicillin and a huge bandage around his chest to stop him from scratching, but the third time it erupted under his jaws and set him scratching from morning until night. The meant another trip to Dr. Roberts, who suggested I make booties for Homer's back paws.

"Booties?" I squawked. Fortunately for my sanity, Tony's Leather Shop was able to make leather booties. Despite his solid ungainly bulk, Homer periodically managed to get rid of them and, with maddening stupidity, would scratch himself raw again. Then Dr. Roberts fashioned a padded Elizabethan collar of tin that fitted around Homer's neck. Now a basset hound is a dolorously funny dog when he is absolutely normal; add an Elizabethan collar and you have a riot.

During his illness, Homer had to be kept in the house so he wouldn't wander away. (We couldn't tie him up as usual, because of his Elizabethan collar.) His constant despairing woofing at night in the basement was driving us almost wacky, so Clive developed a jacket out of an old army duffel bag with a handle on top so he could be tied up outside. This time Homer bore a striking resemblance to a suitcase. But he eventually recovered, and so did we.

Homer's biggest claim to fame, however, had to be his stage appearance.

Home economics teacher Belle Grattan had already produced two highly successful musical fashion shows when in 1961 she decided her third would the *The Boy Friend*, a fast-moving, funny musical of the 1920s.

I'll never forget my astonishment the morning Belle phoned to say: "I need a French poodle for my show, Irene, and I wondered if I could have Homer?"

Homer? "But Homer's a basset hound," I spluttered. She pointed out there were no poodles in town, and she figured our sloppy old beast would fit the bill nicely. And, so help me, when the big night came, there it was on the program: "French poodle played by Homer Stangoe."

Despite misgivings from his family as to whether he might, er, misbehave, Homer, with perfect aplomb, walked out onto the stage with Mlle. Dubonnet (Cheryl Stanchfield), surveyed the audience with sorrowful mien, and although it was not written in the script, disappeared into the tent with Mademoiselle while she was changing into her bathing costume. He brought down the house.

At the end, when the whole cast erupted onto the stage in a wild Charleston number there was Homer in the middle, peering out with a bored, nonchalant expression. Ah, what has Clark Gable got that I haven't got? he seemed to be saying.

Homer loved his family dearly, and after we became accustomed to his face, we loved him dearly too. He died of cancer in 1965.

Our Last Trail Ride

a new story by Eldon Lee

In the first volume of Heart of the Cariboo-Chilcotin, *we featured Dr. Eldon Lee's touching tribute to his younger brother Todd. Growing up together on an isolated ranch in the rugged Central Cariboo region, the two siblings were best friends and true-blue companions, sharing adventures, hijinks and a love of the wildnerness and its denizens that only country boys could really know. In this story, Eldon fondly remembers their last such escapade, a trail ride with Todd in the style of the "Old West," to search for some old Native dwellings and graves.*

Todd and Eldon on Tony and Dickie.

Brother Todd was leaving the Hills and Paul Ranch and the Cariboo for the outside world, just as I had four years earlier.

A last saddle-horse trail ride was in order. Poor Todd, it would be his last ride with his horse Dickie, a faithful companion for the previous 10 years. For me, it would be the last trail ride with Todd—my brother, my buddy, my closest friend. In the back of our minds, we realized that this ride marked the end of our previous lifestyle.

We had heard of some old Indian Keekwullie dwellings and graves on MacIntosh Lakes, 15 miles to the east, close to the road linking the 108 Mile House to Horsefly, 50 miles north. Years before, a Salish Indian tribe west of the Fraser River, when pressed by the Chilcotins, fled to the MacIntosh Lake area, where they survived on the local game, coarse fish from the lake, and roots and berries. Eventually the Chilcotin lost interest and the Salish were able to return to the Fraser and again fish for salmon.

We could have journeyed by road over a lengthy route, but determined instead to ride straight across country, in the style of the Old West.

This was to be a two-day venture, so our first consideration was food. Our supplies were mainly from the ranch: sourdough fixings, smoked ranch ham, potatoes, butter, jam, rolled oats and coffee. We added canned milk from the store and at mother's insistence, packed carrots, dried apples, raisins and a mild, white homemade cheese. These were all laid out on the kitchen floor along with two blankets apiece. When two pots for cooking were added, we realized that, along with our guns, we would need a pack horse.

"We might as well be loading for a girl's outing," said a disgusted Todd. Pat, a quarter horse, was picked to carry the pack saddle and camping gear, and supplies were securely fixed with diamond hitches. At a respectable hour, that is, 9 a.m., we were loaded and goodbyes were said. Todd rode on Dickie; I rode behind him on Tony, with Pat reluctantly bringing up the rear. We passed through the gate at the upper pasture fence and headed north through the pine and fir.

Horses, when reluctant to move, will rub riders against trees, stumble over logs and rocks, and generally make their unhappiness known. Our horses did all these, so with Todd leading Pat, I swung Tony in behind her and gave her a whack on the backside. She gave an angry shake of her head and kicked straight back, catching Tony straight on the chest. This awakened Tony, who in return bit Pat on the flank. After this conniption, all was peaceful and we moved along at a faster pace.

A two-and-a-half-mile ride brought us to the old Felker Trail, which was first cut through from 144 Mile House to join Knife Creek Road at Squawks Lake. This wagon road was still clearly marked with blazes, so we followed it eastward and crossed two small brooks bubbling over gravel bottoms. All three horses drank thirstily. Todd and I were also thirsty, so we lay on the bank and, supporting ourselves with our hands in the shallows, drank deeply. The water was cold and delicious.

Around noontime we reached a small meadow, and it was here we slipped the bits on Tony and Dickie, loosening all the cinches so the horses could graze on the lush grass. Todd and I sprawled out on the grassy cover and ate our lunch too as we lazed and talked in the warm summer sunshine. A lone raven squawked above and circled, eyeing our food. We threw it a bread crust.

At two o'clock we reached Knife Creek Road. The junction with our trail was marked by a large grey rock with the face chipped away on one side and a carved arrow pointing east toward Half Way House. We went in that direction for a mile, then took off on a fir-covered rocky rise following along a cow path to Barney's meadow. Here a tumbledown log cabin and barn lay slowly rotting into earth. One could feel the despair of a pioneer on leaving this failed enterprise.

Our horses picked up the scent of something nearby. With ears forward, they snorted and shied away as we heard twigs breaking and hoof beats in the distance. It sounded huge, but we saw nothing until fresh moose pellets satisfied our curiosity.

The two MacIntosh lakes extended over three miles and were half a mile wide. Much to our surprise, in a small open area along the lake sat a cabin, its roof in poor repair. (Hey, who expected the Hilton?) We unsaddled and tethered the horses; while I unpacked our provisions, Todd mixed up the sourdough in a can.

Evening came and around our open fire we feasted on hot bread baked over coals, potatoes baked in them, ham and chili beans. A special treat was mashed saskatoon berries; it had taken us half an hour to pick a pailful of the dark, delicious fruit from the loaded branches around the clearing.

Darkness found the two of us prepared for rest. Blankets were laid out on the cabin floor, one to cover us and two below, resting on some pine branches. We followed old western tricks, placing our saddles, covered with jackets, at the head of our bed for pillows. All was at peace. Loons sounded across the lake, grebes' garbled shrieks echoed on the surface of the lake and, in the distance, a flock of geese honked companionably.

"What's that?" cried Todd suddenly, rising up. There was a scrabble of claws across the rough floor and up the wall. I lit a match and saw two little eyes shining back at me. Todd said, "Light another match," and then fired a shot at the ceiling, adding a few new holes in it. The rats scrambled away to find peace in a different setting.

We were just dozing off again when our horses began to scream in a blood-chilling crescendo. The sound of a wounded or frightened horse makes a person's hair stand on end. I seized the heavy rifle and looked outside, but could see little by the light of the coals. The horses were staring fixedly at a willow patch on the periphery, so I fired twice at the willow tops, bringing down branches and leaves. Attired only in shoes and shorts, we quieted the horses and ran from one to the other petting each in turn. The animal that spooked the horses was probably a cougar. We built the campfire up with logs and went back to bed. The light of the flames visible through the open door gave little comfort, and we slept poorly until dawn.

The morning was gloriously sunny and with hotcakes, ham, and porridge with saskatoon berries in us, we explored the open area and found three Keekwullie sites. These were circular excavations 10 feet in diameter and one foot deep, with the depression partially filled in with debris. The teepee-like structure that had sheltered the original inhabitants was gone, but our spade unearthed charred coals and bone fragments. One must admire the stoic endurance of hardship by these early residents. With winter temperatures dropping to 50 below zero and two feet of snow covering the ground, the Natives wore only moosehide moccasins on their feet.

We searched some more and found an old boat made of rough boards that was half-filled with water but still serviceable. We paddled across the lake to an open point of land, using paddles we cut from boards with our axe. There on the far shore we found several mounds suggestive of graves. We tested the surface and found some large stones, probably placed there by the Natives to deter wild animals. Their dead were likely buried in sitting positions, as old Bill Squawk was at the mouth of Knife Creek, on the lake still named after him. If so, they, like Bill, had been provided with a fine view.

Our trip back across the lake was alarming because a rising wind caused two-foot-high waves to roll in the from the west. We paddled our leaky vessel and bailed water as fast as we could, happily reaching shore just in time to see a bald eagle swoop down and spear a foot-long mullet from the crest of a wave. Deeply pierced, the fish struggled wildly for a moment and then grew limp. The heavily loaded eagle made his way to his mate and their nest high up in a large fir tree overlooking the lake.

"I bet I can climb up there and have a look at that nest," Todd said, and then proceeded to climb the tree limb to limb until he was within six feet of the eyrie. Well, those eagles were not at all happy to receive a visitor, and they made some fierce dives with claws outstretched. I shouted, "Todd, get down right now!" and he did. The eagles perched in a nearby tree, looking mean and suspicious.

That night's rest was somewhat better, and the next morning we fished and caught several three-pound mullets, a coarse bottom-feeding fish commonly found in Cariboo lakes. Soon it was time to pack and head home. There was a feeling of satisfaction. We had found the Keekwullie sites, and suspected that the mounds across the lake held the early inhabitants. We had also had the sense of living off the land. Our horses felt our mood and galloped across wild meadows, the uncut hay coming up to their bellies. Pat, the pack horse, was let loose to follow on her own and did so, keeping pace. Todd and I, on the other hand, abandoned all common sense, standing up on our saddles on the galloping horses and yelling like maniacs.

Two hours later we pulled up before the barnyard gate of the Hills and Paul Ranch, slid off our horses and hugged each other. We were never to share the joy of such a trail ride again.

Old Nero looked a lot like this huge grizzly.

The Legend of Old Nero

from *The Fire Still Burns:*
A Life of Trail Talk and Contrary Opinions
by Chilco Choate

One day while out riding, Chilco Choate came across the biggest grizzly tracks he'd ever seen. A hunting guide at the time, the astute Choate didn't take long to recognize in this bear his proverbial rich uncle. So began a strange relationship of mutual benefit between a bear with a horse-sized appetite and a man with a very human-sized appetite for making the most of an opportunity.

Steve Johnson was mounted on one of his favourite horses and riding a long way out in front of the boss, which had become the customary place for him to be. I should say this was his favourite horse when there was nothing critical to do: the mare was strictly a show-off piece, a nag that loved to prance along with her head high and her tail cocked up like she was heading for the Williams Lake Stampede. There wasn't a brain in her head. She was virtually useless as a hunting or trail mount, and in our world that pretty well spelled out the probable content of her life to come. Steve broke this mare and, once he'd begun to identify her numerous faults, named her the Bay Bitch, which turned out to be a most appropriate name.

A hundred yards behind, the boss was plodding along on his old reliable, at that time a big bay gelding named John Henry. As was also customary, for reasons now long forgotten, it was the boss's job to drag along the two pack horses carrying our camping and trail gear. Whoever was relegated to that job automatically became the "tail-end-Charlie." It was a well-known fact that Steve Johnson hated leading a pack horse, and the thought had often surfaced in my mind that maybe it was no accident he almost always rode a horse that was unsuited to leading others. In fact, that may have had a lot to do with how he came to be the "guide leading the guide" most of the time. Well, what the hell! He was good at it. So without comment from either of us, that had pretty much become our permanent relationship.

This was the year that I had become a self-employed businessman, which meant that I had elevated myself up, or thought I had, from being someone else's hired hand. I was the new owner, which was supposed to translate into meaning the BOSS, of a hunting and trail-ride guiding operation that I had been working for over the past three years. The previous name of the outfit was the Gang Outfitter. It had never been part of the Gang Ranch, but the "Gang" part of the name was certainly meant to imply that it might be, or, more realistically, to position its operation area on the map. The first thing I did when I became the boss was to drop that title and use my own name instead. That may not have been the wisest decision, but I was only 23 years old and not the brightest person in the country. As time went on I discovered that there were many other things in this world that I was ignorant of. This Gang Ranch that I refer to, if you do not already know, is one of Canada's larger ranches, but by no means the largest, as various owners of it would like the world to think. Geographically it begins west of the Fraser River, 65 miles west of Clinton, B.C., and it holds a grazing licence that covers about a million acres of Crown land.

Steve Johnson, who is often referred to in these stories, was a friend and work partner when the former owners held the camp, and he was still now supposed to be relegated to the position of the "hired hand," but that was a title that often became blurry over the next several years. There was never any doubt in my mind or in the minds of my parents, who lived in Clinton, that given the opportunity, Steve Johnson could easily have run an operation of his own. He was not the only assistant guide of this new operation—there were other short-term assistants—but I will concede that Steve was my top or head guide when I wasn't around. After his death 12 years later, his position was taken over by a friend of both of us, Jimmy Seymour of Canoe Creek. Jimmy worked for me for over 30 years.

On this particular ride-out, during the early fall of 1958, we were in the Gang Ranch area of the Chilcotin and heading up into the high country to do some game scouting. This was the best excuse we could come up with to go there, and when the Chilcotin weather breaks clear in late summer and early fall it's an easy excuse to fall back on. The previous day we had sniffed the air, tossed powder into the wind, and come to the unanimous decision that the time was exactly right to go do it all again. We weren't wrong about that either. First day out and there we were riding down the centre of Hungry Valley, soaking up the glorious scenery and revelling in the feelings of contentment brought on by such days—the kind a person wants to last forever. You drift along in such a wonderfully mellow mood that you can slip your mind to wherever in the universe you want it to go. I've personally experienced thousands of days like that, days we've come to refer to as Indian summer.

Travelling along in this dream-like state, I was jolted back to earth when John Henry came to an abrupt stop in a muddy creek. In the middle of the crossing, the hired hand and his fancy horse were blocking the trail, with Steve turned halfway back so he could face me. There was a big grin on his face when he asked, "Do we need a tag for a sasquatch?" I don't recall the facial expression I was trying to portray, but before I could answer, Steve nodded down toward a track in the mud. "Holy Christ!" I thought. Something with snowshoe-sized feet had recently walked down that creek.

We moved our horses up out of the crossing and both of us bailed off so we could examine the tracks more closely. We knew they weren't from sasquatch, but the size of the imprints was impressive all the same. The tracks were still distinct and created the overwhelming feeling that we'd stumbled onto the trail of what must have been the biggest grizzly in the country. Because they were so much larger than any tracks we'd ever seen, we marked their length and width on an axe handle to be sure there would be no after-fudging of the figures. We cut small notches into the wood so the exact measurements could be verified later with a tape.

We'd remounted and were moving up the trail again when Steve laughed back at me and said, "Think you can handle that one with your .30-30?" He could afford to laugh—he was riding a faster horse and packing a bigger rifle, which happened to be a .30-06. He wasn't dragging a couple of reluctant pack horses along behind him either. But I simply grinned back and replied, "Whoever gets him breaks the record book," and we nodded in agreement.

After that we rode along in silence for a while, our minds returning to their respective realms. Mine went back to memories of conversations with Gus Piltz, who still owned the Sky Ranch over near Big Creek. The first time I met Piltz, three years earlier, he'd mentioned something about a huge grizzly, one that had taken to visiting the Sky Ranch calving grounds almost every spring in the previous few years. These veal forays proved sufficiently costly that Gus had apparently been offering a $500 reward to anyone who could bring the marauder to justice. I heard a couple of other fellows in the area, Jim Russell and Jim Bishop, mention something about this offer, but so far nobody had been able to cash in on the reward.

Because of the way Gus described his unwelcome visitor, especially its size and cleverness in avoiding its just desserts, I'd taken the whole story with at least a few grains of salt. But now, having seen those tracks, the implications were enough to make me wonder. Pretty soon there wasn't the slightest doubt in my mind that such an enormous bear really did exist, and this realization made me begin to reconsider some of Gus's other stories as well, tales that, at the time, I had perhaps not taken seriously enough. A person has to be careful about things like that.

Putting aside Piltz's problems and offer for a moment, it seemed to me there might be a way to exploit this new situation and turn it into a figure somewhat larger than $500—even though most people would have considered that to be a great deal of money in 1958. It was to me, especially since I'd only that year gone into the outfitting business. As a consequence of that decision my finances were strung out on such a thin, tight shoestring that the twang often woke me up at night. That $500 was sure tempting, but the allure was tempered by the knowledge that turning those tracks into quick cash was by no means a sure bet.

And so it was that with a slightly devious mental turn I began seeing those tracks leading not so much toward a bear, but toward something more like the goose that lays the golden eggs. Do you believe in killing that kind of goose? Well, I don't either. So I shifted my thinking into higher gear and more than likely added quite a few years to this goose-bear's life.

By the end of the day's ride, which had brought us up to our cabin in Lost Valley (or Dash Creek as it's named on the maps), a plan had pretty well jelled in my mind. It was simply this: to leave the bear as he was in the hope that he would continue living within my allotted guiding area and keep making lots of those platform-sized tracks along the trails. Being a hunter myself, and realizing what the sight of those pad prints had done to both Steve and me, it wasn't hard to imagine how they would stir up our hunting dudes. Perhaps the tracks by themselves could be turned into trails of gold or, more literally, the continuous cash flow my banker kept harping on about and that I clearly did not yet have.

At that time I was charging $500 for a two-week hunting trip. The way the seasons were laid out, there was room for two trips in the spring and two in the fall. Because of sheepherders' poison and ranchers like Gus, however, there really weren't enough grizzlies left to warrant such liberal seasons. This was especially so if every hunter expected to be successful. With things as they stood it seemed the government was, in actuality, selling sportsmen hunting opportunity rather than high success rates. And if that's legal for the government, then why not for others, too?

Viewed from this perspective, it only required lots of those huge tracks and ongoing luck on the bear's part and there could be a bonanza for both of us. So that's the way it was decided. See how easy it is to ride up a sunny Chilcotin trail and become rich as you are doing it? It can be rainbows and pots all the way!

Later on that evening, secure in our Lost Valley cabin, we measured the marks on the axe handle and recorded the bear's paw size. The length of the hind foot was 17 inches, and both the front and back feet were 11 inches across. The largest tracks we had ever recorded prior to that were 14 inches by 8 inches. This platter-foot specimen—so long as its body size related to its feet—was going to be a great deal bigger than any bear we had ever seen before. In all probability it would make it into the record book, assuming, that is, that some hunter was lucky enough to kill it.

With all these factors fresh in mind, I decided it was time to run my business plan by somebody else to see how it might take. Steve being the only other person in the valley, it didn't take much to figure out whose ears should receive the first pitch. I saw my opening and laid it on him as he was chewing on a steak bone and gazing out the window. When I was done he didn't say anything for a few moments, and it was obvious he was mulling the idea over in his own mind. Finally, though, he nodded in agreement. "That's a pretty good plan," he said. "And anyway, any bear that has lived as long as this one has, and eaten as many Gang Ranch cattle as it has, deserves to be allowed to die of old age." (Since Steve had done a stint or two as a Gang Ranch cowboy, he and I shared several like-minded opinions about the value of cattle in wilderness areas, not to mention our further lack of appreciation for the ranch owners and their new manager.)

Thus far in agreement, I then began relating some of the stories that Piltz had told me about what I assumed was the same bear. From the stories we'd heard, and the figures we had to play around with, we tried to figure out how old that bear might be. In the end we decided it must be somewhere around 30 years old, which we knew was getting on for a wild bear. That night, as we lay in our bunks being entertained by the overly friendly mosquitoes, we were still hyped up and talking about this bear, a prize grizzly that was at that moment somewhere close by. Steve told me a story he had recently read about a similar-sized bear, one that had led ranchers and bounty hunters on a merry chase through the U.S. cattle country for years before someone finally killed it. That American bear had been given a name (which I have now forgotten), and, winding up the story, Steve suggested we lay a name on this one, too, as it might make the sales promotion easier to pitch. Well, that made good sense to me. So we lay there for a while and lobbed different names back and forth. We debated names like Bigfoot, Squatch, Beefeater, and even Old Gussy (in honour of Gus Piltz), any one of which would have been appropriate. In the back of my mind, though, there was an epic story of a Roman rebel, and I kept trying to remember his name. This Roman had been a renegade slave, had escaped to the mountains, and from there had turned on his masters and made Rome tremble. This bear being an obvious rebel, it seemed to me that the story was a good fit and that the Roman's name might serve well.

That night the only name I could dredge up from memory was Nero, even though something kept haunting me, telling me he was not the right Roman. When I suggested the name and history to Steve, he didn't take to it at all. His rationale stemmed from the high probability that a) this bear had never been to Rome and b) nobody over there would even know what a grizzly was. So why try to draw them falsely together? But I'd made up my mind and, being the boss of our outfit, I pulled rank.

The following morning some Gang Ranch cowboys dropped in to

visit, and in the course of conversation I tested the entire bear story on them, complete with its new name. These fellows were a good bunch of cowboys and saw the entire plan for what it was: a good lark for Choate to lay on "those rich Yankee hunters." At the same time, they warned us that if they saw the bear first, they intended to collect Gus Piltz's bounty. As of that moment, Old Nero of the Gang Ranch/Big Creek country became formally recognized and named into our vocabulary.

About a month later I tried the story and pitch on one of my best client-friends, "a rich Yankee hunter" who went by the name of Bill Norton, from Seattle. Bill began to laugh as he informed me, "Aw, hell! The Roman you're trying to remember is Hannibal." And of course, he was right. For a while after that we tried renaming our gold pot to the more appropriate name, but it was too late. By then the story was spreading all by itself, so the huge bear remained sort of misnamed.

As it turned out, my plan was a good one, at least from our perspective, because it eventually became every bit as lucrative as we'd imagined. I do not recall exactly how many hunters came and paid their dues for a sporting chance at trying to collect that world-record golden hide. Over the next several years there were well in excess of 30, but as fate would have it, luck was always on the side of the bear and the outfitter. There were even those odd occasions when we made a little more effort towards actually bagging the bruin. Since several of our clients had become good friends, we naturally had qualms, like: "Should a person do this to a friend whose booze you are then partaking in?" But such thoughts we usually rationalized away by convincing ourselves that the hunters were getting a sporting chance at meeting Nero. At least sort of ... Well, think about it this way. Considering we were all out there in the same bush, there was always the possibility that the bear might just walk out in front of us, even walk into camp. Things like that. And that would have landed the rainbow straight into the hunter's pot.

In the end, though, we were able to sell a lot of sizzle and keep the steak, and Piltz's bounty turned out to be a paltry sum compared to the way we conducted matters. In 1958, for instance, I was charging $500 for a Nero hunt. A few years later, after inflation began setting in, the price went up to US$3,000. Hell, it got to the point that I even used to consider Nero part of the family, a rich uncle who was sharing the wealth and that sort of thing. Would you cash in your rich uncle before it was necessary? So there you are!

Over the ensuing 14 years, Nero's reputation grew with every cow that died or was killed in the high country. The Gang Ranch cowboys gave him full credit for most of the deaths, even though over in our camp it was common knowledge that there were other marauding bears doing some of the killing. And we knew that far more cattle died from ingesting poisonous weeds than from bear attacks. Beyond that, bog holes and outright quicksand take a high toll, too. In those days, though, cowboys refused to acknowledge such losses. When bears got the credit the cowboys were encouraged to go bear hunting, which is a lot more exciting than packing salt, fixing fences, and other such chores. Sometimes they hunted for bounty, too, because the Gang had gotten into the act as well.

The first person from our camp who set eyes on Nero was one of my assistant guides and a long-time friend, Jimmy Seymour. He was guiding a pair of moose hunters up in Lost Valley at the time. The year would have been 1961 or '62. I was hunting out of the same camp, and my hunter was the one who had come looking for bear (you can guess which one). This hunter's name was Dan. One afternoon, about halfway through Dan's hunt, we decided to take the rest of the day off. Although we'd seen lots of nice tracks, we had not sighted a single grizzly, much less Nero, and Dan was growing weary from hunting what he was beginning to describe as "phantom bears."

We rode into the yard and the first thing that caught my attention was that Jimmy had his entire horse string all tied up and saddled. It looked as if he was getting ready to pack up and pull out, even though there was still a week left on this hunting trip. There was no sign that his hunters had bagged their moose either, so the situation appeared strange at first glance. It gave me an odd feeling, knowing there'd been no previous plans to split up the party.

After tying up our own horses, Dan and I walked over to the cabin, opened the door, and, looking inside, saw Jimmy and his two hunters finishing their lunch. I noted their three bedrolls were all rolled up and ready for packing—proof they were preparing to leave. Jimmy never said a word and barely moved, other than sticking his head deeper into his soup bowl. But those two moose hunters jumped right up and proceeded to give me a tongue-lashing. Let me tell you, those two guys were steaming mad. According to their account, "This Indian guide you left us with goddamn near got all of us wiped out by the biggest grizzly in the world." They did not seem to be the least bit impressed by the fact that they'd become a couple of God's chosen few just to have met such a bear and been allowed to survive the encounter. Even after I tried to reason out a few like-minded suggestions for them, their hype was not dampened one little bit. The old standby—assuring them that "if you don't bother a griz, the griz won't bother you"—didn't work either, as one of the moosers retorted back, "Like hell they won't! Down in the States those goddamn things kill several people in Glacier and Yellowstone parks every year!"

By this time Dan could no longer contain himself and jumped into the conversation on my side. "Yeah," he said, "but up here it's a different situation because you guys have a pair of .300 magnums that will make sure things like that don't happen to you. Why, hell, man, you guys missed an opportunity to collect what might be the world's record grizzly." That didn't help matters much, though. One of the moosers now turned on Dan, laying a finger up against his chest and replying, "Look, you big fuckin' fool, my brother and I aren't up here on some kind of power trip like some other people are. All we came here for was to bag a truckload of meat, so we're getting the hell out of this valley. As far as we're concerned, you and Chilco can stay right here and you're both welcome to our share of every fuckin' bear in the country."

The mooser then turned to me and said in a calmer voice, "So right now, Chilco, you are going to explain to Jimmy where he can take us so we are not going to be meeting up with one of those goddamn things again." He turned back to Dan and began appealing to us in a more rational way. "Why, that goddamn bear we saw is big enough to peel the door off this cabin with one swipe of its paw."

If he was trying to scare Dan down to his own level it didn't work, because Dan's reply to that was, "Well, I sure as hell hope he comes and does it because my ass is getting saddle sore from riding around looking for him." The quip was lost on the moosers. One of them started getting fired up all over again and he challenged Dan and me with a kind of hypothetical-wish comeback. "Well, I hope you stupid bastards walk right into that thing on the path to the shithouse tonight!"

The conversation went round and round that way, with nobody giving ground, until I knew for sure there was no way those two moosers could be talked into reconsidering their plans to move out of the valley. We agreed the next best thing was to have Jimmy pack them down into a lower valley, either Hungry Valley or our base camp at Gaspard Lake. Jimmy opted to go all the way to Gaspard, and I suspected that choice was because my wife, Carol, was there, and she would then be doing the cooking and camp chores for them. Jimmy hated cooking for other people.

I suggested they stay in Hungry Valley—there was a better chance of bagging a bullmoose because of the lesser hunting pressure. Both moosers had been quietly listening to Jimmy and me discussing these options, and one of them now butted in, asking whether there was any chance of bumping into a grizzly down in Hungry Valley. "They never cross the mountain range between here and there," I assured him. At that point, Jimmy, being the loyal hand he was, ducked his head deeper into his soup bowl to hide the grin on his face. One of the moosers turned to his brother and, nodding in obvious satisfaction, reset the tone of the discussion by stating, "Okay then, Hungry Valley it is. We'll meet up down there with whatever is left of these guys at the end of the week." And that was what we all agreed to do.

When we had finished our lunch and the conversation had cooled to more civil levels, Jimmy and the two moosers treated Dan and me to the story of how they had come upon the grizzly. It went something like this.

Early that morning they had been riding up a small brushy creek, looking for bullmoose, when Jimmy, being in the lead, stopped his horse and began focusing his binoculars on something farther up the valley. He quickly dismounted, tied his horse to a tree, and while doing so, silently signalled the others to do the same. The hunters at this point assumed they were about to begin stalking a moose that was somewhere up ahead. Jimmy was not carrying a rifle, but he did have a 28-inch axe that all our guides carry in a scabbard on their saddle. When the hunters saw him withdraw it, they did likewise with their rifles, chambered a round, and set their safety catches. Not a word was spoken. Jimmy stepped right into the creek and motioned the hunters to do the same. Very cautiously, he proceeded to lead his crew up the creek. Every once in a while he would stop, motion the hunters to stay low, and sneak another peek through the binocs at whatever it was they were stalking. Apparently he never did offer the hunters the opportunity to look for themselves, and they never pressed the issue, instead letting Jimmy make all the decisions.

They had waded up the creek a fair distance before one mooser's curiosity began to overpower his caution, and since he had never seen a bullmoose, he decided he wanted to get a look at one before the shooting started. So at Jimmy's next reorienting peek through the binocs, this mooser decided to take a peek too. Because his feet were now freezing in the water filling his boots, he was thinking of taking a longer-range shot to get out of that creek as soon as he possibly could. When he saw Jimmy slide back down into the creek and go into a sneaky sort of crawl, he figured that between his freezing feet and the power of his .300 magnum, they had to be close enough to the moose to get him. And anyway, his brother was there as backup.

So the mooser stuck his head up to take a look, and what he saw was clearly not what he had come all the way up here to collect. Right up ahead, less than 100 yards away, was a huge dark-coloured creature feeding on a dead cow that was lodged in the creek. At that moment the enormous thing must have sensed something was amiss, because it reared up on its hind legs and came eyeball to eyeball with the hunter. Rather than the horn spread he was hoping for, the mooser saw a large piece of rotten flesh hanging out of a gaping mouth that contained rows of remarkably big teeth. "Oh, God! For a split second I felt like I was going to sit down in the creek and shit my pants," the hunter admitted. "Why, that goddamn thing was standing 12 feet tall and looking straight down on us. Not only that, it was only about four big jumps away, too."

Fighting the compelling urge to sink backwards into the creek, he managed to reach out, touch his brother, and, using sign language, quickly make him understand what was about to happen. Jimmy was by now too far ahead to signal, and the mooser said he was afraid if they called out to him the bear might attack. So as silently as they had gone up the creek, they turned and retreated back down it. "If the goddamn guide wanted to see a bear killed, he could damn well tackle it himself," he said. "After all, he still had that fuckin' axe."

Jimmy told me his version of events later, when we were alone. "I was guidin' my hunters up to this really big grizzly bear, and I figured to get them real close so they can't miss it. We was doin' really good, too, because when I got up to about 50 yards, I figures it's close enough. So I turns around to signal them hunters to start shootin', but I ain't got no hunters. I see those bastards is all the way back to the horses and gettin' ready to leave me there with nothin' but my axe.

"So I stuck my head up to look again, and I see the bear is watching them hunters and not me, so maybe the bear don't know I'm there. So I sits down behind a bush and waits. When them hunters get onto their horses and start to leave for camp, the bear, he grabs a big piece of cowhide and takes off the other way. So I went back to my horse and come back to camp too, because my feet is damn near froze." Jimmy shook his head in disbelief and lamented, "All that goddamn work for nothin'. Goddamn chickenshit hunters!"

That being the story, I had to quiz him further about the bear. "Jimmy," I said, "everybody talks about how big this huge bear is, but how big is he, really?" As I asked, I stretched my arms out, inviting Jimmy to demonstrate just how high and long the bear might be. Jimmy thought for a moment, then sort of shook his head and replied, "Oh, he's big all right. Big as a bull!" I knew he was referring to the domestic Angus bulls the Gang Ranch were at that time ranging in the area, and at first it seemed a ridiculous comparison. On the other hand, I'd read about grizzlies shot in earlier days that had topped the 1,800-pound mark, which would certainly put them in the same weight range as domestic bulls. In my mind, I compared bears we had taken on other hunts, whose paws measured 8 inches wide, with the 11-inch width of this one. After considering all the angles, it was easy to conclude that we had a *very* big bear for a neighbour.

But that was it for that hunting trip. The two moosers and Jimmy moved down into Hungry Valley, where they were able to bag a bullmoose without being challenged by Nero or any other bears. Dan and I stayed up in Lost Valley and watched over the dead cow for another week, but the only bear that came near it was a black bear. Dan shot it instead, and dreamed of Nero for another year.

I didn't actually see Nero myself until the following summer, when I returned to Lost Valley alone to cut the season's firewood and tighten up the pasture fence before the cattle arrived. This would have been about mid-June, and I was working on the woodpile when a small herd of cattle came walking past the cabin, heading down into the lower part of the valley. Their arrival was early as there was not much feed for them, and yet it was not that uncommon because Gang Ranch cattle control was still almost non-existent.

Once the cattle were turned out of the winter feed yards onto the open grassland, the stronger and wilder ones usually began roaming in an upward direction, following the higher edge of the green grass line in the same way migratory wild ungulates do.

This might also have had something to do with the wilder and smarter cows wanting to keep their new calves far away from the cowboys' branding irons and cutting knives for as long as they possibly could. By fall, cows don't seem as protective of their calves as they do when they are younger; perhaps they figure it's time for their kids to begin fending for themselves. That's pure speculation on my part, of course, as it's debatable how smart cows are. I do know for sure that only a few are natural leaders, the rest are followers. (So are cows like us, or are we like cows?)

Anyway, this small herd of cows arrived ahead of the main herd, choosing to compete with their natural enemies rather than the two-legged ones that were following along two weeks behind them. Since all of this had happened many times before, there was no reason for me to be particularly surprised to see these early arrivals, but I always took note of when, where, and sometimes why these things happened the way they did. In this case there were about 20 cattle, some of them with small calves following, which made them wary of me. All the same, they drifted right on by, clearly heading down into the lower end of the valley.

I forgot about them till about an hour later, when the same herd came stampeding back up the hill, charged past me, and headed up the trail towards Hungry Valley. Some of the cows were sweated up, too, with their tongues hanging out. This was a strange sight, enough so that it raised my curiosity to the point where I stopped working and began backtracking, trying to discover what their problem might be. I was fully expecting to discover that a bear or wolf attack had started the stampede; there seemed to be nothing else that could make cattle behave that way. I collected the only gun in camp—a .22 rifle we used for clearing packrats out of the cabins—slung my binocs around my neck, called my big collie, Kim, and set off down the hill.

Cattle running over soft ground through the timber made easy tracking for about a mile. There the trail reached the edge of the open valley of Dash Creek, and I walked out onto a high, open ridge. It was a perfect lookout over the valley, and directly below was a pair of huge grizzlies feeding on a recently killed adult cow. The distance between us was only about 150 yards, but Kim and I had the advantage of height, wind, and noise from the creek, as well as cover from the timber.

We immediately ducked under a thick, bushy pine tree that had branches right down to the ground. It took only a moment or two to convince Kim that he did not have to chase the bears away to protect me, and he dug himself a cozy nest in the squirrel shavings piled up under the tree and curled up in them. Making myself comfortable in the shavings alongside, I loaded a few more cartridges into the magazine of the .22, just in case. A .22 is almost useless in a bear attack unless the barrel is actually shoved down the animal's throat and fired, but it can serve as a noisemaker. I know from personal experience that if a bear is inclined to be turned away by noise, there is nothing better than a gunshot to do the job. I would rather have a .22 than an axe or a club, that's for sure. An even bigger gun is better by far, but you have to make do with what's available. On this occasion, rather than a bigger gun, I wished I'd had a camera. Without one, eyes and memory were left to do all the recording.

Luckily for Kim and me, the two grizzlies were totally engrossed, tearing the cow carcass into smaller pieces. They seemed to be in a race with each other for what they must have considered the choicest pieces of the dead animal's guts, because those were the parts they devoured first. Closer examination made me realize that describing these bears simply as "huge" was an understatement, especially when you think of normal bears. The larger of the two was a dark brown colour, almost black, and it likely would have appeared black from a greater distance, with only a tinge of frosty silver on its neck and shoulders. He was obviously male, or a boar as they are sometimes called. The other griz was about three-quarters the size, a beautiful, mottled, brown-to-brown sow. She showed much more silver than the boar, displaying the typical grizzly frosting over her face, neck, and all down her back—as beautiful a blonde as I have ever seen, but perhaps not one to meet on a dark trail.

The claws on both bears were long enough to be seen without aid of binoculars. From the size and colouring of the boar, I thought he might well have been a drifter from the coastal inlets. Bella Coola, Bute Inlet, and Knight Inlet, where the world's largest grizzlies have been recorded, are only about 80 miles west of that part of the Chilcotin. Wildlife biologists have told me that grizzlies from those areas are almost colour-coded for identification. That said, from my first sighting of those two bears below me that day, I knew instantly that I had finally met Old Nero.

That was the first time in my life that I'd had such a grandstand view of grizzlies behaving as they naturally do, and all in broad daylight! So woodpile be damned: Kim and I just hunkered down for the day because I knew there might never be another one like it. It did not take the bears long to get the cow well laid out, and like dogs do with a fresh kill, they frequently rolled all through the sloppiest parts of the innards. They were enjoying themselves in all the blood and guts. They played around with their food the way small children do and showed no aggression toward each other at all.

They were having so much fun that I even began thinking thoughts like, "What a nice thing it would be if Kim and I were to go down there and join them." But I quickly realized that it might not be such a wise thing to try, and we stayed put. Just the same, the sight and the feelings emanating from the bears were contagious. Up to that time I never would have suspected that bears are such social creatures, but they sure as hell are. For me, this was a kind of "continuing education" course that was worth whatever it cost, because the way they fed and played was only part of what they taught me.

These two bears were also mating. When a person watches something like that it's only natural to compare it with your own feelings under similar circumstances. I was able to watch them go through the love up to the full sex act, which was an eye-opener. It surprised me that grizzlies enjoy the ritual just as much as we do, and do it all pretty much the same way, too. Having witnessed other animals going through the sexual act, I'd learned that for most wildlife it's fast, sometimes violent, and makes you wonder why they even bother with it. But these bears soaked into it for 20 minutes to half an hour at a time, and even then it wasn't over. Then they sat back on their haunches, wrapped their forelegs around each other, and proceeded to lick all that gucky, gutty, gooey stuff off each other's faces and necks. Not all that different from what you or I might do in the shade of a cherry tree on a nice summer day.

Those bears displayed other human characteristics as well, showing off and trying to impress each other with demonstrations of strength. The cow they had killed was about four years old and must have weighed more than 1,000 pounds before they opened it up and drained most of the juices. Yet several times Nero took a good mouth hold into the centre of its back and proceeded to lift the entire carcass clear off the ground. He would give it a good shaking, throwing more blood and guts all over both of them. Every time he did this, Blondie was so impressed she would bounce right over and lick all the goo off Nero's face, neck, and ears, and her appreciation was such that it usually started the two of them into that other ritual again.

Once, when Blondie was trying to tear a front leg and shoulder off the carcass and it would not come apart for her, she just sat there in what looked like a pleading pout. Soon enough, Nero walked over and took hold of the opposite leg and they proceeded to have a tug-of-war until one of the shoulders did tear loose. That made a strange sound. Even at 150 yards or so it was loud enough to wake Kim up, and he acted like he wanted to head down there and help them out. Luckily I was able to grab him and quietly persuade him to go back to sleep.

Then there must have been a change in the wind or something, because both bears suddenly stopped feeding and reared up onto their hind legs to sniff the breeze. They didn't seem to detect anything alarming, but that moment gave me a true estimate of how high a big bear stands and, by God, let me tell you again, it is impressive. Looking through a pair of 7-power binoculars at 150 yards on a clear day left me in little doubt that Old Nero stood well over 10 feet to the top of his head. By stretching his neck and pushing his nose up in the air, there was no question that he could reach another two feet higher. Old Nero sure was a lot of bear.

It still seems hard to believe, but by the end of that day there was so little of the cow left that Nero and Blondie were satisfied enough to simply wander off in separate directions, leaving the scraps to a flock of ravens that had been gathering. She went down the valley and he headed up, and from my last sight of Nero, I swear he had a swagger. He was projecting such an air of complete confidence that I could only assume what he wanted next was either a good fight or another female.

The following day I went back to inspect the site for any further information that might be gleaned from the experience. All that was left of the cow was a large piece of hide that had been licked clean, along with the skull, backbone, leg, and shoulder bones. Most of the ribs had been snapped off and eaten, likely by coyotes that packed them off during the night. Other than that, the only evidence of what had taken place was the large piles of "bear sign." From the size of them, it seemed both those bears must have had bungholes the size of stovepipes.

So that was my introduction to old Nero, and I've never felt disappointed by it.

Over the next few years, a steady procession of hunters who wanted to put their names into the record book were lured here by those huge tracks or by the stories they heard about them. And there were the Gang Ranch cowboys to take into account—they would have shot

Old Nero on sight at any time of year. Considering that several other people I know had also seen Nero at one time or another, I eventually came to the conclusion that he was more lucky than smart. On several occasions even I could have shot him legally.

A number of moose hunters came within range under almost the same conditions as the hot-tempered brothers I've already told you about, but every time Nero left himself exposed, it seemed always to be for the benefit of moosers who weren't interested. Whenever we had a hunter who wanted nothing more than to nail that bear's hide to the wall, Nero seemed to become nocturnal, because his tracks simply disappeared. Maybe he was telepathic or something. Whatever it was, he got the message and left the area for a while.

Sometimes he was gone for long periods, but that didn't surprise us. Wildlife biologists, using radio tracking collars, have confirmed that boar grizzlies often establish a circular range that can be as much as 200 to 300 miles long, and they might only pass through a given part of it once or twice a year. This is especially true in the dry Interior country, where natural bear food tends to be scarce. Grizzlies are continually on the prowl for a feed, a fight, and in midsummer, for satisfaction of that other basic urge. If you and I will admit to the honest truth for a moment, it all comes down to realizing just how similar their lives are to ours.

Some later experiences will give you a better idea of just how smart (or lucky) this old bear was, and you can judge for yourself. Like I said, there were times when we did make a serious effort to help our hunters tag Old Nero. Bob and Rocky, client-friends from Portland, Oregon, came on at least four occasions to try their luck. On one of their later hunts we knew from his tracks in mud that we'd lured Nero to a horse we'd killed for bait (at that time it was legal). Even with the bait laid out in a perfect location, though, things were still not going as we'd hoped. It was turning out to be another of those times when Nero was acting "oh so clever!"

On this occasion he decided to become a midnight snacker. We arrived at the bait site every morning before daylight, and returned in the evening to keep watch until full darkness, but Nero eluded us every time. As a matter of fact, we never even caught a glimpse of him, although there was plenty of evidence that he'd been there: our bait was rapidly disappearing from one location and reappearing in another in the form of huge piles of bear sign. After his third successful feeding, we knew we had to come up with a better plan or this hunt was going to end up like all the previous ones. Another of those "chalk up one for Nero, zero for the hunter" deals again. Since Bob had been on three other "zero" bear hunts with me in the past, he was beginning to get cheesed off. The impending probability that this one was going to turn out the same way had both him and Rocky getting vocal on the subject.

Late evenings in the cabin they would lean on me a bit to, perhaps, bend a few rules and laws so the odds might turn in our favour. Their major proposal centred around Bob's big, six-cell flashlight, and they had a couple of good, rational arguments why we should use it. One was that if one of my paying clients (such as Bob, for instance) did not collect Nero's hide soon, then one of the Gang Ranch cowboys was bound to luck out ahead of us and collect the ranch bounty that was still on offer. We all knew from direct conversation with the cowboys that they had no qualms about bending any rule in the book. They were all packing guns, but hardly any of them bothered buying a licence, much less a bear tag. Paperwork and game wardens were mostly a big joke in the cow camps. All of this was hard to dispute.

The other argument, a kind of thinly veiled threat, was the suggestion that continuing to take influential hunters out on zero hunts could do damage to an outfitter's reputation. Furthermore, Bob would reason, when I was finally ready to accept the light of economic reality, what other hunter could I think of who was more entitled to this bear than he was? The way they had it figured, they already had about US $20,000 invested in Nero, so it was about time Choate mended his ways and dropped the charade of being so goddamn prudish. After all, everybody knows laws and rules have always been made to control other people, they'd reason, and if they aren't bent once in a while, game wardens, cops, and lawyers would soon be out of their jobs. They might even have to find real, honest work for a change!

You might think such lines of thought are put forward in jest, but when you have one of your best client-friends with his hand on your shoulder and the other keeping your glass filled with nothing but the best, it becomes mighty easy to finally see the pure, white light of reality. So my decision was made.

The next afternoon we made up a stack of sandwiches for supper and the following day's breakfast, then rode up to the meadow where what was left of the bait still lay. We also took along our sleeping bags as it was mid-fall and the night temperature at an elevation of 6,000 feet can be nippy. We picketed the horses about a half mile away on a lower meadow, then walked up to a good ambush site. There we got well positioned and bedded down for the coming vigil, which we referred to as the "bear watch." The hunters each had a rifle, while I had the six-cell light, my skinning knife, and a hunting axe. With something just over a smidgen of luck, before the week was over Nero would be relocating 600 miles south, down to Portland, Oregon.

Peering out in silence, all three of us stayed awake until well after midnight, but there was no sign of movement across the meadow. If anything approached, especially an animal as big as a bear, there was enough natural starlight to see it. The intense watching was beginning to tire our eyes, however, so we decided to take our turns at the bear watch, allowing the other two to catnap. We settled on two-hour shifts, mine being the last, which would take us through to daylight. I soon dozed off, leaving the other two to keep tabs on what might be going on across the meadow. It was agreed that under no circumstances was anybody to use the flashlight until we knew for certain that it was time to do so. A misfire would surely spook a bear like Nero, and in all likelihood he would never return again.

When I awoke later on in the night I discovered both hunters snoring logs off. Perhaps that was what woke me up. Bob was a big-bellied man and could really do justice to that type of job. Soon we were all sort of half-awake, and we could hear the horses down at their end of the meadow snorting and whistling. We could tell from the sound that they were alarmed, and that woke us up in a hurry. As I got the six-cell positioned, I could hear the other two checking the safety catches on their rifles. There we lay, tense and at the ready for about an hour, but with no sign of movement across the meadow. I eventually drifted off to sleep again. At 5 A.M., a hand shook me awake to announce the beginning of my official watch. The others assured me that during my snooze nothing had moved across the meadow. I lay there expectantly: I was sure this was the time of day when the action was most likely to begin. But as my watch ticked on and nothing appeared, it was beginning to look like we would be repeating the whole procedure again the following night. Oh well, that's the way it goes, I thought, consoling myself with the notion that if success comes too easily it's not really appreciated. This could all be viewed as whetting the appetite.

With the greying of daylight, which at that time of year happens about 6:30 A.M., visibility comes slowly. By straining my eyeballs through Bob's 7 x 50 mm Bausch & Lomb, night-and-day binoculars (at that time the best money could buy), I could see that things across the meadow did not appear the way I remembered them from the previous evening. When I cautiously stood up in my sleeping bag to get a better view, I learned for sure that they had changed for the worse. I awoke the other two and they jumped up with rifles at the ready, but the silent shake of my head told them that wasn't necessary. A sighting through their rifle scopes confirmed what I already knew— that somehow, some way, we were already too late. It was now light enough to sidle over to where the bait was, but the evidence there only confirmed what we already suspected: we had no bait to watch over. Apparently that goddamn bear had snuck in sometime during the night and dragged the remainder of the horse carcass about 200 yards back into the thick timber. He then proceeded to clean the last meal off those bones at his leisure, and the game was up.

I had no doubt that the hunters' snoring was to blame for spooking the bear, and I told them so with no mincing of words. But Bob was not about to buy that theory. The way he had it figured, our failure had more to do with the sleepy-headed guide, and he emphasized this in a number of ways, such as informing the guide that he was beginning to wonder what the hell he was paying the guide for anyway! As we were saddling our horses and preparing to head back to the shack, he gave me his parting shot. "This is the fourth horse that I've paid a hundred dollars for to feed your goddamn bears and coyotes and it's the last one I'm buying, too. If I ever come back here to try for this smart son of a bitch again, then we'll just feed him a couple more Gang Ranch cows."

Another bear hunt season ended, and Nero was once more scratching his marking tree with symbols that meant "another horse, another year."

The following year I laid out a horse for a different hunter in exactly the same place, but this time I was smarter about it. It was another one of those years and hunts when I was leaning in favour of the hunter. Perhaps it was time somebody collected this trophy, or at least got a shot at him, I thought. I bought a bigger horse this time and laid it farther out into the meadow where it would be clear of the early morning and late evening shadow from the trees. After only a few days, tracks and signs appeared and it was clear that the first bear to the bait was none other than Nero himself. The trip was rapidly shaping up to be a memorable hunt.

Unless you come across it by accident, a bear's first feeding on bait should be granted as a freebie. It seems that bears need that first feed to take possession of bait. After that, many become so possessive they will not run off at all, although not all bears react that way. Whether it's intelligence or just plain hunger that makes the difference, we still do not know. In any event, we never began any bear watch until the quarry had that first free meal.

We'd gathered this bait intelligence over the years by observing other bears that were neither as lucky nor as intelligent as Nero, because we had stretched out a few lesser grizzlies. Some of them happened purely by accident, some through planned baiting that worked like a textbook case, and a few by hair's breadth luck on our part. When I say hair's breadth, I'm referring to instances where the bear seemed as wily as Old Nero, but in the end it was still the hunter's luck that took the field. When our efforts focused entirely on Nero, we always felt that we were dealing with The Old Man of the Mountains. That being the case, he was always the teacher and we were the students.

On this occasion we didn't expect him to return to the bait the next night: bears seldom do. Usually they'll take a huge feed off a carcass and then wander off for a few days, returning to feed at intervals until the carcass is finished. This time, though, Nero did return the following night for a second nocturnal feeding. And once again he dragged what was left of the carcass back to his favourite dining spot in the thick timber. By the time we located it, there was still at least 1,200 pounds of carcass left, and it was all Steve and I could do to get our saddle horses to drag that carcass back out into the meadow. Considering that Nero had taken possession of this carcass, we took our chances handling it. We drove a wooden stake three or four feet into the ground and tied the dead horse's back feet to it with a halter shank. With that much human scent around, we were sure that a bear as wise as Nero would this time take a few days before returning to feed. He certainly would not reappear out of pure hunger, because he had already eaten and spread out about 500 to 600 pounds of horsemeat and guts.

The following morning we all went moose hunting, planning to check the bait each afternoon when we returned on horseback from our moose excursions. That turned out to be another poor decision. The first afternoon, even as I rode up, I could see that—lo and behold—there was no bait! It was not hard to discover why. The Mountain Man had simply pulled the stake out of the ground and dragged horse and stake together back to exactly the same dining spot as the day before. By this time the carcass had been whittled down to about 1,000 pounds, and the only good thing about that was it made it easier to drag it back to the meadow again. By now we, too, were getting smarter, and this time we tied the bait to a good-sized tree. We began the bear watch in earnest, but as the hunter hadn't pressured me into using the six-cell system that year, we reverted back to rising earlier, going to bed later, and not sleeping on the meadow with the bait.

The honest truth of it is that I have never, to this day, killed an animal by pit lamp, and I don't relish the idea at all, especially when you're dealing with an animal of grizzly bear calibre. Aside from the possible legal consequences, my attitude stems more from the safety aspect. In the dark, even using a light, it is not easy to make a sure and deadly first shot, and it is unlikely there will be a decent chance of a well-placed second shot. Since the behaviour of a wounded grizzly is well recorded, it doesn't take much to imagine the danger of that situation when you throw in a hyped-up hunter—one who is probably nowhere near as experienced or brave as he implied before the shooting started. It could all too easily wind up in an erratic case of buck fever, with disastrous consequences for both hunter and guide. (I'll have a few things to say about that subject later on.)

Suffice to say, I still much prefer any type of daylight hunting to a shady midnight affair. And, of course, with the illegality of six-cell hunting, trouble is never far away. Even back in the deep bush, a hunter would do well to consider the value of his wallet and, maybe, his freedom before being so tempted. There's always a big risk when there's a witness. My philosophy is that when two people (and read that as *any* two people) know a secret, then there is no secret. Shifty things seem to have devious ways and reasons for somehow leaking out.

So there we were, trying our best, and yet the tied-to-the-tree system didn't work either. Three nights later Nero returned to the bait, and this time he simply chewed off the rope and once again dragged the carcass back to his preferred feeding area. By now we didn't even have to follow the drag marks, but rode straight to where we knew the carcass was going to be. Given that both time and bait were running out on us, we were becoming a little concerned. The bait, in particular, was a worry as it was now down to about 800 pounds. On the upside, it only took one saddle horse to drag it back to the same tree, and this time we tied it there with heavy fencing wire.

But that didn't seem to be the answer either. It was as if he were always watching us from some vantage point. Two mornings later, when daylight arrived, the two hind legs were all that was still wired to the tree, and there was only enough meat left attached to them for raven pickings. Again, we rode directly to where we knew the rest of the carcass was going to be, only this time there was an astounding surprise awaiting us. That huge bear let us come crashing up to within 50 yards of him—and there were two other large grizzlies with him.

The three of us saw Nero plain as day—he was standing in a reared-up position—but the other two were more nervous and waited only long enough to take a good look at us. Then they took to their heels. Nero acted almost as if he were going to challenge us, but when his buddies left he slowly dropped down on all fours and followed them. That was a lucky thing for us, because we were in thick timber and our horses were spooked. If one of the bears had charged, we would have been in serious trouble. By the time we'd dismounted and drawn our rifles from their scabbards, the bears were long gone. It made for a few exciting moments—coming upon three huge bears at a 50-yard distance does give your heart a flutter or two. Especially when it's all over and you know that events could have ended with drastic consequences.

After we'd calmed down and taken stock of our circumstances, we discovered that the carcass was all but completely cleaned up. It had been torn into several pieces and scattered all over the bush area, so there wasn't enough left to serve as bait anymore. It appeared to be all over for another Nero hunt. This time, though, the hunter did at least get a good look at him—almost eyeball to eyeball—and that was enough to bring him back to try another year. Unsuccessfully, of course. That's the way "fair chase" hunts go sometimes, but it's not all so bad, because the outfitter and guides get paid just the same, and that's what it's all about, isn't it?

Jimmy Seymour had a different sort of amusing go-round with Nero when he was once again guiding a mooser. We were all hunting out of the same cabin in Hungry Valley at the time. Since the cabin is located right in the centre of the 25-mile-long valley, when there is more than one guide, we divide the territory: one of us hunts to the east and the other to the west, or north. This time Jimmy had a single hunter and it was his turn to go east, so I went west, both of us hunting only for moose. I received most of this story from the hunter himself, a dentist from Seattle, but Jimmy was sitting there listening to the hunter's rendition and he never disputed a word of it.

According to the dentist's version of events, they rode down the valley about four miles to where there is a large brushy meadow that runs right up into the mountain. The Lost Valley trail follows the edge of this meadow for quite a distance. When Jimmy arrived there he decided to hunt on foot, since parts of the meadow are too brushy and noisy for hunting on horseback. So he stopped and tied the horses to some trees. The idea was to circle the meadow and return to the horses, a route that would take a couple of hours. The mooser loaded his rifle, Jimmy grabbed his axe, and off they went.

It was early morning and there were still a few patches of fog and mist swirling over parts of the meadow as they drifted along, examining each section as they came to it. There are areas where you can see quite far across the meadow, but in other places the willow brush is high and dense—places where a hunter can easily miss seeing an animal, even one as big as a moose. Since a moose can suddenly appear out of nowhere, you have to hunt slowly and cautiously. Jimmy had his binoculars and was scanning the meadow methodically, but he was having no luck locating a moose. The mooser, meanwhile, was relying on the naked eye, which at those distances in poor light makes for poor hunting ability. Yet as the mooser studied one of the larger meadows, he noted a low mound over on the far side. It was covered with some windfalls that had a large, dark-coloured stump in the centre. He couldn't see the stump too clearly at first, but the mist was now lifting. As visibility improved, each time he saw the stump anew he was surprised (and laughed to himself) at how much that stump resembled his daughter's big teddy bear. And wasn't it amazing that although his viewpoint kept changing as they moved along, every time he took another look from a fresh angle that teddy bear stump always seemed to be looking directly at them?

The mooser found all this to be very amusing, the way his sight and mind were playing tricks on him. Finally, just as they were about to enter the timber, he reached out and touched Jimmy on the shoulder, pointing to the stump and whispering, "Jimmy, what does that stump look like to you?"

Jimmy raised his binoculars, peered through, slowly lowered them again, and returned his gaze to the mooser. "You wanna shoot a grizzly bear?"

"No, I don't," the mooser advised him.

Jimmy nodded. "Well then, let's get the hell out of here." And that's exactly what they did.

Judging from the way Nero had been standing there observing them for so long, if that hunter had wanted his name in the record books it would've taken only a "duck soup" shot to put it there.

Instead, the Bear God smiled and respected Nero's powerful totems.

Old Nero lived to a ripe old age. The last time I saw him was during the spring bear hunt of 1972. As before, we were hunting out of the Hungry Valley cabin. By then he must have been getting past his mental prime because he came about as close to getting measured as we ever heard.

It was an early June morning and I was guiding a fellow by the name of Bud Westgate, who was hunting for the big, dark phantom. On that particular day there were three other non-hunting riders tagging along. For some reason I can no longer recall, we were out on a rather "la-di-da" ride, more for pleasure than hunting expectancy. The three others were Julia the cook, Bud's son Jerry, and a sometime assistant guide of mine who went by the name Cactus Kind.

We hadn't gone far from the cabin, still riding along the fence line of the horse pasture, when I noticed what appeared to be a moose browsing in the brush on the north side of the valley. The distance would have been about half a mile. At that time of year in those days Hungry Valley was literally crawling with moose—we were used to seeing between 20 and 30 every day. So I didn't pay much attention to this one, other than keeping it in the corner of my eye, until I noticed something curiously different about the way this animal moved. Just before we entered the timber, heading towards another meadow, I stopped my horse and slid from the saddle.

Well, Holy Christ, there it was!

Not only a grizzly, but *the* grizzly: Old Nero. And he was right out there in the open, too. Preparing a fast war plan with Cactus, we decided that he and the other two non-hunters should remain where they were to keep an eye on the bear, while Bud and I would make the stalk on horseback. The plan was practical and made sense. To get over to where he was we'd have to go around a swampy area and cross a creek that runs high in the spring runoff period, which it then was. All that ground in the springtime is just one small step away from being pure muskeg. We all knew that it was going to be nip and tuck to catch up with the bear. We could see that he was slowly feeding his way towards a dense, burned-over area.

This was our idea: Cactus would remain on a high point of land where he could see the bear and we could see him. He would give us hand signals if the bear moved off and at those times when we lost sight of it, because we were going to have to dip down into a shallow ravine to cross the creek. It was a perfect plan, even though as much speed as possible was needed. Bud and I took off as fast as our horses could move through that muck.

Once we'd crossed the ravine, we couldn't immediately get a resighting of Nero, but we knew he was still quite a way ahead of us. With the ends of our halter ropes we encouraged a little more speed from our horses and headed straight for the timbered area where I figured the bear was heading. We still had a bit of a problem, though: a goddamn wire fence and the island of trees that straddled it. It took us about 10 minutes to get to where, without the fence, we could have been in three or four. At that moment I would have been willing to trade my left nut for a pair of wire cutters, but seeing as there were none on offer it was the long route for us. The island of trees was only an acre or two in size, but it was big enough to obstruct our view until we circled the fence line. By the time we'd done that there was no sign of the bear.

We were able to get up onto some slightly higher ground near the island of trees, and from there we could see across the entire meadow, all the way back to our spotters. Still there was no sign of Nero. We sat there on our horses and discussed the situation for a few minutes. Scanning with my binocs, I suddenly saw our spotters jumping up and down. It looked as if they were pointing directly at us, which seemed strange. I figured they must be pointing to someplace past us up in the timber, so we rode over to the edge of the trees, looking for bear tracks that should have been easy to spot in all that mud. There were no tracks and no other signs of the bear.

The situation had my mind spinning, wondering whether I was losing my hunting skills, trying to conjure up an explanation. There was no sense even trying to hunt in the densely timbered area; it would have been impossible to approach a bear in there, much less one as wise as we knew Nero to be.

We sat dumbfounded on our horses, silently shaking our heads over being beaten again. It does not bolster a guide's ego much to be continually outsmarted by what some people consider a "dumb" animal. With thoughts like that running through my mind, I led the way back past the island of trees and along the fence to rendezvous with our spotters, who we could now see making fast tracks towards us. We met up at the creek, and did they have a story to tell.

They told us that when Bud and I dropped down into the creek gully and lost sight of Nero, something seemed to have spooked him. But instead of running for the burned timber area, he had turned back towards us and gone into the island of trees. As far as any of us could tell, he was in there the whole time we were between that island and the burn. He was evidently able to maintain his nerve and keep from bolting—not just once, but both times we rode close to that island. He must have been watching us all the time, and the distance between us would have been no more than 150 yards. He'd stayed put until we headed back to the creek to meet the others. Then, while our backs were turned, he'd used the island as a screen and made a dash to the heavy timber on the edge of the valley. Old Nero had once again proved that his totem was stronger than mine.

There were many other Nero hunts, but luckily for him and me they all ended pretty much the same way. Both of us were able to bank considerable wealth simply from the hype that was created by his tracks. I banked money and Nero banked fat, because over the 14 years that we trailed him around these hills, he was able to eat his fill from the better part of 20 head of those bear-bait horses we laid out for him. He had other grizzlies helping him with that chore, too, and it eventually became an undisputed fact that we had some of the fattest and sleekest bears in this part of the country.

Unable to tag Nero, our hunters were nevertheless able to stretch out a few of his buddies, and a couple of them had skulls measuring more than 24 inches. As far as we know, though, no other hunter in this area ever got the measure of Old Nero.

A Pig Makes a House Call

from *Don't Shoot From the Saddle:*
Chronicles of a Frontier Surgeon
by D.A. Holley

In the first volume of Heart of the Cariboo–Chilcotin, *we
met some of the colourful characters who were the patients
and friends of Dr. Al Holley, a surgeon who practised in the
Cariboo from the 1930s to the 1960s and later wrote about his
experiences. There are no patients in the following excerpt from
the same book, just a few overly helpful, eager friends with a
weird mission: to get the Doc a pig—a live one. The scene when
that mission is accomplished is chaotic and, of course, hilarious.*

" ... I heard this gawdawful commotion. Jed was at the back door, clutching a half-grown pig."

In between the various catastrophes, tragedies and high-tech procedures, we seemed to have time for the occasional prank or party when things were quiet. With some of the friends I had, I didn't need enemies—like when my wife discovered a live pig turned loose in our living room.

I had solicited the help of some neighbour friends to help me bring a piano. After we got it in from Jed's pickup truck, Jed Campbell, Buzz Heinzelman, Fred Kirsh and I finished putting the piano in place, and one of them remarked on what a nice big fireplace we had in our living room. He said, "It's big enough to roast a pig in."

I said, "You bring the pig, and we'll roast it." As soon as I said it I knew these were the wrong guys to give such a challenge to.

Six months later, in mid-July, I came home from the operating room at one in the morning.

My wife told me, "Don't bother going to bed. Jed has a pig in his wife's car and he's bound to give it to you. He's had a few drinks." I agreed that that he was unlikely to give up on the venture. Within a few minutes I heard this gawdawful commotion. Jed was at the back door, clutching a half-grown pig.

Mike, our big black lab, was trying to get it by the throat; our little wire-haired terrier was trying to screw it; and the pig was squealing bloody murder, all under a full moon and starlit sky.

In order to keep the neighbours from shooting us all, I told Jed to bring the pig and we'd have a drink. We barricaded the pig in the laundry room at the back door with kitchen chairs, where it settled down quietly. My brother-in-law was staying with us, so he got out of bed and joined us for a drink.

Jed and RCMP sergeant John Stinson had been trying all summer to get a pig to bring us. They had come home covered with mud and pig shit many nights before Jed successfully ran this pig down on his way home from Prince George, scooped it up, tossed it in the trunk of the car, and kept on going.

After awhile we all said goodnight and went our separate ways to bed. The pig was quiet.

The first thing I saw in the morning was my wife standing in the bedroom doorway with a .22 repeating rifle in her hands, saying, "I don't know whether to shoot that damned pig or Jed Campbell. You should just see what the pig has done to our new dining room carpet." It had rooted things up quite a bit, but it wasn't irreparable.

Jed and his whole family, along with their car, were nowhere to be seen. Another neighbour told me they had gone to Beavermouth for the weekend. When my brother-in-law got back from morning goose shooting, he and I caught the pig and took it down in the basement, where we shot it, skinned and dressed it out, and took it over to Campbells' outdoor barbecue. We invited Stinson and one or two others and had a nice pork barbecue. Stinson brought a bottle of Crown Royal that he had been given and we liberally basted the pork with it while it was roasting; the flavour was delicious.

Cariboo Gold

first published in the *British Columbia Almanac*, edited
by Mark Forsythe
by Ann Walsh

*Alabama-born Ann Walsh had an unusual childhood. She
didn't meet her father (separated from her expectant mother
by World War Two) until she was four, when her parents were
reunited in South Africa. Walsh started school there, and
continued her education wherever her parents moved next:
England, Holland, Kansas, Saskatchewan and finally B.C.,
where she attended university in Vancouver.*

*Walsh married and settled in the Cariboo–Chilcotin to
raise a family. She began her career as a writer after attending
a workshop in Wells with Robin Skelton. Best known for her
highly acclaimed children's and young adult novels, many of
which are set during the Cariboo's gold rush, Walsh has also
published stories and articles for adults in magazines around the
world. The following story is about motherhood. It speaks in rich
metaphors—of children and flowers, loss and return.*

The Cariboo's sunflower, the arrow leaf balsam root, blooms in May,
painting the hillsides with gold.

Mother's Day will always mean sunflowers to me. Not the dinner-plate-sized, heavy, nodding plants the rest of the world knows as sunflowers, but Cariboo sunflowers.

They aren't really sunflowers at all, but a plant with an unpronounceable proper Latin name that has been shortened to balsam root, or arrow leaf balsam root. But to those of us who live in the interior of B.C.'s Cariboo region, their technical name doesn't matter; they are known simply as sunflowers and they bloom in May, painting the hillsides with gold.

The flowers are yellow, rather like a large daisy in shape and size, and they never reach the height of true sunflowers. On sunny slopes they seem to spring up overnight, nodding on their thick hollow stems, head bowed in the spring breeze, cradled by many pale green, slightly fuzzy leaves.

My association of sunflowers with Mother's Day began before we had children. I can't remember the first time a Sunday drive in May ended with us struggling for footholds on steep roadside embankments as we picked armfuls of the flowers.

Later, in the years of the children, those trips to find the sunflowers became a tradition. The first springtime picnic, wonderful not only for being the first, but also for being the only picnic all season that would be mosquito-free, would always be on Mothers' Day.

On the way home we would pull to the side of the road and I would watch nervously as dirt-smudged, hot-dog-stuffed children scrambled up the hillsides and returned, smiling and proud, with armloads of yellow sunflowers. "For you, Mum. We picked them just for you."

For days after Mother's Day those flowers filled the house—in jars, bottles, jugs; on tables, desks, counters. They gave off only a faint scent of dusty vanilla, but after the long winter months they were a heady perfume for the eyes. Spring is here. Rejoice.

Still later in the child-raising years, the Mother's Day picnic became, in itself, my husband's gift to me. He would pack the hamper, fill the containers with juice, find and re-outfit the first-aid kit and unearth the rubber boots.

Then he would take the children on a picnic, leaving me with a gift beyond price—a whole day for myself. I remember treasured hours spent luxuriating in a bath, reading a new book, taking an afternoon nap.

When they returned, my husband weary, the children smeared with toasted marshmallow, the dog thick with last summer's burrs, they brought me armloads of yellow sunflowers: "For you, Mum."

The first year that no children lived in our home, I picked my own sunflowers. I set them in nearly every room of the house, but they didn't look the same, not until the phone rang. "Yes," I said. "The sunflowers are blooming. Yes, I miss you, too." Then I cried.

The strange thing about Cariboo sunflowers is that although they cover the hillsides in the early spring, by July there is not a trace of them. Their thick leaves vanish shortly after the blooms themselves are finished, slipping back into the earth as if they had never left it. You can tramp the open fields for hours, and never come across the slightest remnant of the plants.

It is hard to believe that they ever existed, harder yet to believe that they will return next spring. But the root of the Cariboo sunflower is so tenacious, so permanent, that it always comes back, strong, joyous, welcoming—rather like the love between a child and a mother. Even when we think that it has died, that it was a springtime illusion, a withered childhood need, even then the root of that love still lives beneath the surface, waiting. Waiting for tears to water it, smiles to warm it and forgiveness to lend it strength to grow tall.

And, given the chance, that love will grow again, no matter how long it has been buried. Just as the soft rain and warm sun bring the balsam root back to life even though the flower has left no trace of itself, the love between a mother and child, no matter how dead we think it is, can bloom again.

It's Mother's Day once more, and once more the sunflowers are golden on the hills. I knew they would come back.

Preg-testing

a new story by Heidi Redl

On Heidi Redl's and her husband Tom's ranch near Williams Lake, "preg-test" day is when the vet pays a visit to let them know how many of their cows are pregnant. The pregnant ones are kept and fed over the winter, and those that aren't are slaughtered for their meat. Redl's account of how one of these days unfolds offers a colourful insight, from a woman's perspective, into the nitty-gritty business of cattle ranching. Redl grew up on a cattle ranch that her grandfather pioneered about eight miles up the road from her current home. She and Tom are raising their three children and a lot of cows and calves on Redl Ranch, an environment that she loves. She reckons "you can take the girl out of the ranch, but you can't take the ranch out of the girl."

"When I reach the corrals, the cows quieten just long enough to eye me up."

November 1. A pale blue sky arches over branches of silver lace. The thermometer reads six degrees below zero Celsius. Half an inch of fresh snow cloaks the ground. Dead grasses and weeds are silvered into fairy wands, their frosty stems sparkling in the morning sunlight. It's an enchanted world out there, one that tricks naive people into falling in love with it.

I hear the stentorian, dissonant bawling as soon as I step out of the house. The noise has risen to billow over the forest and echo in the hills behind me. It surrounds me as I tromp down the hard road in my black rubber boots, stinging my ears much as the clear, cold morning air stings the linings of my nostrils.

When I reach the corrals, the cows quieten just long enough to eye me up. Deciding I'm not of any consequence, they resume bellowing, their rough voices raspy around the edges of the baritone notes. Now that I am here, I can hear the answering cries from their calves. The calves have rejected the freedom offered by the open field and turned back toward the corrals and their mothers, but their higher-pitched bleating comes from outside the fence. They are still free to leave anytime they want, but each calf has identified its lone mother's voice out of the 300-strong choir and is staying as long as it can hear her.

Plugging my fingers into my ears, I scan the herd to see what their condition is after a summer out on the range. They've been walking miles through the forest and the thick underbrush, rustling for grass and drinking from creeks while providing milk for their calves the whole time. They're all in good shape. The first animals I notice are the all-white Charolais, the large-framed French breed. Providing a sharp visual contrast are the smaller-boned, shiny, black Angus cattle, a breed that originated in Britain. Their skinny, long tails with the black, fluffy tip remind me of slender paintbrushes. Then I see the meaty, red-brown Herefords with their white faces and bellies, a shorter, stocky breed, also from Britain. Mixed throughout are the tan-and-white coloured, big-eared Simmentals from continental Europe, a favourite in German herds. While the cows show their bloodlines in their colouring, their calves outside the corral wear various mixed and mottled shades of gray and brown. Our bulls aren't colour-prejudiced during breeding season.

I climb up the boards, lean over and shout into a hairy face, "It's preg-test day. You'll be back together with your baby by tonight. Don't you remember this from last year?"

The answering roar is almost forceful enough to knock me off the boards.

"All brawn, no brain," I chide her, climbing down again.

My feet are cold and I stomp them hard against the frozen ground while I walk around the corral, looking for the guys. I know that we have a full complement of family here today to help out. My father-in-law Ed never misses a chance to be involved in any work to be done on the ranch and my nephew Travis would far rather ride his horse and help with moving the cows around than be in school. My husband Tom left the house before I did and is busy around here somewhere too. The first person I see, though, is my brother-in-law Barrie, rolling an empty, oil-stained, blue diesel drum toward me.

"When's the vet coming?" I ask.

"Should be here 'round eight."

"Ready?"

"Nope."

"Let's get a move on, then." I'm kidding, but he frowns at me.

"I've had a move on since 5:30 this morning."

I'm at a loss for a good, quick retort so I go get the other barrel instead. We've got them set up on end and are pushing a piece of plywood over top to make a table when I hear a truck motor chugging up the driveway behind me. I give our new table an experimental push and the plywood slides off to one side, taking one of the barrels over with it. This time, I get *the look* from Barrie, along with the frown.

"Oops."

The little red pickup with the battered canopy on the back pulls in beside us, and Bruce, the vet, steps out.

"Morning!"

"Hi, Bruce. How's it goin'?"

"We're busy. Like normal this time of year." Bruce is grinning but then, he always is. From long experience I know he may be the only one still smiling at the end of this day.

While he's talking, he's sized up the situation in the corral, realized we're almost ready and opened the canopy back and tailgate of his truck. He hauls about half a dozen boxes out onto the flat space made by the opened tailgate. Then he unpacks a huge, black workman's toolbox filled with syringes, needles and objects I don't recognize. I decide not to ask about them; some things I really don't want to know. In my opinion, this type of day is the grossest part of being a vet. But there's always the chance I could be wrong.

Bruce wears well-washed, faded blue work clothes that seem designed for amputees. One sleeve of his work shirt is cut short above the elbow and neatly hemmed. The heavy coveralls he puts on over top are made by the same designer (himself), and goosebumps appear on the bare arm moving around outside the warm clothes. He dusts powdered disinfectant over his arm and hand, then slides them into a brown rubber glove, wiggling his fingers into its fingertips. This is a serious glove; it expands up his arm, over his shoulder and ends in a harness across his upper back and chest. I do up the buckles on the harness for him.

"What did you bring for us today?" My husband Tom has joined us and is examining the pharmacy on the tailgate.

"Just the usual. Ivomec, Tasvax, 7-Way."

We nod knowingly. Mine's fake. I can never remember which medicine is which. Hang on, Ivomec's the delouser, that leaves the other two. One of them is an annual vaccination against bovine diseases and it occurs to me that I haven't heard the third name before. I tell myself it's only important that I remember which one gets injected where; it doesn't really matter what they do.

"Did you get the inoculation job again?" Bruce is looking at me, still grinning.

"Yup." One monosyllable with a world of meaning behind it.

The first time I came out to help on preg-test day, my new husband thought I was there to take over writing down the ear tag numbers as the cows came through. In what I'm sure was a diplomatic way, I explained that I wanted something more useful to do than secretarial duties. I got *the look* that day too. (*The look* is an inherited trait. Like his brother, my husband has it in his genes.) I didn't get the secretarial job, though. They don't even try that one on me anymore. We all share writing down the numbers.

The bawling picks up behind me and I turn to watch the first batch of cows coming up the fenced-in laneway that runs between the corral and the chute. Travis, riding tall on his horse, is behind them. He's cut this first group of 20 out of the herd and now he's bawling too, discouraging any of them from turning around in the narrow lane and going back. A gate slams shut behind the cows and they're trapped in the holding pen.

"They look good," I offer.

Barrie grunts in acknowledgement as he levers a heavy, green, metal gate behind the cows' rumps, pushing them into the crowding tub that heads up the chute's runway.

While Bruce is double-checking his supplies, I briefly debate campaigning for a mobile job. My cold toes feel hard. They're icy chunks in my rubber boots that rub stiffly against each other when I wiggle them. I'm already dreading the pain that will accompany their thaw tonight. Then again, maybe they'll just drop off as solid, pathetic little pieces when I take off my boots. I stomp my feet again, making a futile effort to encourage the blood to circulate down there, and wonder why on earth I can't remember this scenario from year to year. My breath puffs in a frosty cloud in front of me as I consider my options. Eventually I reach the conclusion that if I ask for a lateral promotion to cow mover, I'd be admitting that I didn't wear an extra pair of socks on a morning this cold. Pride wins out and I stay put.

When cows are made to move against their will, they employ a universal strategy to show their objection. As a result, it's not long before the heavy, unmistakable tang of fresh manure wafts over us. Today I actually welcome it: the warm fumes take the sharp sting out of the cold winter air.

Bruce's voice calls me to work, "Hey, I've set this syringe to dispense two ccs. This medication is thick at the best of times, and it gets thicker when it's cold. You might have a hard time refilling your syringe when you run it out today, so just keep this refill bottle warm in your pocket, inside your jacket."

"Right next to my heart," I murmur, pushing the bottle into my shirt pocket. "Damn, that's cold."

Bruce laughs.

The first cow leaves the group in the crowding tub and moves up the runway, encouraged along by the stick that one of the guys keeps prodding her with. Then she sees the freedom offered between the open doors at the head of the chute and picks up speed, charging toward it on those skinny legs, her full-blown belly and udder swaying from side to side. She's got her neck stretched out for the finish line, thinking she's won, when the gates bang shut, grabbing her neck just behind the ears. She comes to a dead stop, surprised. With a grin, Ed lets go of the lever he's just pulled at the top of the chute and says, "It's all in the timing."

"Good one, Dad." I grin back at him, enjoying his enthusiasm.

The cow snorts in disgust, but she's older and in the dim recesses of her brain she remembers being here and knows she's stuck. This chute, a tall cage made of green-painted iron bars, is designed to hold a 2,000-pound animal in place.

"Hey." I turn and see Bruce holding up another heavy syringe whose sharp needle tip is covered by a white plastic tube with a hole in the end. "This one goes up their nose."

"Yeah, right. Nice try, Bruce." Why isn't he smiling?

"C'mon Bruce, you're not serious?"

Now he's smiling.

"The guys wanted to try a dewormer this year. The nasal spray is the best way to do it. You give them a shot up into each nostril. If you can time it for when they're inhaling, they'll get a good dose. If they're blowing out when you do it, they'll give you a free shower. On the bright side, you won't get any worms this winter."

"You okay with that?" My brother-in-law is finally grinning too, the bastard.

Little does he know *the look* can be learned, as well as inherited. I practise it on him while I keep my voice very nonchalant: "No big deal."

"What's your cut-off date?" Bruce adroitly changes the subject.

"I want a calf out of them by mid-April." Barrie's answer is hollered over the back of the next cow, who's being prodded up the runway.

"Okay, Bossy, let's get this show on the road," I mutter, marching toward the chute, the needle ready in my right hand. I take a firm grip of the black, wiry hair on the cow's neck with the fingers of my left hand, and tug. Nothing happens. The cow doesn't move, neither does the skin of her neck. I grab a whole fistful of hair and try again. This time a pocket of skin pulls away from the neck. Not enough to jab a needle into, though. The cow isn't moving; she doesn't even feel this. I brace my frozen feet and haul back with my arm, bringing skin and hair with it. Now the needle won't go in.

"Jab it," Bruce encourages me. "Use your whole arm if you have to. Remember, this is the stuff they make leather out of."

I do have to use my whole arm, swinging it to get the needle to penetrate the tough hide. With a feeling of relief I watch the needle shank disappear under the black hair and I pull the stiff trigger. As soon as I pull the needle back out, I rub the injection site with my fingers, dispersing the hard little ball of medication that sits there.

In the meantime, Bruce has taken up his station at the back of the cow. While I was distracting her with my needle, he reached that long glove into the cow, under her tail. His hand went in first, then his arm. When his upper arm disappeared halfway to his shoulder, his fingers went to work. Now his face wears a look of deep concentration, his eyes focused miles away as his brain interprets what his fingers are feeling.

"She's good," he says tersely, and pulls his arm back out. Tom shuffles by in heavy work boots and notes her number down in the log book with a "P" beside it. Then he hooks a white, plastic backpack with a hose and a plastic pistol hanging from it to the top of the chute.

"You'll have your hands full with those other two shots; I'll handle the delouser." He thinks he's being generous and no doubt has good reason to be surprised when *he* gets *the look*. But why should I be gracious when he picked the easy job, the one that looks like fun? He picks up the pistol and holds it over the cow's shoulders as the feeder line from the white backpack fills with blue fluid. When he squeezes the trigger and pulls the pistol down along the cow's back, the delouser sketches a steady, straight line down her backbone before dribbling down her sides.

"They do look good," he affirms. "Doesn't look like they picked up the usual load of lice out in the woods this summer."

By now, I'm returning to the front of the chute, the new needle gripped in my hand. "This is going to be easy," I insist to myself. Not. This stuff is a whole different story.

As soon as she sees me coming, the cow, who has been standing quietly until now, starts blowing, snorting snot and banging her head from side to side. I hadn't thought she was smart enough to be scared at the sight of the needle.

"Cover her eye with your left hand—if she can't see you she'll settle down," Bill calls out helpfully from the cow's other end. That does help a bit to keep the cow from swinging her head around, but it seems like I have to wait forever for her to stop snorting and start inhaling. I know that the first cow always takes the longest; it takes a few cows before we get into our rhythm and the pace picks up. I also know that this is the first of 300 cows and we want to finish before dark. More importantly, we don't eat and I can't take off these goldarn boots until we're done. I pull the trigger.

A sticky, nasty mixture of snot and medication plasters my cheek, my hair and my arm.

"Christ!" I wipe my face with my dry hand. "I guess I won't get worms now."

No one laughs. They don't dare.

Barrie hurries past us to open the head gate. The first cow ambles out of the chute and down the outside laneway. Unlike me, she looks unchanged by the recent events. My nephew opens the gate at the bottom end and she joins the calves in the field. As soon as she finds hers, the wall of noise around us diminishes by one tiny particle.

By the time I've turned around again, the second cow has been captured in the chute. My technique with the neck shot is better and my end of the cow goes fairly smoothly—even the nasal spray. I've simply resigned to getting wet. Bruce is having problems at his end, though, the business end of the cow. He can't fit his whole arm in this time.

He inserts his hand, grunts, then pulls out a handful of steaming manure that spatters in a pile on the ground and over his boots. As he scoops more and more manure out, putting his arm in deeper with each handful he extracts, he notices my expression. "I have to clean out the canal," he says, "otherwise I can't reach up to feel the buttons."

"I remember," I tell him. "I just have to see it every year to believe it, otherwise I'd convince myself I dreamt it. By the way, don't lick your lips, you've grown something that looks like a new mole at the side of your mouth."

"Have a look at that chart, will you, the one on the table there. I've reached the uterus and these buttons are about two centimetres wide. I can't remember offhand if this calf is old enough to be born before your cut-off date."

Tom beats me to the chart. "She'll make it, just." He checks her tag number. "She's young, we'll keep her another year. I'll risk getting a smaller calf out of her because she's in good shape to keep going for few more years." He writes a "P" down beside her number while I get my worm shower.

The next cow is not in a co-operative mood. She jumps from side to side, banging against the chute's bars. The pulling of another lever cures that as the sides of the chute fall inwards, with a matching clang. The cow is now clamped into place, squeezed, unable to move her body in any direction.

"She's open."

That's not good news, this early in the proceedings. We're hoping that over 90 percent of the cows are pregnant.

"What are the slaughter prices like right now?" I ask.

"Not great," Barrie answers with a frown. "There's lots of these types of cows being sold this month, the supply's pretty well outweighing the demand."

I have a sudden, almost hysterically gleeful, insight, "I guess I don't need to give her the shots."

"Nope. Save the money."

"Hmmmm. Maybe this isn't such a bad thing after all."

"Come on, you shithead!"

I jump in indignation, but the summons isn't for me. Another cow should be coming up the runway, but she's backed up instead and has pinned Barrie against the crowding tub's solid metal side. He whacks her across her bony tail head with a stout stick, and she jumps forward. A sharp thwack clangs on the metal wall as she kicks back in retaliation.

"Jeez, I'm glad that missed you." It's true; I know a kick like that could break a human leg.

"I'm glad she's not any heavier than she is, it feels like she squeezed my ribs closer together." Barrie grimaces as he hobbles up the runway.

"Watch out, will ya? We need all the manpower we've got today. Can't afford anybody getting laid up," says Tom. There is brotherly concern hidden deep beneath that brusque comment.

By the fourth cow, our team rhythm is starting to flow. One cow after another passes through the chute to the regular, repetitive notes of "git up there," gates opening and closing on oil-deprived hinges, the clop of hooves on frozen ground, the splash of hooves through steaming, fresh manure, and the odd "Jesus Christ!"

Their bodies are warm and the heat that radiates up through their rough hair warms my cold fingers while I work on them. I contemplate pulling my boots off and warming my feet on a broad side, but only for a split second. The smell that comes with the heat isn't something I want on my socks. It's not that unpleasant—not as bad, say, as wet dog hair, but it's strong enough.

Most of the cows are quiet when the needle goes in, but the odd one bellows and makes me feel guilty. The nasal spray, however, is a recurring problem with each cow. While they stand quietly for Bruce and even for the neck jab, none of them will stand for having liquid blown up their nose. I have to be mighty quick with the trigger to get the spray off in the half-second that the cow isn't exhaling. By covering one of her eyes, I can get close enough to reach the needle into each nostril but for all that, I don't get even one "clean" shot. Personally, I think they have their priorities wrong. If I were them, I'd be very irate with Bruce and a lot less co-operative back there.

Partway through the morning my attention wavers for a moment and I smack the needle against one of the chute's iron bars. I hold it up against the bright blue sky and squint. Its sharp end is blunted and twisted. "Aw, I'm sorry Bruce. I've wrecked one of your syringes."

"No problem," he grins at me. He clumps over to the table and takes a whole package of needles out of his workbox. With his deft, quick fingers he takes the old one off, drops it into a garbage bag and replaces it with a new one.

"Thanks, I was worried I'd wrecked the whole thing."

"Just like magic, eh? I can make it look like it never happened." He's still got that smile.

"Hey, don't do that too often," someone yells up from the depths of the crowding tub, "we have to pay for those."

"Please, fire me!" I encourage the invisible challenger. There's no response.

Time and cows pass by and the early afternoon sunshine melts the rime that last night imposed on our world. The wooden fences and metal structures around us glisten wetly and the ground starts sucking at my boots as I wear a path between chute, table, head gate, table. We're all keeping that steady, relaxed rhythm going—especially me: I'm working like a pro. Grab the hair, pull out hard, push the needle in, squeeze the trigger ... what is that white stuff on the cow's neck?

"Oh my God, I put the needle through her skin on both sides, oh, the poor thing."

"She's going to feel like a pincushion," Bruce laughs. "Don't worry, I've seen that done before too. Give her another shot. In a different spot."

"Just when I thought I was getting good."

Too many hours and too many cows later, I finally hear the sweetest phrase on earth: "This is the one we were looking for, the last one."

I raise my head stiffly from the second-last one and listen. It must be true. I can only hear two cows bawling. The noise diminished so slowly, I hadn't even noticed it disappearing.

As the last tail swishes through the head gate, I set my heavy syringes down and admire my snot-wet thighs. "I got a lot more of it than they did."

"They all got some of it," Bruce answers generously. "They got enough to keep them healthy, and I've seen people come out of that job a lot wetter than you are. Come to think of it, I've seen people wear rain gear for that job."

"You couldn't have told me that before I started?" I help him unfasten his buckles anyway.

"You'll remember for next year."

"Yeah," I grumble, "Sure. Just like I'll remember to wear extra socks and warmer boots." Then I eye him up, notice how gingerly he's moving. "What am I complaining for? You started out wearing blue. You're the same colour as the calves now. You even smell the same."

Barrie appears again, this time dragging a yellow hose. "Shower time."

Bruce stands with his eyes shut as his gloved arm, fingers and then boots are doused. A slow-moving trickle of yellow-brown water rolls down the driveway behind him. Tom arrives with a bucket of warm, soapy water and we all dive in, revelling in the feeling of clean warmth on our red faces and wind-chapped hands.

"Who has to do your laundry, Bruce?"

"Oh, I throw it in a separate machine every night. Sometimes I'm so tired at the end of one of these days I'd rather skip that step, but I know the rules. Clean clothes for each new place. I don't want to be responsible for spreading any diseases, you know, in case something's hidden in one of the cows. Are you going to feed me now?"

"Chili's on. I'll ride back with you." Barrie jumps into Bruce's truck.

Tom and I meander back through the herd on the way to our own house, checking that all the cows and calves have found each other. The day is finally quiet. The calves are nursing, bunting their poor mothers to get warm milk, while the cows are eating too. Their heads are lowered to the cold ground, tearing up hunks of the yellowed grass, chewing on it greedily as they make up for their day-long fast in the corral. We stop and I watch them, my frozen feet temporarily forgotten. It's been a good, long day after all.

"What's the percentage?" Tom needs to know. He saw me adding up the numbers in the log book after the last cow had gone through and doing some very fast math.

"We made 92 this year. A few open. None sick."

They all look content. Even the one that still has her tail sticking straight out behind her is concentrating on her cud as she wanders around the field.

The big, multicoloured herd stands in sharp contrast to the mounds of snow that drifted into the hollows last night and stayed today, looking like white punctuation marks on the dying, yellow grass. The daylight is fading; the sun has slipped halfway down behind the treetops on the far hill. Evening's deep purple is coming up behind us, pushing against the red and gold clouds over our heads. The sun's flaming disk is mirrored in the pale face of the moon, just rising over the eastern hills.

I do love this. Call me naive.

Looking for Horses

from *Tell me a good lie: Tales from the Chilcotin Country*
by Paul St. Pierre

*One of Canada's best-known raconteurs, Paul St. Pierre, who
wrote about ranching in the first volume of this series, is back
with a story about a long-standing tradition of the Cariboo–
Chilcotin. Like many traditions rooted in the necessities of a
different time, looking for horses may have outlived its more
practical purposes. So why are a lot of people in the Chilcotin
still looking for horses? In the following story, St. Pierre joins
Duane Witte on one such expedition, hoping to get to the
bottom of this intriguing question.*

Looking for horses is an esoteric custom of the Cariboo.

BIG CREEK—A few days ago, when it was 12 below up at the Teepee Heart Ranch, Duane Witte suggested that we go looking for horses. Well, I was delighted, of course. As a matter of fact, I didn't really mind very much. Here was a chance to take part in one of the esoteric rites of the Cariboo: looking for horses.

In the Cariboo, it does not matter where a stranger comes to rest, or why. He may be in a moose camp or a duck blind. He may be prospecting or taking pictures of kigli holes. If he but waits a little while, a rider will come by and this rider will say that he is looking for horses.

Sometimes I have told these riders that yes, I did see some horses that day, and have described the horses. Sometimes I have been able to describe the brand. Sometimes I have not seen any horses. One answer appears to please a rider as much as another. He is very grateful for the information, and says, "thank you," and then says that he must be off again looking for horses, and he leaves.

So last Thursday, for the first time, I was introduced to this mystery as a rider, one of the people who ask the questions.

Shortly after noon, when it was warm, we left the ranch. Duane and his wife, Marian, rode young paints and I was on an elderly bay, sometimes used to pack moose. The snow lay deep and crusted, and the moose, who were rustling for food in the horse pasture, paused in brushing the snow away with their long forelegs and watched us go by. They appeared to wonder what we were doing. But moose have a naturally puzzled expression, anyway, and possibly they were not really interested at all.

By 1:30 P.M. we had seen two Stellar's jays, three chickadees, one whisky-jack, and a Franklin's grouse cock, who came out from beneath the horse's feet with a blast of powdered snow, more like a cannon than a rocket. At 2:00 P.M. we sighted half a dozen horses on one of the long buckbrush meadows of Duane's ranch. They were pawing in the snow for feed, as the moose had been doing—and, like the moose, they paused to look at us as we went past. They were Duane's horses. Unfortunately, they were not the ones he was looking for.

We saw coyote track, lynx track, rabbit track, moose track, and squirrel track. Even our stirrups left tracks as our horses walked through the deeper snows.

There were some of Duane's horses on the meadow that we reached at 3:00 P.M. But these also were not the ones that he was looking for.

Duane rode right to look over a spruce swamp, and Marian and I went to the Big Meadow. We found horses in both places. But these too were not the right ones.

We rode by an old corral built by wild-horse hunters. (Hunting horses is much different from looking for horses. But that is another story.) We rode through the little grove of trees where the rustlers had camped a few years ago. They had stolen 30 horses from Duane and are believed to have driven them north to the roadless ranges above his ranch.

When it was late in the afternoon, an east wind began to cut at our cheekbones with little pieces of broken razor blade, and we came home to the ranch house. We had seen, oh, quite a lot of horses, I would say, although not one of those that we had set out to look for. And that is what it is all about.

The only thing I forgot to find out was why we were looking for them. The thought did not occur to me until a day later, when I was hours away on the road out to Hanceville.

Come to think of it, in all the years of meeting riders in the Cariboo, I have never met one who found his horses, nor one who said why he wanted to find them. What an opportunity was mine! I could have penetrated to the very heart of the mystery! There I was, riding with the man. He was there. An expert. All I had to do was ask the question. But I never asked him.

That is the way a man fritters away the great opportunities of life.

Looking for Horses Again

from *Tell me a good lie: Tales from the Chilcotin Country*
by Paul St. Pierre

Paul St. Pierre was unable to penetrate the mystery of why all those Chilcotin characters are out looking for horses. In this next story, he gives it one more shot.

"We were looking for horses. I don't know why."

Big CREEK—The last couple of days have been spent at Duane Witte's Teepee Heart Ranch in the Cariboo. We were looking for horses. I don't know why. But there is, no doubt, some reason.

Duane's place is at the Eight Mile Meadow. It is eight miles beyond what was traditionally considered the end of the road. However, it is now possible to drive a car to Duane's except for some periods of spring, winter, summer, and fall. A couple of days ago, it was possible—and there, in the yard of his ranch, was Duane. He was fixing the tractor and thinking about horses.

"I am pretty sure," he said, "that my good team is up at the Long Jim Meadow."

The Long Jim being only 20 miles distant, we decided to ride over there to look for the team. What we would do if we found them he did not say. Drive them down to the corral where we could have a good look at them before turning them loose again, perhaps. Something of that sort.

First, however, to save a day's ride, we made a trip down the trail to the Bell Ranch. Sherwood Henry is on the Bell Ranch. Sherwood probably had been in touch with Lynn Bonner of the Deer Creek Ranch. Lynn has a plane. Possibly he had been flying over the range. Possibly he had seen Duane's horses. Possibly he had told Sherwood about it. Think of the time we'd save.

So we drove out of Eight Mile and went down the road and didn't get stuck until we hit the hill on Jack's Mountain. We had to put chains on, and this took two hours because the chains didn't fit. Putting small chains on large wheels requires a great deal of perseverance, deep in the night with no flashlight, and we were very late waking up Sherwood at the Bell Ranch. It didn't matter, however, because although Lynn had been flying, he hadn't flown over the Long Jim Meadow, so there wasn't a thing that Sherwood could tell us about Duane's horses.

This ended the first day of the horse hunt.

On the second day, many people had collected at the Teepee Heart Ranch. Harold Nickson of the Old Hutch Place had come to fix Duane's tractor. Lonnie Russel of the Anvil Mountain Ranch, another neighbour, had come to help. Thus, there were plenty of riders—ample to hunt for horses on the Long Jim. However, there weren't enough saddle horses in the corral for all of us. So before riding up to Long Jim to hunt horses, we had first to hunt Duane's saddle horses. They were feeding nearby on Wild Horse Range and Big Opening.

I declined this exercise. Harold, Lonnie, Duane, and his wife, Marian, went out for the saddle horses shortly after noon. Harold, Lonnie, and Marian were home by dark. They hadn't found the saddle horses. The horses had moved for some reason. Why, nobody knew.

Duane got home at nine. His spurs jingled like Santa Claus' bells when he stepped on the porch, but he wasn't noticeably cheerful. His face had been cut by brush. It is hard to chase horses through Jack pine in the dark of a moonless winter night. He had cut track. His saddle horses were moving west for some reason. They were probably heading for Bald Mountain. He didn't know why.

Duane was riding Colonel Ambleman, his Tennessee-walking horse stud. The stud could detect the stepping holes of the other horses in the snow long after Duane had lost sight of them. But eventually even Colonel Ambleman couldn't follow the trail any longer, so they had come home.

On the third day of the horse hunt, Duane, Harold, and Lonnie set out to find the saddle horses with which we were to look for the other horses, which were possibly up at Long Jim Meadow. The saddle horses are probably on Bald Hill Mountain. Either that or they have gone over the watershed to Paxton Valley. If they are in Paxton Valley, it will take—oh, a long time—to get them back.

Unfortunately, I can't wait. I must pull out tonight. However, I am in the third day of hunting horses and I have not yet had to climb aboard a single knot-headed cayuse. It is one of the best horse hunts I have ever attended. And just as productive as any other.

Born to Buck

from *Chilcotin: Preserving Pioneer Memories* by The Witte
Sisters
by Duane Witte with Veera Bonner

*Cowboy, rancher, guide-outfitter, mail deliverer, enthusiastic
accordian player. Always willing to lend a hand and share his
extensive knowledge of the Chilcotin. Hospitable, fun-loving
and as witty as his name suggests—these are some of the
things that made Duane Witte one of the area's best-known
personalities. Born in 1920 in Hanceville, he was a grandson
of Tom and Nellie Hance, whose pioneer story was told in the
first volume of* Heart of the Cariboo–Chilcotin. *Witte was
also the original owner of the Teepee Heart Ranch and alpine
trail-riding business, friend to Paul St. Pierre, and the kind
of cowboy who always seemed to be looking for horses. In the
preceding two stories, St. Pierre never got to the bottom of
why his friend occupied himself with this apparently fruitless
pastime. Perhaps the following tale by the man himself will
shed light on the mystery. Witte's story was set down by his
sister, Veera Bonner. He "went over the big mountain," as
Harry Marriott would say, in 1988. Wherever Witte is now, no
doubt he is looking for horses. Perhaps one horse in particular:
a horse named Alamando.*

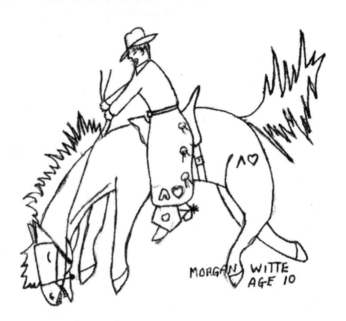

A horse named Alamando.

I had a real pretty mare once long ago that I named Alamando after a famous racehorse in Washington, USA. She had a big round white spot in her forehead, black points, and two white feet behind. When she was about four years old I got her in with the rest of the bunch to break her to lead. She was wild and snorty. When I rode into the horse corral and threw a loop over her head she made a high dive, tripped on a flat rock and smashed all her front bottom teeth out, except one that I had to pull so that she could close her jaws to eat. After she was broke to lead I turned her out on the range again. When I got her back in after a couple of months she was good and fat—she was managing okay without those bottom front teeth.

About this time, Dad and I and a young fellow named Harold Coburn were planning a trip through the mountains to look for hunting territory. I decided to take Alamando along as a spare saddle horse. I had ridden her a few times in the corral and figured the trip would do her good.

I led her for the first few miles to kind of get the kinks out of her back and Dad took the pack horse. Going up the mountain to Dick Meadow, we stopped and I switched my rigging onto Alamando and got on her—the first time outside a corral. She bucked a little but not bad. I rode her the rest of that day and off and on during the trip. She seemed to be gentling down and coming along fine. I used a snaffle bit on her to start with but by the time we got back I was using my loose-jawed spade bit. I always wore spurs. Horses like the sound of them and you can "talk" to a horse without using them rough or mean. I always had good spurs and liked two-and-one-half inch rowels with lots of points on them, as they very seldom hurt a horse. Dad and I used tapedaros over our stirrups in those days. They keep your feet dry and protect your boots from brush and sticks. A lot of horses are scared of them though, hanging down below your boots. They make extra weight on your feet so you have to be careful with your spurs.

After we got back from the mountain trip, I turned Alamando in the pasture as I had a good stud at the time and wanted to raise a colt from the two of them. Some time later I needed to make a ride to Siwash Meadow to look for horses. When the mount I was intending to use turned up lame, I took Alamando. After I saddled her up and stepped on in front of the house she lit right into bucking. This bucking surprised me, as she had been coming along so well.

She went high and wide, then sunfished so low I could touch the ground with my hand. Pretty soon she bucked me off—and my hand wasn't the only thing touching the ground! Leo Diehl, who was helping me for a few days, was watching. I picked myself up, caught her and led her up to the bronc corral. My knee was bothering me—it sometimes went out of joint—and I was riding a longer stirrup than usual. I shortened my stirrup leathers a hole and got on her in the corral. Encouraged by her success in the yard she went at it again, but this time I stayed with her. When she quit bucking I opened the gate and headed towards Siwash Meadow. Leo mounted and headed out to cross Big Creek and look for some other horses we needed.

For me and Alamando it was a rough day. Alamando bucked with me 17 times on that 15-mile ride. She just wouldn't quit. And that mare could buck! It took me all my time to stay with her. A sunfishing horse is hard to ride—when they parallel the ground it throws you off balance and gives you the feeling they're going to flop right over on top of you.

When we finally got as far as the meadow I kind of forgot about horse hunting. I was played out and felt too sick to go any farther. My insides were so shook up I was spitting blood and began to wonder how I'd ever make it home. I got off and tied the mare up and lay down under a tree for a half hour or so. The thought of riding her home gnawed at my twisted innards. I took my taps off and cached them behind a log—I thought that might help. Then I climbed on her and turned back the way we'd come. Her mouth was getting sore by now, and maybe because we were headed in the right direction, she only bucked with me three times.

A few miles from home a young fellow named Hugh MacDonald caught up to me in a pickup and stopped to talk. "That's sure a good-looking horse you're riding," he said. "Do you want to sell her?" He didn't ask about her disposition. I'd have been happy to sell her on the spot, but thinking I shouldn't act too anxious, I answered kind of slow: "Yeah, I guess so. If you give me $85." That was a good price for a horse then. He said he wanted her, and came up the next day to clinch the deal and take her away.

He came into the house first and paid me. Then we went up to the corral and Hugh threw his saddle on the handsome bay and got on. Her mouth was sore from all that bucking the day before, and she walked around the corral quiet enough. Then he rode over to where I was standing and asked if he could borrow my spurs to wake her up a bit. I said, "Sure!"

When he mounted her again and touched her with the spurs, she threw him so high and so fast she didn't even get to sunfishing. He came down hard and decided not to get back on. He never did ride her. She went back on the range and one spring, years later, I found her bones. I could tell her skull because of those missing teeth on the lower jaw. I hung that jaw in a little Jack pine tree at a meadow we called Seven Mile. Every time I rode by I thought of Hugh's $85 and a tough little mare called Alamando that was born to buck. She could have earned her living coming out of the rodeo chutes—and I would loved to have seen her—but instead spent her life running free in the Chilcotin hills.

Photo Credits

Front and back cover image by Chris Harris

Sage Birchwater, p. 54; Karen Piffko, p. 62; Robert Keziere, p. 68; Chris Harris, p. 92; Diane Labombarbe, iStock photo, p. 100; Mikael Rinnan, iStock photo, p. 112; Michelle Muntau, p. 120 top; Witte family, p. 120, bottom; Douglas Cowell, p. 128; Richard Harrington, p. 138 top and bottom (courtesy of Cathy Hobson); Collier family, p. 152; Richard Harrington, p. 164 (courtesy of Veera Bonner); *Williams Lake Tribune*, pp. 172, 176; Eldon Lee, p. 182; Len Tillim, iStock photo, p. 188; Clint Scholz, iStock photo, p. 220; oil painting by Sonia Cornwall, p. 224; Jill Fromer, iStock photo, p. 228; drawings by Hazel Henry Litterick, pp. 242, 246; drawing by Morgan Witte, p. 250

Heritage Collection: pp. 12, 38, 44, 74, 80, 88, 106

Acknowledgements

Earl Shaw Baity, "A Land Primeval" from *Wilderness Welfare: An epic of frontier life*, published by Mitchell Press Limited, Vancouver, BC, 1966.

Sage Birchwater, "Neighbours." Copyright © 2007 by Sage Birchwater.

Chilco Choate, "The Legend of Old Nero" from *The Fire Still Burns*, published by Heritage House Publishing Company Ltd., Surrey, BC, 2001. Copyright © 2001 by Chilco Choate.

Eric Collier, Chapter Fourteen from *Three Against the Wilderness*, reprinted by TouchWood Editions, 2007. Copyright © Veasy Collier. Reprinted by permission of Veasy Collier .

Alan Fry, "Rodeo" from *The Ranch on the Cariboo*, first published by Doubleday, New York, 1962, reprinted by TouchWood Editions Ltd., Victoria, BC, 2002. Copyright © 2002 by Alan Fry. Reprinted by permission of TouchWood Editions Ltd.

Bill Gallaher, excerpt from *The Promise*, published by TouchWood Editions, Victoria, BC, 2001. Copyright © 2001 by Bill Gallaher. Reprinted by permission of TouchWood Editions Ltd.

Bill and Joyce Graham, "Those Cariboo Stampedes!" from *Pioneer Days in British Columbia, Volume One*, edited by Art Downs, first edition published by Heritage House Publishing Company Ltd. 1973, reprinted 1991.

Richmond P. Hobson Jr., "Pan Meets a Girl" from *Grass Beyond the Mountains: Discovering the Last Great Cattle Frontier on the North American Continent*, published by McClelland & Stewart Ltd., Toronto, ON, 1951, reprinted 1998. Copyright © 1951 by Richmond P. Hobson Jr. Reprinted by permission of McClelland & Stewart Ltd.

D.A. Holley, "A Pig Makes a House Call" from *Don't Shoot From the Saddle: Chronicles of a Frontier Surgeon*, published by Heritage House Publishing Company Ltd., Surrey, BC, 2000. Copyright © 2000 by D.A. Holley.

Eldon Lee, "Our Last Trail Ride." Copyright © 2007 by Eldon Lee.

Todd Lee, "Lady of the Lakes" from *Stories from the Cariboo: He Saw With Other Eyes*, published by The Caitlin Press, Prince George, BC, 1992. Copyright © 1992 by Todd Lee. Reprinted by permission of the Lee estate.

Olive Spencer Loggins, "Danger Dodges Us as the Ice Breaks Up" from *Tenderfoot Trail: Greenhorns in the Cariboo,* published by Sono Nis Press, Victoria, BC, 1983. Copyright © 1983 by Olive Spencer Loggins. Reprinted by permission of Sono Nis.

Fred. W. Ludditt, excerpt from "Jolly Great Rabbit" from *Campfire Sketches of the Cariboo,* published by author, Union Bay, BC, 1974. Copyright © 1974 by Fred. W. Ludditt.

Harry Marriott, "George Harrison and I Start the OK" from *Cariboo Cowboy,* first Heritage edition published by Heritage House Publishing Company Ltd., Surrey, BC, 1994, reprinted 2001. Copyright © 1994 estate of Harry Marriott.

Karen Piffko, excerpt from "Early Life in the Chilcotin" from *The Life and Times of Texas Fosbery: The Cariboo and Beyond,* published by Heritage House Publishing Company Ltd., Surrey, BC, 2000. Copyright © 2000 by Karen Piffko.

Hilary Place, "Pete Colin" and "Alkali Lake Hockey Team." Copyright © 2007 estate of Hilary Place. Printed by permission of Martin Place.

Heidi Redl, "Preg-Testing." Copyright 2007 © by Heidi Redl.

Bill Riley and Laura Leake, "First Williams Lake Stampede" from *History and Events of the Early 1920s,* published by Vantage Press, New York, NY, 1980. Copyright © 1980 by William Riley.

Robin Skelton, excerpt from "The Cariboo Road" in *They call it the Cariboo,* published by Sono Nis Press, Victoria, BC, 1980. Copyright © 1980 by Robin Skelton. Reprinted by permission of Alison and Brigid Skelton.

Jean E. Speare, ed., "The Story of the Surgeon" from *The Days of Augusta,* first published by J.J. Douglas Ltd., Vancouver, BC, 1973, reprinted by Douglas & McIntyre Ltd., Vancouver, BC, 1992. Copyright © 1973, 1992 Augusta Evans and Jean E. Speare. Reprinted by permission of Douglas & McIntyre Ltd.

Irene Stangoe, "The Day We Hanged W.A.C. Bennett" and "The Tail End" from *History and Happenings in the Cariboo–Chilcotin: Pioneer Memories,* published by Heritage House Publishing Company, Surrey, BC, 2000. Copyright © 2000 by Irene Stangoe.

Paul St. Pierre, "Looking for Horses" and "Looking for Horses Again" from *Tell Me a Good Lie: Tales from the Chilcotin Country,* published by Douglas and McIntyre Ltd., Vancouver, BC, 2001. Copyright © 2001 by Paul St. Pierre. Reprinted by permission of Douglas & McIntrye Ltd.

Mark S. Wade, "The Nugget Pin" from *The Cariboo Road,* published by The Haunted Bookshop, Victoria, BC, 1979. Reprinted by permission of Enid Wade.

Ann Walsh, "Cariboo Gold." Copyright © 2001 by Ann Walsh. First published in the *British Columbia Almanac,* Arsenal Pulp Press, Vancouver, 2001. Reprinted by permission of Ann Walsh.

Duane Witte with Veera Bonner, "Born to Buck" from *Chilcotin: Preserving Pioneer Memories,* published by Heritage House Publishing Company Ltd., Surrey, BC, 1995, reprinted 2005. Copyright © 1995 by Veera Bonner, Irene E. Bliss, and Hazel H. Litterick.

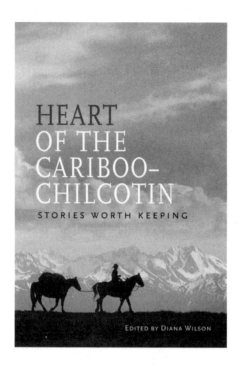

Heart of the Cariboo–Chilcotin: Stories Worth Keeping

The spirited stories in this first volume of the *Heart of the Cariboo–Chilcotin* series are straight-shooting and straight from the heart. Occasionally shocking and always entertaining, they capture the severity and grace of the distinct pioneer culture that resides in British Columbia's rugged central Interior.

ISBN 13: 978-1-894974-08-0
ISBN 10: 1-894974-08-5
6 x 9 sc; 240 pages
$19.95

visit www.heritagehouse.ca for more great titles